DOCUMENTS

ILLUSTRATING THE REIGNS OF

AUGUSTUS & TIBERIUS

DOCUMENTS
ILLUSTRATING THE REIGNS OF
AUGUSTUS & TIBERIUS

COLLECTED BY

VICTOR EHRENBERG

AND

A. H. M. JONES

SECOND EDITION

OXFORD

AT THE CLARENDON PRESS

Oxford University Press, Ely House, London W. 1

OXFORD LONDON GLASGOW NEW YORK
TORONTO MELBOURNE WELLINGTON CAPE TOWN
IBADAN NAIROBI DAR ES SALAAM LUSAKA ADDIS ABABA
KUALA LUMPUR SINGAPORE JAKARTA HONG KONG TOKYO
DELHI BOMBAY CALCUTTA MADRAS KARACHI

ISBN 0 19 814819 4

First edition 1949
Second (enlarged) edition 1955
Reprinted (with Addenda) as paperback 1976

Printed in Great Britain
at the University Press, Oxford
by Vivian Ridler
Printer to the University

INTRODUCTION TO REPRINT OF SECOND EDITION

THIS reprint has been made possible by a generous grant from the Board of the Faculty of Literae Humaniores of the University of Oxford. The opportunity has been taken to include a limited amount of new material. (These addenda are printed at the end of the book as Nos. 365–79 and are not subdivided as to subject-matter or arranged in chronological order: the choice of what to include or exclude was to some extent governed by trying to calculate what would most economically fit into the small space available.) To have done more would have meant having to charge a price far above what the undergraduates for whose use this collection was intended could be expected to afford.

The selection has been made after seeking the advice of historians and epigraphists at Oxford and Cambridge. The responsibility for the final choice is mine.

It should be noted that number 105, now generally accepted as Flavian in date, has been omitted from this reprint, and the space used to reproduce the important Paphos oath.

D. L. STOCKTON

BRASENOSE COLLEGE, OXFORD
June 1975

PREFACE TO SECOND EDITION

WE have taken the opportunity of a second edition to make some corrections and additions which will we hope increase the usefulness of the collection. In the first place, we have added forty-two new items. Many of them are texts which have appeared since the first edition; others are previously published documents which we or our friends thought would make the collection more complete and representative. We wish to thank our friends for their suggestions, and in particular Professor Grant for providing a selection of coins from which we were able to strengthen the numismatic evidence. The new items have been inserted in their appropriate places, but to avoid confusion the numbering of the first edition has been left unaltered (with the exception of the *Tabula Hebana*, which has ceased to be an *addendum* as 365, and gone to its proper context as 94a), and the new documents have been given a and b numbers. One item (no. 22) has been replaced by a similar but better-preserved inscription. Secondly, we have made a number of corrections. Here again we wish to thank our friends and our reviewers for calling our attention to errors and oversights. Finally, we have relegated to the Comparative Table references to the *Année épigraphique*, Bruns, *Fontes*[7], *Acta divi Augusti*, and Grueber, substituting in the text references to a fuller or better publication. We have also added to the Comparative Table the *CIL*. number of inscriptions cited from *ILS*. By this arrangement we hope that our readers will be able more easily both to go back to the original or best publication of a document, and to find in our book a document cited in a variety of ways.

We are grateful to Dr. Scullard for having shared in the task of proof-reading.

LONDON AND CAMBRIDGE
October 1954

PREFACE TO FIRST EDITION

WE embarked on this work with the idea of reprinting a number of important documents belonging to the reigns of Augustus and Tiberius which have not hitherto been readily accessible. As the work progressed it became evident that its usefulness would be greatly increased if more were included. In times like these, when books are frequently hard to come by, even a reprint of the *Res Gestae* seemed desirable, especially since during the last two decades its text has undergone some important corrections. Thus we decided to expand our scheme into a fully representative selection of documents, including many already published in well-known collections such as Dessau's *Inscriptiones Latinae Selectae*. We have strictly adhered to the true conception of documents, most of which are, of course, inscriptions; in addition there are a number of coins, a few papyri, and some documents preserved in literary sources. The Fasti and Calendars, though not printed in the form of the original documents, are based on epigraphical evidence.

We have endeavoured to illustrate all important aspects of the reigns of Augustus and Tiberius, and to do so by contemporary evidence only; one document of undoubtedly later date, the *lex de imperio Vespasiani*, has been included as an appendix. The 'reign' of Augustus has no definite beginning; we generally reckon it from his first consulship (43 B.C.), but a few items belong to the time immediately preceding that year. While we hope that the imperial administration as a whole is adequately illustrated, we thought it better to exclude the peculiar administrative system of Egypt.

Any such selection of documents will inevitably be to some extent arbitrary, and many readers will no doubt deplore the absence of some favourite document. We hope, however, that nothing of outstanding importance has been omitted. A purely chronological order would be both confusing and, since many items cannot be precisely dated, impracticable; we have therefore grouped the documents under rough subject-headings and arranged them under each heading as the case seemed to demand, chronologically, geographically, or according to different persons or types. Many documents would fit equally well into more than one group; we have given cross-references under each heading which, we hope, will mitigate this difficulty.

We owe thanks for valuable help and critical suggestions to Messrs. H. Mattingly, R. Meiggs, R. Syme, and E. G. Turner. We also wish to thank the Delegates of the Clarendon Press for the readiness with which they accepted the book, and the compositors and readers for their skill and speed in performing what was anything but an easy task.

LONDON

February 1949

CONTENTS

ABBREVIATIONS AND SYMBOLS

ADOA.	*Archives d'histoire du droit oriental et revue internationale des droits de l'antiquité.*
AJA.	*American Journal of Archaeology.*
AJP.	*American Journal of Philology.*
Ann. ép.	*L'année épigraphique.*
APont.	*Atti della pontifica accademia romana di archeologia (rendiconti).*
Arch. Anz.	*Archäologischer Anzeiger.* Beiblatt zum *Jahrbuch des Deutschen Archäologischen Instituts.*
Ἀρχ. Ἐφ.	*Ἀρχαιολογικὴ Ἐφημερίς.*
Ath. Mitt.	*Mitteilungen des Deutschen Archäologischen Instituts in Athen.*
BCH.	*Bulletin de correspondance hellénique.*
BFC.	*Bolletino di filologia classica.*
BGU.	*Ägyptische Urkunden aus den Museen zu Berlin. Griechische Urkunden.*
BMC.	*British Museum Catalogue.*
BSA.	*Annual of the British School at Athens.*
Bull. Comm.	*Bulletino della commissione archeologica comunale di Roma.*
CIG.	*Corpus Inscriptionum Graecarum.*
CIL.	*Corpus Inscriptionum Latinarum.*
CP.	*Classical Philology.*
CRAcInscr.	*Comptes rendus de l'académie des inscriptions et des belles-lettres.*
FIR.	*Fontes iuris Romani antejustiniani,* ed. S. Riccobono and others. Second edition. Vol. I.
Grant, *Asp.*	M. Grant, *Aspects of the Principate of Tiberius.*
Grant, *FITA.*	M. Grant, *From Imperium to Auctoritas.*
Grueber	H. A. Grueber, *Coins of the Roman Republic in the British Museum,* Vol. II.
Head, *HN.*[2]	B. V. Head, *Historia Nummorum.* Second edition.
Heiss	A. Heiss, *Description générale des monnaies antiques de l'Espagne.*
IBM.	*Ancient Greek Inscriptions in the British Museum.*
IG.	*Inscriptiones Graecae.*
IGRR.	*Inscriptiones Graecae ad res Romanas pertinentes,* ed. R. Cagnat and others.
ILS.	*Inscriptiones Latinae Selectae,* ed. H. Dessau.

IPEux.	B. Latyschev, *Inscriptiones antiquae orae septentrionalis Ponti Euxini.* Vol. II.
ISyr.	L. Jalabert and R. Monterde, *Inscriptions grecques et latines de la Syrie.*
ITrip.	J. M. Reynolds and J. B. Ward Perkins, *The Inscriptions of Roman Tripolitania.*
JdS.	*Journal des savants.*
JRS.	*Journal of Roman Studies.*
Mattingly	H. Mattingly, *Coins of the Roman Empire in the British Museum.* Vol. I.
MemAmAcR.	*Memoirs of the American Academy in Rome.*
NdS.	*Notizie degli scavi di antichità.*
OGIS.	*Orientis Graeci Inscriptiones Selectae*, ed. W. Dittenberger.
PdP.	*Parola del passato.*
PIR.[2]	*Prosopographia Imperii Romani.* Second edition.
RA.	*Revue archéologique.*
REG.	*Revue des études grecques.*
RFil.	*Rivista di filologia e d'istruzione classica.*
RhM.	*Rheinisches Museum.*
RPh.	*Revue de philologie.*
SEG.	*Supplementum Epigraphicum Graecum.*
Sydenham	E. A. Sydenham, *The Coinage of the Roman Republic.*
TAPA.	*Transactions of the American Philological Association.*
Vives	A. Vives, *La Moneda Hispánica*, Part IV.

[ ] enclose letters supposed to have been originally in the text.

( ) enclose letters added to complete a word abbreviated in the text.

⟨ ⟩ enclose letters either omitted or wrong in the text.

{ } enclose letters which are superfluous in the text.

A dot under a letter (ṇ) indicates that its reading is not quite certain.

(*vac.*) indicates a vacant space in the original text.

| marks the beginning of a line,

|| that of every fifth line.

I

RES GESTAE DIVI AUGUSTI

Text based on the critical edition by H. Volkmann, *Bursians Jahresbericht*, Suppl. vol. 276, 1942. Cf. also E. Gottanka, *Philol.* 1942, 230, and Volkmann, *Historia* iii (1954), 81.

The Latin text is printed according to the lines of the *Monumentum Ancyranum*. In both the Latin and the Greek texts the Roman and Arabic numbers in the margin indicate the columns and lines of the *Monumentum Ancyranum*. Letters in square brackets are missing in all surviving copies of the *Res Gestae*.

rerum gestarum divi Augusti, quibus orbem terra[rum] imperio populi Rom[a]ni subiecit, et impensarum, quas in rem publicam populumque Romanum fecit, incisarum in duabus aheneis pilis, quae su[n]t Romae positae, exemplar sub[i]ectum.

c. 1.

annos undeviginti natus exercitum privato consilio et privata impensa comparavi, per quem rem publicam a dominatione factionis oppressam in libertatem vindicavi. **2** eo [nomi]ne senatus decretis honorif[i]cis in ordinem suum m[e adlegit C. Pansa et A. Hirti]o consulibus con[sula]rem locum s[ententiae dicendae tribuens, et i]mperium mihi dedit. **3** res publica n[e quid detrimenti caperet], me propraetore simul cum consulibus pro[videre iussit. **4** p]opulus autem eodem anno me consulem, cum [cos. uterqu]e in bel[lo ceci]disset, et triumvirum rei publicae constituend[ae creavit].

c. 2.

qui parentem meum [trucidaver]un[t, eo]s in exilium expuli iudiciis legitimis ultus eorum [fa]cin[us e]t postea bellum inferentis rei publicae vici b[is a]cie.

c. 3.

[b]ella terra et mari c[ivilia ex]ternaque toto in orbe terrarum s[aepe gessi] victorque omnibus v[eniam petentib]us civibus peperci. **2** exte[rnas] gentes, quibus tuto [ignosci pot]ui[t, co]nservare quam excidere m[alui].

μεθηρμηνευμέναι ὑπεγράφησαν πράξεις τε καὶ δωρεαὶ Σεβαστοῦ θεοῦ, ἃς ἀπέλιπεν ἐπὶ Ῥώμης ἐνκεχαραγμένας χαλκαῖς στήλαις δυσίν.

c. 1.

ἐτῶν δεκαε[ν]νέα ὢν τὸ στράτευμα ἐμῆι γνώμηι καὶ | ἐμοῖς ἀν[αλ]ώμασιν ἡτοί[μασα], δι' οὗ τὰ κοινὰ πρά|γματα [ἐκ τῆ]ς τ[ῶ]ν συνο[μοσα]μένων δουλήας | [ἠλευ]θέ[ρωσα. ἐπὶ ο]ἷς ἡ σύνκλητος ἐπαινέσασά || [με ψηφίσμασι] προσκατέλεξε τῆι βουλῆι Γαΐωι Πά[νσ]α<ι> | [καὶ Αὔλωι Ἱρτίωι ὑ]π[ά]το[ι]ς, ἐν τῆι τάξει τῶν ὑπατ[ευσά]ν|[των τ]ὸ σ[υμβου]λεύειν δοῦσα, ῥάβδου[ς] τέ μοι ἔδωκεν. | [περ]ὶ τὰ δημόσια πράγματα μή τι βλαβῆι, ἐμοὶ με|[τὰ τῶν ὑπά]των προνοεῖν ἐπέτρεψεν ἀντιστρατήγωι || [ὄντι. ὁ δ]ὲ δ[ῆ]μος τῶι αὐτῶι ἐνιαυτῶι ἀμφοτέρων | [τῶν ὑπάτων ἐν π]ολέμωι πεπτω[κ]ότων ἐμὲ ὕπα|[τον ἀπέδειξ]εν καὶ τὴν τῶν τριῶν ἀνδρῶν ἔχον|[τα ἀρχὴν ἐπὶ] τῆι καταστάσει τῶν δ[η]μοσίων πρα|[γμάτων] ε[ἵλ]ατ[ο]. ||

c. 2.

[τοὺς τὸν πατέρα μου φονεύ]σ[αν]τ[α]ς ἐξώρισα κρί|[σεσιν ἐνδί]κοις τειμω[ρ]ησάμε[ν]ος αὐτῶν τὸ | [ἀσέβημα κ]αὶ [με]τὰ ταῦτα αὐτοὺς πόλεμον ἐ|[πιφέροντας τῆι πα]τ[ρ]ίδι δὶς ἐνείκησα παρατάξει. |

c. 3.

[πολέμους καὶ κατὰ γῆν] καὶ κατὰ θάλασσαν ἐμφυ||[λίους καὶ ἐξωτικοὺς] ἐν ὅληι τῆι οἰκουμένηι πολ|[λάκις ἐποίησα νεικ]ήσας τε πάντων ἐφεισάμην | [τῶν ἱκετῶν πολειτῶν. τ]ὰ ἔθνη, οἷς ἀσφαλὲς ἦν συν|[γνώμην ἔχειν, ἔσωσα μ]ᾶλ[λον] ἢ ἐξέκοψα. μυριάδες | Ῥωμαίων στρα- II

3 millia civium Roma[no]rum [sub] sacramento meo fuerunt circiter [quingen]-
ta. ex quibus dedu[xi in coloni]as aut remisi in municipia sua stipen[dis emeri]-
tis millia aliquant[o plura qu]am trecenta, et iis omnibus agros a[dsignavi]
aut pecuniam pro p[raemis mil]itiae dedi. 4 naves cepi sescen[tas praeter]
eas, si quae minore[s quam trir]emes fuerunt.

c. 4.

[bis] ovans triumphavi et tri[s egi] curulis triumphos et appella[tus sum v]iciens et
semel imperator, [decernente plu]ris triumphos mihi senatu, qu[ibus]
[omnibus su]persedi. l[aurum de f]asc[i]bus deposui in Capi[tolio, votis quae]
quoque bello nuncupaveram [sol]utis. 2 ob res a [me aut per legatos]
meos auspicis meis terra ma[riqu]e pr[o]spere gestas qui[nquagiens et q]uin-
quiens decrevit senatus supp[lica]ndum esse dis immortalibus. dies a[utem],
[pe]r quos ex senatus consulto [s]upplicatum est, fuere DC[CCLXXXX. 3 in triumphis]
[meis] ducti sunt ante currum meum reges aut r[eg]um lib[eri novem. 4 consul]
[f]ueram terdeciens, cum [scribeb]a[m] haec, [et eram se]p[timum et] tricen[simu]m
tribuniciae potestatis.

c. 5.

[dic]tat[ura]m et apsent[i e]t praesent[i mihi delatam et a popu]lo et a se[na]tu
[M. Marce]llo e[t] L. Arruntio [cos.] non rec[epi. 2 non sum] depreca[tus] in s[umma]
[f]rum[enti p]enuria curatio[n]em an[non]ae, [qu]am ita ad[min]ist[ravi, ut intra]
die[s] paucos metu et periclo p[r]aesenti civitatem univ[ersam liberarem]

τ[εύ]σ[ασ]αι ὑπ[ὸ τὸ]ν ὅρκον τὸν ἐμὸν | ἐγένοντ[ο] ἐνγὺς π[εντήκ]ο[ντ]α· [ἐ]ξ ὧν κατή[γ]αγον εἰς | τὰ[ς] ἀπο[ι]κίας ἢ ἀ[πέπεμψα εἰς τὰς] ἰδία[ς πόλεις] ἐκ|π̣λ̣[ηρωθέντων τῶν ἐν]ι̣[αυτῶν τῆς] στρατε̣[ίας] μ[υρι]ά̣δ̣α̣ς || [ὀλίγω]ι̣ π[λείους ἢ τριάκοντα καὶ αὐ]τ̣[οῖς πᾶ]σ̣[ιν ἀγρ]ο̣[ὺς | ἐμέρισα] ἢ̣ [χρήματα ἀντὶ δωρεῶν στρατείας ἔ]δ[ωκα]. | ν̣[α]ῦ̣ς εἷ̣[λον ἑξακοσίας ἐκτὸς τούτων εἴ τινες ἥσσονες | ἢ τριήρεις ἐγένοντο.] |

c. 4.

δὶς πεζ[ὸν ἐθριάμβευσα καὶ] τρὶς [ἐ]φ' ἅρματος, εἰκο||σά[κις καὶ ἅπαξ προσηγορεύθην αὐτο]κράτωρ, τῆς | [συνκλήτου ἐμοὶ πλείους θριάμβου]ς ψηφισσ[αμέ|νης, ὧν πάντων ἀπεσχόμην. ἀπὸ τῶν ῥάβδ]ων τὴν [δά|φνην ἀπέθηκα ἐν τῶι Καπιτωλίωι, τὰ]ς εὐχάς [ἃς ἐν] | τῶ[ι πολέμωι ἑκάστωι ἐποιησάμην ἀποδ]ούς. [διὰ τὰς ἐμὰς || πράξεις ἢ τὰς τῶν πρεσβευτῶν τῶν ἐ]μ[ῶν, ἃς αἰσίοις | οἰωνοῖς καὶ κατὰ γῆν καὶ κατὰ θάλασσαν] κατώρθω|σα, π̣[εντ]ηκοντάκις [καὶ] πεντά[κις ἐψ]ηφίσατο ἡ | σύ[νκλητ]ος θεοῖς δεῖ[ν] θύεσθαι. [ἡμ]έραι οὖν αὗ|[τα]ι ἐ[κ συ]ν[κλήτου] δ[ό]γματ[ο]ς ἐγένοντο ὀκτα[κ]όσιαι ἐνενή|||[κοντα]. ἐν [τ]οῖς ἐμοῖς [θριάμ]βοις [πρὸ το]ῦ ἐμοῦ ἅρ|μ[ατος βασι]λεῖς ἢ [βασιλέων παῖ]δες [προήχθ]ησαν | ἐννέα. [ὑπάτ]ε[υ]ον τρὶς καὶ δέκ[ατο]ν, ὅτε τ[αῦ]τα ἔγραφον, | καὶ ἤμη[ν τρια]κ[οστὸ]ν καὶ ἕβδομ[ον δημαρχ]ικῆς | ἐξουσίας. | III

c. 5.

αὐτεξούσιόν μοι ἀρχὴν καὶ ἀπόντι καὶ παρόντι | διδομένην [ὑ]πό τε το̣ῦ δήμου καὶ τῆς συνκλήτου | Μ[άρκ]ωι [Μ]αρκέλλωι καὶ Λευκίωι Ἀρρουντίωι ὑπάτοις || ο[ὐκ ἐδ]εξά̣μην. οὐ παρη‹ι›τησάμην ἐν τῆι μεγίστηι | [τοῦ] σ[είτ]ου σπάνει τὴν ἐπιμέλειαν τῆς ἀγορᾶς, ἣν οὕ|[τως ἐπετήδευ]σα, ὥστ' ἐν ὀλίγαις ἡμέρα[ις το]ῦ παρόντος | φόβου καὶ

[impensa et] cura mea. 3 consul[atum] quoqu[e] tum annuum e[t perpetuum]
[mihi] dela[tum non recepi].

c. 6.

[consulibus M. Vinicio et Q. Lucretio] et postea P. Lentulo et Cn. L[entulo et tertium]
[Paullo Fabio Maximo et Q. Tuberone senatu populoq]u[e Romano consen]-
[tientibus] ut cu[rator legum et morum summa potestate solus crearer],
[nullum magistratum contra morem maiorum delatum recepi. 2 quae tum per me]
[geri senatus] v[o]luit, per trib[un]ici[a]m p[otestatem perfeci, cuius potes]tatis
conlegam et [ips]e ultro [quinquiens a sena]tu [de]poposci et accepi.

c. 7.

[tri]umv[i]rum rei pu[blicae c]on[s]ti[tuendae fui per continuos an]nos [decem].
2 [p]rinceps s[enatus fui usque ad e]um d[iem, quo scrip]seram [haec],
[per annos] quadra[ginta. 3 pon]tifex [maximus, augur, XV vir]um sacris fac[iundis],
[VII virum ep]ulon[um, frater arvalis, sodalis Titius,] fetialis fui.

c. 8.

patriciorum numerum auxi consul quintum iussu populi et senatus. 2 sena- II
tum ter legi. et in consulatu sexto censum populi conlega M. Agrippa egi.
lustrum post annum alterum et quadragensimum fec[i]. quo lustro civium Romanorum censa sunt capita quadragiens centum millia et sexa-
g[i]nta tria millia. 3 tum [iteru]m consulari cum imperio lustrum
[s]olus feci C. Censorin[o et C.] Asinio cos., quo lustro censa sunt

κι[νδ]ύνου ταῖς ἐμαῖς δαπάναις τὸν δῆμον | ἐλευθερῶσα[ι]. ὑπατείαν τέ μοι τότε δι[δ]ομένην καὶ || ἐ[ν]ιαύσιον κα[ὶ δ]ι[ὰ] βίου οὐκ ἐδεξάμην. |

c. 6.

ὑπάτοις Μάρκωι Οὐινουκίωι καὶ Κοίντωι Λ[ουκρ]ητ[ίωι] | καὶ μετὰ τα[ῦ]τα Ποπλίωι καὶ Ναίωι Λέντλοις καὶ | τρίτον Παύλλωι Φαβίωι Μαξίμωι καὶ Κοίν[τωι] Του|βέρωνι τῆς [τε σ]υνκλήτου καὶ τοῦ δήμου τῶν || Ῥωμαίων ὁμολογ[ο]ύντων, ἵν[α ἐπιμε]λητὴς | τῶν τε νόμων καὶ τῶν τρόπων ἐ[πὶ με]γίστηι | [ἐξ]ουσ[ίαι μ]ό[νο]ς χειροτονηθῶ{ι}, ἀρχὴν οὐδε|μ[ία]ν πα[ρὰ τὰ πά]τρ[ια] ἔ[θ]η διδομένην ἀνεδε|ξάμην. ἃ δὲ τότε δι' ἐμοῦ ἡ σύνκλητος οἰ||κονομεῖσθαι ἐβούλετο, τῆς δημαρχικῆς ἐξο[υ]|σίας ὢν ἐτέλε[σα. κ]αὶ ταύτης αὐτῆς τῆς ἀρχῆς | συνάρχοντα [αὐτ]ὸς ἀπὸ τῆς συνκλήτου π[εν]|τάκις αἰτήσας [ἔλ]αβον. |

c. 7.

IV τριῶν ἀνδρῶν ἐγενόμην δημοσίων πραγμάτων | κατορθωτὴς συνεχέσιν ἔτεσιν δέκα. πρῶτον | ἀξιώματος τόπον ἔσχον τῆς συνκλήτου ἄχρι | ταύτης τῆς ἡμέρας, ἧς ταῦτα ἔγραφον, ἐπὶ ἔτη τεσ||σαράκοντα. ἀρχιερεύς, αὔγουρ, τῶν δεκαπέντε ἀν|δρῶν τῶν ἱεροποιῶν, τῶν ἑπτὰ ἀνδρῶν ἱεροποι|ῶν, ἀ[δε]λφὸς ἀρουᾶλις, ἑταῖρος Τίτιος, φητιᾶλις. |

c. 8.

τῶν [πατ]ρικίων τὸν ἀριθμὸν εὔξησα πέμπτον | ὕπατ[ος ἐπιτ]αγῆι τοῦ τε δήμου καὶ τῆς συνκλή||του. [τὴν σύ]νκλητον τρὶς ἐπέλεξα. ἕκτον ὕπα|τος τὴν ἀπ[ο]τείμησιν τοῦ δήμου συνάρχον|[τ]α ἔχων Μᾶρκον Ἀγρίππαν ἔλαβον, ἥτις ἀπο|[τείμη]σις μετὰ [δύο καὶ] τεσσαρακοστὸν ἐνιαυ|τὸν [σ]υνε[κ]λείσθη. ἐν ἧι ἀποτειμήσει Ῥωμαίων || ἐτει[μήσ]α[ντο] κεφαλαὶ τετρακό[σιαι ἑ]ξήκον|τα μυ[ριάδες καὶ τρισχίλιαι. εἶτα δεύτερον ὑ]πατι|κῆι ἐξ[ουσίαι μόνος Γαΐωι Κηνσωρίνωι καὶ]|| Γαΐωι [Ἀσινίωι ὑπάτοις τὴν ἀποτείμησιν ἔλαβον]· | ἐν [ἧι] ἀπο[τει-

civium Romanorum [capita] quadragiens centum millia et ducen- ta triginta tria m[illia. 4 et tertiu]m consulari cum imperio lustrum conlega Tib. Cae[sare filio] m[eo feci] Sex. Pompeio et Sex. Appuleio cos., quo lustro ce[nsa sunt] civ[ium Ro]manorum capitum quad- ragiens centum mill[ia et n]onge[nta tr]iginta et septem millia. 5 legibus novi[s] m[e auctore l]atis m[ulta e]xempla maiorum exolescentia iam ex nostro [saecul]o red[uxi et ipse] multarum rer[um exe]mpla imi- tanda pos[teris tradidi].

c. 9.

vota p[ro valetudine mea susc]ipi p[er cons]ules et sacerdotes qu[in]to qu[oque anno senatus decrevit. ex iis] votis s[ae]pe fecerunt vivo m[e ludos aliquotiens sacerdotu]m quattuor amplissima colle- [gia, aliquotiens consules. 2 pr]iva[ti]m etiam et municipatim univer[si] [cives unanimite]r con[tinente]r apud omnia pulvinaria pro vale- [tu]din[e mea s]upp[licaverunt].

c. 10.

nom[en me]um [sena]tus c[onsulto inc]lusum est in saliare carmen, et sacrosan- ctu[s in perp]etum [ut essem et, q]uoad viverem, tribunicia potestas mihi [esset, per lege]m s[anctum est. 2 pontif]ex maximus ne fierem in vivi [c]onle- [gae mei l]ocum, [populo id sace]rdotium deferente mihi quod pater meu[s] [habuer]at, r[ecusavi. qu]od sacerdotium aliquod post annos, eo mor- [t]uo q[ui civilis] m[otus o]ccasione occupaverat, cuncta ex Italia

μήσει ἐτειμήσαντο Ῥωμαί]||ων τετ[ρακόσιαι εἴκοσι τρεῖς μυριάδες καὶ
τ]ρι[σ]|χίλιοι. κ[αὶ τρίτον ὑπατικῆι ἐξουσίαι τὰς ἀποτειμή]|σε[ι]ς
ἔλα[βο]ν, [ἔχω]ν [συνάρχοντα Τιβέριον] | Καίσαρα τὸν υἱόν μο[υ
Σέξτωι Πομπηΐωι καὶ] | Σέξτωι Ἀππουληίωι ὑπάτοις· ἐν ἧι ἀπο- V
τειμήσει | ἐτειμήσαντο Ῥωμαίων τετρακόσιαι ἐνενήκοντα | τρεῖς
μυριάδες καὶ ἑπτακισχείλιοι. εἰσαγαγὼν και|νοὺς νόμους πολλὰ ἤδη
τῶν ἀρχαίων ἐθῶν κα||ταλυόμενα διωρθωσάμην καὶ αὐτὸς πολλῶν |
πραγμάτων μείμημα ἐμαυτὸν τοῖς μετέπει|τα παρέδωκα. |

c. 9.

εὐχὰς ὑπὲρ τῆς ἐμῆς σωτηρίας ἀναλαμβάνειν | διὰ τῶν ὑπάτων καὶ
ἱερέων καθ' ἑκάστην πεν||τετηρίδα ἐψηφίσατο ἡ σύνκλητος. ἐκ τού|των
τῶν εὐχῶν πλειστάκις ἐγένοντο θέαι, | τοτὲ μὲν ἐκ τῆς συναρχίας τῶν
τεσσάρων ἱερέ|ων, τοτὲ δὲ ὑπὸ τῶν ὑπάτων. καὶ κατ' ἰδίαν δὲ καὶ |
κατὰ πόλεις σύνπαντες οἱ πολεῖται ὁμοθυμα||δ[ὸν] συνεχῶς ἔθυσαν
ὑπὲρ τῆς ἐμῆς σω[τ]ηρίας. |

c. 10.

τὸ ὄν[ομ]ά μου συνκλήτου δόγματι ἐνπεριελή|φθη εἰ[ς τοὺ]ς σαλίων
ὕμνους. καὶ ἵνα ἱερὸς ὦ{ι} | διὰ [βίο]υ [τ]ε τὴν δημαρχικὴν ἔχω{ι}
ἐξουσίαν, | νό[μωι ἐκ]υρώθη. ἀρχιερωσύνην, ἣν ὁ πατήρ || [μ]ου
[ἐσχ]ήκει, τοῦ δήμου μοι καταφέροντος | εἰς τὸν τοῦ ζῶντος τόπον, οὐ
προσεδεξά|μ[η]ν. [ἣ]ν ἀρχιερατείαν μετά τινας ἐνιαυτοὺς | ἀποθανόν- VI
τος τοῦ προκατειληφότος αὐ|τὴν ἐν πολειτικαῖς ταραχαῖς ἀνείληφα,
εἰς | τὰ ἐμὰ ἀρχαιρέσια ἐξ ὅλης τῆς Ἰταλίας τοσού|του πλήθους

[ad comitia mea] confluen[te mu]ltitudine, quanta Romae nun-[q]uam [fertur ante i]d temp[us fuisse], recep[i] P. Sulpicio C. Valgio consulibu[s].

c. 11.

aram [Fortunae] R[educis a]nte aedes Honoris et Virtutis ad portam Cap[enam pro] red[itu me]o senatus consacravit, in qua ponti-[fices et] vir[gines Ve]stal[es anni]versarium sacrificium facere [iussit eo] di[e, quo co]nsul[ibus Q. Luc]retio et [M. Vi]nic[io] in urbem ex [Syria redieram, et diem Augustali]a ex [c]o[gnomine] nos[t]ro appellavit.

c. 12.

[ex senatus auctoritat]e pars [praetorum e]t tribunorum [plebi cum consule Q.] Lu[cret]io et princi[pi]bus viris [ob]viam mihi mis[s]a e[st in Campan]iam, qui honos [ad ho]c tempus nemini prae-ter [m]e e[st decretus. **2** cu]m ex H[isp]ania Gal[liaque, rebu]s in iis provincis prosp[e]-re [gest]is, R[omam redi] Ti. Nerone P. Qui[ntilio consulibu]s, aram [Pacis A]u[g]ust[ae senatus pro] redi[t]u meo consa[c]randam [censuit] ad cam-pum [Martium, in qua ma]gistratus et sac[er]dotes [vi]rgines-[que] V[est]a[les] [anni]ver[sarium sacrific]ium facer[e iussit].

c. 13.

[Ianum] Quirin[um, quem cl]aussum ess[e maiores nostri voluer]unt, cum [p]er totum i[mperium po]puli Roma[ni terra marique es]set parta vic-toriis pax, cum, pr[iusquam] nascerer, [a condita] u[rb]e bis omnino clausum [f]uisse prodatur m[emori]ae, ter me princi[pe senat]us clauden-dum esse censui[t].

συνεληλυθότος, ὅσον οὐδεὶς || ἔνπροσθεν ἱστόρησεν ἐπὶ Ῥώμης γεγονέναι, Πο|πλίωι Σουλπικίωι καὶ Γαΐωι Οὐαλγίωι ὑπάτοις. |

c. 11.

βωμὸν Τύχης Σωτηρίου ὑπὲρ τῆς ἐμῆς ἐπανόδου | πρὸς τῆι Καπήνηι πύληι ἡ σύνκλητος ἀφιέρωσεν, | πρὸς ὧι τοὺς ἱερεῖς καὶ τὰς ἱερείας ἐνιαύσιον θυ||σίαν ποιεῖν ἐκέλευσεν ἐν ἐκείνηι τῆι ἡμέραι, | ἐν ἧι ὑπάτοις Κοίντωι Λουκρητίωι καὶ Μάρκωι | Οὐινουκίωι ἐκ Συρίας εἰς Ῥώμην ἐπανεληλύ|θει[ν], τήν τε ἡμέραν ἐκ τῆς ἡμετέρας ἐπωνυ|μίας προσηγόρευσεν Αὐγουστάλια. ||

c. 12.

δόγματι σ[υ]νκλήτου οἱ τὰς μεγίστας ἀρχὰς ἄρ|ξαντε[ς σ]ὺν μέρει στρατηγῶν καὶ δημάρχων | μετὰ ὑπ[ά]του Κοίντου Λουκρητίου ἐπέμφθη|σάν μοι ὑπαντήσοντες μέχρι Καμπανίας, ἥτις | τειμὴ μέχρι τούτου οὐδὲ ἑνὶ εἰ μὴ ἐμοὶ ἐψηφίσ||θη. ὅτε ἐξ Ἱσπανίας καὶ Γαλατίας, τῶν ἐν ταύ|ταις ταῖς ἐπαρχείαις πραγμάτων κατὰ τὰς εὐ|χὰς τελεσθέντων, εἰς Ῥώμην ἐπανῆλθον | Τιβερίωι [Νέ]ρωνι καὶ Ποπλίωι Κοιντιλίωι ὑπάτοις, | βωμὸν Ε[ἰρ]ήνης Σεβαστῆς ὑπὲρ τῆς ἐμῆς ἐπαν- VII
ό|δου ἀφιερωθῆναι ἐψηφίσατο ἡ σύνκλητος ἐν πε|δίωι Ἄρεως, πρὸς ὧι τούς τε ἐν ταῖς ἀρχαῖς καὶ τοὺς | ἱερεῖς τάς τε ἱερείας ἐνιαυσίους θυσίας ἐκέλευσε ποιεῖν. ||

c. 13.

Πύλην Ἐνυάλιον, ἣν κεκλῖσθαι οἱ πατέρες ἡμῶν ἠθέλησαν | εἰρηνευομένης τῆς ὑπὸ Ῥωμα‹ί›οις πάσης γῆς τε | καὶ θαλάσσης, πρὸ μὲν ἐμοῦ, ἐξ οὗ ἡ πόλις ἐκτίσθη, | τῶι παντὶ αἰῶνι δὶς μόνον κεκλεῖσθαι ὁμολογεῖ|ται, ἐπὶ δὲ ἐμοῦ ἡγεμόνος τρὶς ἡ σύνκλητος ἐψη||φίσατο κλεισθῆναι. |

c. 14.

[fil]ios meos, quos iuv[enes mi]hi eripuit for[tuna], Gaium et Lucium Caesares
honoris mei caussa senatus populusque Romanus annum quin- tum et deci- III
mum agentis consules designavit, ut [e]um magistratum inirent post quin-
quennium. et ex eo die, quo deducti [s]unt in forum, ut inter- essent consiliis
publicis decrevit sena[t]us. **2** equites [a]utem Romani universi principem
iuventutis utrumque eorum parm[is] et hastis argenteis dona- tum ap-
pellaverunt.

c. 15.

plebei Romanae viritim HS trecenos numeravi ex testamento patris
mei et nomine meo HS quadringenos ex bellorum manibiis consul
quintum dedi, iterum autem in consulatu decimo ex [p]atri- monio
meo HS quadringenos congiari viritim pernumer[a]vi, et consul
undecimum duodecim frumentationes frumento pr[i]vatim co- empto
emensus sum, et tribunicia potestate duodecimum quadringenos
nummos tertium viritim dedi. quae mea congiaria p[e]rvene- runt
ad [homi]num millia nunquam minus quinquaginta et ducenta.
2 tribuniciae potestatis duodevicensimum, consul XII, trecentis et
viginti millibus plebis urbanae sexagenos denarios viritim dedi.
3 et colon[i]s militum meorum consul quintum ex manibiis viritim
millia nummum singula dedi; acceperunt id triumphale con- giarium
in colonis hominum circiter centum et viginti millia. **4** consul ter-

c. 14.

υἱούς μου Γάϊον καὶ Λεύκιον Καίσ[α]ρας, οὓς νεανίας ἀ|νήρπασεν ἡ τύχη, εἰς τὴν ἐμὴν τειμ[ὴ]ν ἥ τ[ε] σύνκλη|τος καὶ ὁ δῆμος τῶν Ῥωμαίων πεντεκαιδεκαέτεις | ὄντας ὑπάτους ἀπέδειξεν, ἵνα μετὰ πέντε ἔτη || εἰς τὴν ὕπατον ἀρχὴν εἰσέλθωσιν· καὶ ἀφ' ἧς ἂν | ἡμέ[ρα]ς εἰς τὴν ἀγορὰν κα[τ]αχθ[ῶ]σιν, ἵνα [με]τέχω|σιν τῆς συ[ν]κλήτου ἐψηφίσατο. ἱππεῖς δὲ Ῥω|μαίων σύν[π]αντες ἡγεμόνα νεότητος ἑκάτε|ρον αὐτῶν προσηγόρευσαν, ἀσπίσιν ἀργυρέαις || καὶ δόρασιν [ἐτ]είμησαν. |

c. 15.

δήμωι Ῥωμαίων κατ' ἄνδρα ἑβδομήκοντα π[έντ]ε | δηνάρια ἑκάστωι ἠρίθμησα κατὰ δια|θήκην τοῦ πατρός μου, καὶ τῶι ἐμῶι ὀνόματι | ἐκ λαφύρων [π]ο[λέ]μου ἀνὰ ἑκατὸν δηνάρια || πέμπτον ὕπατος ἔδωκα, VIII
πάλιν τε δέ[κατο]ν | ὑπατεύων ἐκ τ[ῆ]ς ἐμῆς ὑπάρξεως ἀνὰ δηνά|ρια ἑκατὸν ἠρίθ[μ]ησα, καὶ ἑνδέκατον ὕπατος | δώδεκα σειτομετρήσεις ἐκ τοῦ ἐμοῦ βίου ἀπε||μέτρησα, καὶ δημαρχικῆς ἐξουσίας τὸ δωδέ|κατον ἑκατὸν δηνάρια κατ' ἄνδρα ἔδωκα· αἵτ[ι]|νες ἐμαὶ ἐπιδόσεις οὐδέποτε ἧσσον ἦλθ[ο]ν ε[ἰ]ς | ἄνδρας μυριάδων εἴκοσι πέντε. δημα[ρ]χικῆς ἐ|ξουσίας ὀκτωκαιδέκατον, ὕπατ[ος] δ[ωδέκατον], || τριάκοντα τρισ[ὶ] μυριάσιν ὄχλου πολειτικ[οῦ ἑ]ξή|κοντα δηνάρια κατ' ἄνδρα ἔδωκ[α, κα]ὶ ἀποίκοις στρα|τιωτῶν ἐμῶν πέμπτον ὕπατος ἐ[κ] λαφύρων κατὰ | ἄνδρα ἀνὰ διακόσια πεντήκοντα δηνάρια ἔδ[ωκα]· | ἔλαβον ταύτην τὴν δωρεὰν ἐν ταῖς ἀποικίαις ἀν||θρώπων μυριάδες πλ[εῖ]ον δώδε[κα.

tium dec[i]mum sexagenos denarios plebei, quae tum frumentum publicum accipiebat, dedi; ea millia hominum paullo plura quam ducenta fuerunt.

c. 16.

pecuniam [pr]o agris, quos in consulatu meo quarto et postea consulibus M. Cr[a]sso et Cn. Lentulo Augure adsignavi militibus, solvi municipis. ea [s]u[mma s]estertium circiter sexsiens milliens fuit, quam [p]ro Italicis praedis numeravi, et ci[r]citer bis mill[ie]ns et sescentiens, quod pro agris provincialibus solvi. id primus et [s]olus omnium, qui [d]eduxerunt colonias militum in Italia aut in provincis, ad memoriam aetatis meae feci. 2 et postea Ti. Nerone et Cn. Pisone consulibus itemque C. Antistio et D. Laelio cos. et C. Calvisio et L. Pasieno consulibus et L. Le[nt]ulo et M. Messalla consulibus et L. Caninio et Q. Fabricio co[s.], milit[i]bus, quos emeriteis stipendis in sua municipi[a dedux]i, praem[i]a numerato persolvi, quam in rem sestertium q[uater m]illiens cir[cite]r impendi.

c. 17.

quater [pe]cunia mea iuvi aerarium, ita ut sestertium milliens et quing[en]tie[n]s ad eos, qui praerant aerario, detulerim. 2 et M. Lepido et L. Ar[r]unt[i]o cos. in aerarium militare, quod ex consilio m[eo] co[ns]titutum est, ex [q]uo praemia darentur militibus, qui vicena [aut plu]ra sti[pendi]a emeruissent, HS milliens et septing[e]nti[ens ex pa]t[rim]onio [m]eo detuli.

ὕ]πατος τ[ρι]σ|καιδέκατον ἀνὰ ἑξήκοντα δηνάρια τῶι σειτομετρου-| μένωι δήμωι ἔδωκα· [οὗ]τος ἀριθμὸς πλείων εἴκο|σι μυριάδων ὑπῆρχεν. |

c. 16.

χρήματα ἐν ὑπατείᾳ[ι] τετάρτηι ἐμῆι κα[ὶ] μετὰ ταῦτα ὑ||πάτοις Μάρκω[ι] Κράσσω[ι] καὶ Ναΐωι Λέντλω[ι] Αὔγου|ρι ταῖς πόλεσιν ἠρίθμησα ὑπὲρ ἀγρῶν, οὓς ἐμέρισα | τοῖς στρατ[ιώ]ταις. κεφαλαίου ἐγένοντο ἐν Ἰτ[α]λίαι | μὲν μύριαι π[εντακι]σχε[ίλιαι μυ]ριάδες, τ[ῶ]ν [δὲ ἐ]παρ|χειτικῶν ἀγρῶν [μ]υ[ριάδες ἑξακισχείλ]ιαι πεν[τακό]σ[ιαι]. || τοῦτο πρῶτος καὶ μόνος ἁπάντων ἐπόησα τῶν | [κατα]γαγόντων IX ἀποικίας στρατιωτῶν ἐν Ἰτα|λίαι ἢ ἐν ἐπαρχείαις μέχρι τῆς ἐμῆς ἡλικίας. καὶ | μετέπειτα Τιβερίωι Νέρωνι καὶ Ναΐωι Πείσωνι ὑπά-|| τοις καὶ πάλιν Γαΐωι Ἀνθεστίωι καὶ Δέκμωι Λαι|λίωι ὑπάτοις καὶ Γαΐωι Καλουισίωι καὶ Λευκίωι | Πασσιήνωι [ὑ]πάτο[ι]ς καὶ Λευκίωι Λέντλωι καὶ Μάρ|κωι Μεσσάλ[αι] ὑπάτοις κ[α]ὶ [Λ]ευκίωι Κανινίωι καὶ | Κοίντωι Φαβρικίωι ὑπάτοις ‹τοῖς› στρατιώταις ἀπολυ||ομένοις, οὓς κατήγαγον εἰς τὰς ἰδίας πόλ[ει]ς, φιλαν|θρώπου ὀνόματι ἔδωκα μυριάδας ἐγγὺς [μυρία]ς. |

c. 17.

τετρά[κ]ις χρήμασιν ἐμοῖς ὑπέλαβον τὸ αἰράριον, εἰς ὃ | κατήνενκα ‹τρισ›[χ]ειλίας [ἑπτ]ακοσίας πεντήκοντα | μυριάδας. καὶ Μάρκωι Λε[πίδωι] καὶ Λευκίωι Ἀρρουν||τίωι ὑπάτοις εἰς τὸ στρατιωτικὸν αἰράριον, ὃ τῆι | [ἐμῆι] γ[ν]ώ[μηι] κατέστη, ἵνα ἐξ αὐτοῦ αἱ δωρεαὶ τοῖς | ἀπολυομένοις στρατ[ι]ώταις δίδωνται, ο[ἳ εἴκ]ο|σιν ἐνιαυτοὺς ἢ πλείονας ἐστρατεύσαντο, μυρι|άδας τετρα[κ]ισχειλίας διακοσίας πεντήκοντα || ἐκ τῆς ἐμῆς ὑπάρξεως κατήνενκα. |

c. 18.

[ab eo anno, q]uo Cn. et P. Lentuli c[ons]ules fuerunt, cum deficerent
[ve]ct[i]g[alia, tum] centum millibus h[omi]num tum pluribus multo fru-
me[ntarios et n]umma[rio]s t[ributus ex horr]eo et patr[i]monio m[eo]
edidi.

c. 19.

curiam et continens ei Chalcidicum templumque Apollinis in IV
Palatio cum porticibus, aedem divi Iuli, Lupercal, porticum ad circum Flaminium, quam sum appellari passus ex nomine eius, qui pri-
orem eodem in solo fecerat, Octaviam, pulvinar ad circum maximum,
2 aedes in Capitolio Iovis Feretri et Iovis Tonantis, aedem Quirini,
aedes Minervae et Iunonis Reginae et Iovis Libertatis in Aventino,
aedem Larum in summa sacra via, aedem deum Penatium in Velia,
aedem Iuventatis, aedem Matris Magnae in Palatio feci.

c. 20.

Capitolium et Pompeium theatrum utrumque opus impensa grandi refeci
sine ulla inscriptione nominis mei. 2 rivos aquarum compluribus locis
vetustate labentes refeci, et aquam, quae Marcia appellatur, duplicavi
fonte novo in rivum eius inmisso. 3 forum Iulium et basilicam,
quae fuit inter aedem Castoris et aedem Saturni, coepta profligata-
que opera a patre meo, perfeci et eandem basilicam consumptam incendio, ampliato eius solo, sub titulo nominis filiorum m[eorum i]n-

c. 18.

[ἀπ' ἐκ]είνου τ[ο]ῦ ἐνιαυτοῦ, ἐξ οὗ Ναῖος καὶ Πόπλιος | Λέντλοι ὕπατοι ἐγένοντο, ὅτε ὑπέλειπον αἱ δη|μόσιαι πρόσοδοι, ἄλλοτε μὲν δέκα μυριάσιν, ἄλ|[λοτε] δὲ πλείοσιν σειτικὰς καὶ ἀργυρικὰς συντάξεις || ἐκ τῆς ἐμῆς ὑπάρξεως ἔδωκα. | X

c. 19.

βουλευτήριον καὶ τὸ πλησίον αὐτῶι Χαλκιδικόν, | ναόν τε Ἀπόλλωνος ἐν Παλατίωι σὺν στοαῖς, | ναὸν θεοῦ Ἰουλίου, Πανὸς ἱερόν, στοὰν πρὸς ἱπ||ποδρόμωι τῶι προσαγορευομένωι Φλαμινίωι, ἣν | εἴασα προσαγορεύεσθαι ἐξ ὀνόματος ἐκείνου Ὀκτα|ουΐαν, ὃς πρῶτος αὐτὴν ἀνέστησεν, ναὸν πρὸς τῶι | μεγάλωι ἱπποδρόμωι, ναοὺς ἐν Καπιτωλίωι | Διὸς Τροπαιοφόρου καὶ Διὸς Βροντησίου, ναὸν || Κυρείνου, ναοὺς Ἀθηνᾶς καὶ Ἥρας Βασιλίδος καὶ | Διὸς Ἐλευθερίου ἐν Ἀουεντίνωι, ἡρώων πρὸς τῆι | ἱερᾶι ὁδῶι, θεῶν κατοικιδίων ἐν Οὐελίαι, ναὸν Νεό|τητος, ναὸν Μητρὸς θεῶν ἐν Παλατίωι ἐπόησα. |

c. 20.

Καπιτώλιον καὶ τὸ Πομπηΐου θέατρον ἑκάτερον || τὸ ἔργον ἀναλώμασιν μεγίστοις ἐπεσκεύασα ἄ|νευ ἐπιγραφῆς τοῦ ἐμοῦ ὀνόματος. ἀγωγοὺς ὑ|δάτω[ν ἐν πλεί]στοις τόποις τῆι παλαιότητι ὀλισ|θάνοντας ἐπεσκεύασα καὶ ὕδωρ τὸ καλούμενον | Μάρτιον ἐδίπλωσα πηγὴν νέαν εἰς τὸ ῥεῖθρον || [αὐτοῦ ἐποχετεύσ]ας. ἀγορὰν Ἰουλίαν καὶ βασι-|λικήν, ἥτις ἦν μετα[ξὺ τ]οῦ τε ναοῦ τῶν Διοσκό|[ρω]ν καὶ τοῦ Κρόνου, προκαταβεβλημένα ἔργα ὑπὸ τοῦ | [πατρός μου, ἐτελείωσα] καὶ τὴν αὐτὴν βασιλικὴν | [κατακαυθεῖσαν ἐν αὐξηθέντι] ἐδάφει αὐτῆς ἐξ ἐπι||γραφῆς ὀνόματος τῶν ἐμῶν υἱῶν ὑπ[ηρξάμη]ν, | καὶ εἰ μὴ αὐτὸς XI

cohavi et, si vivus non perfecissem, perfici ab heredibus [meis ius]si. 4 duo et octoginta templa deum in urbe consul sex[tu]m ex [auctori]tate senatus refeci nullo praetermisso quod e[o] tempore [refici debeba]t. 5 consul septimum viam Flaminiam a[b urbe] Ari[minum refeci pontes]que omnes praeter Mulvium et Minucium.

c. 21.

in privato solo Martis Ultoris templum [f]orumque Augustum [ex ma]n[i]biis feci. theatrum ad aedem Apollinis in solo magna ex parte a p[r]i[v]atis empto feci, quod sub nomine M. Marcell[i] generi mei esset. 2 don[a e]x manibiis in Capitolio et in aede divi Iu[l]i et in aede Apollinis et in aede Vestae et in templo Martis Ultoris consacravi, quae mihi constiterunt HS circiter milliens. 3 auri coronari pondo triginta et quinque millia municipiis et colonis Italiae conferentibus ad triumpho[s] meos quintum consul remisi, et postea, quotienscumque imperator a[ppe]llatus sum, aurum coronarium non accepi decernentibus municipii[s] et colonis aequ[e] beni[g]ne adque antea decreverant.

c. 22.

ter munus gladiatorium dedi meo nomine et quinquiens filiorum meorum aut n[e]potum nomine, quibus muneribus depugnaverunt hominum ci[rc]iter decem millia. bis athletarum undique accitorum spectaculu[m] p[o]pulo pra[ebui me]o nomine et tertium nepo[tis] mei no-

τετελειώκ[ο]ι[μι, τ]ελε[ι]ω[θῆναι ὑπὸ] | τῶν ἐμῶν κληρονόμων ἐπέταξα. δ[ύ]ο [καὶ ὀγδο]|ήκοντα ναοὺς ἐν τῆι πόλ[ει ἕκτ]ον ὕπ[ατος δόγμα]||τι συνκ[λ]ήτου ἐπεσκεύασ[α] ο[ὐ]δένα π[ε]ριλ[ιπών, ὃς] | ἐκείνωι τῶι χρόνωι ἐπισκευῆς ἐδεῖτο. [ὕ]πα[τος ἕ]|βδ[ο]μον ὁδὸν Φ[λαμινίαν ἀπὸ] Ῥώμης [εἰς Ἀρίμινον] | γ[εφ]ύρας τε τὰς ἐν αὐτῆι πάσας ἔξω δυεῖν τῶν μὴ | ἐπ[ι]δεομένων ἐπ[ι]σκευῆς ἐπόησα. ||

c. 21.

ἐν ἰδιωτικῶι ἐδάφει Ἄρεως Ἀμύντορος ἀγοράν τε Σε|βαστὴν ἐκ λαφύρων ἐπόησα. θέατρον πρὸς τῶι Ἀπόλ|λωνος ναῶι ἐπὶ ἐδάφους ἐκ πλείστου μέρους ἀγο|ρασθέντος ἀνήγειρα ἐπὶ ὀνόματος Μαρκέλλου | τοῦ γαμβροῦ μου. ἀναθέματα ἐκ λαφύρων ἐν Καπι||τωλίωι καὶ ναῶι Ἰουλίωι καὶ ναῶι Ἀπόλλωνος | καὶ Ἑστίας καὶ Ἄ[ρεω]ς ἀφιέρωσα, ἃ ἐμοὶ κατέστη | ἐνγὺς μυριάδω[ν δι]σχε[ι]λίων πεντακ[οσίων]. | εἰς χρυσοῦν στέφανον λειτρῶν τρισ[μυρίων] | πεντακισχειλίων καταφερούσαις ταῖς ἐν Ἰταλί||αι πολειτείαις καὶ ἀποικίαις συνεχώρη[σ]α τὸ [πέμ]|πτον ὑπατεύων, καὶ ὕστερον, ὁσάκις αὐτοκράτωρ | προσηγορεύθην, τὰς εἰς τὸν στέφανον ἐπαγγε|λίας οὐκ ἔλαβον ψηφιζομένων τῶν π[ολειτει]ῶν | καὶ ἀποικιῶν μετὰ τῆς αὐτῆς προθυμίας ὡς τὸ || α[ὐτὸ πρὶν ἐψηφίσαντο]. | XII

c. 22.

[τρὶς μ]ονομαχίας ἔδωκα τῶι ἐμῶι ὀνόματι καὶ | πεν[τάκις τῶν υἱῶν μου ἢ υἱ]ωνῶν, ἐν αἷς μονο|μαχίαις ἐπύκτευσαν ὡς μύρι[ο]ι. δὶς ἀθλητῶ[ν] παν||τ[όθεν] μετακεκλημένων τὴν τοῦ ἀγῶνος θέαν | τῶι δήμ[ωι π]αρέσχον τ[ῶι ἐ]μῶι ὀνόματι καὶ τρίτον | τοῦ ἐμοῦ

mine. **2** ludos feci m[eo no]m[ine] quater, aliorum autem m[agist]ratuum vicem ter et viciens. [pr]o conlegio XV virorum magis[ter con]legii collega M. Agrippa lu[dos s]aeclares C. Furnio C. Silano cos. [feci]. [c]onsul XIII ludos | Mar[tia]les pr[imus fec]i, quos p[ost i]d tempus deinceps ins[equen]ti[bus] | annis [s. c. et lege fe]cerunt [co]n[su]les. **3** [ven]ation[es] best[ia]rum Africanarum meo nomine aut filio[ru]m meorum et nepotum in ci[r]co aut in foro aut in amphitheatris popul[o d]edi sexiens et viciens, quibus confecta sunt bestiarum circiter tria m[ill]ia et quingentae.

c. 23.

navalis proeli spectaclum populo de[di tr]ans Tiberim, in quo loco nunc nemus est Caesarum, cavato [s]olo in longitudinem mille et octingentos pedes, in latitudine[m mille] e[t] ducenti. in quo triginta rostratae naves triremes a[ut birem]es, plures autem minores inter se conflixerunt. q[uibu]s in classibus pugnaverunt praeter remiges millia ho[minum tr]ia circiter.

c. 24.

in templis omnium civitatium prov[inci]ae Asiae victor ornamenta reposui, quae spoliatis tem[plis i]s, cum quo bellum gesseram, privatim possederat. **2** statuae [mea]e pedestres et equestres et in quadrigeis argenteae steterunt in urbe XXC circiter, quas ipse sustuli exque ea pecunia dona aurea in aede Apollinis meo nomine et illorum, qui mihi statuarum honorem habuerunt, posui.

c. 25.

mare pacavi a praedonibus. eo bello servorum, qui fugerant a V dominis suis et arma contra rem publicam ceperant, triginta fere millia capta

υἱωνοῦ. θέας ἐποίησα δι' ἐμοῦ τετράκ[ις], | διὰ δὲ τῶν ἄλλων ἀρχῶν ἐν μέρει τρὶς καὶ εἰκοσάκις. | ὑπὲρ τῶν δεκαπέντε [ἀνδρ]ῶν ἔχων συνάρχοντα || Μᾶρκον Ἀγρίππαν θέας τὰς διὰ ἑκατὸν ἐτῶν γεινο|μένας ὀν[ομαζομένα]ς σαικλάρεις ἐποίησα Γαΐωι | Φουρνίωι καὶ Γαΐωι Σε[ι]λανῶι ὑπάτοις. ὕπατος τρεισ|καιδέκατον θέας Ἄρει πρῶτος ἐποίησα, ἃς μετ' ἐ|κεῖνο[ν χ]ρόνον ἑξῆς [τοῖς μ]ετέπειτα ἐνιαυτοῖς || δόγματι συνκλήτου καὶ νόμωι ἐπόησαν οἱ ὕπα|[τοι. θηρομαχίας τῶι δήμωι τῶν] ἐκ Λιβύης θηρίων ἐ|μῶι ὀνόματι ἢ υἱῶν ἢ υἱων[ῶν ἐν τῶι ἱπποδρόμωι | ἢ ἐν τῆι ἀγορᾶι ἢ ἐν τοῖς] ἀμφιθεάτροις ἔδωκα | ἑξάκις καὶ εἰκοσάκις, ἐν [αἷς κατεσφάγη θηρία] || ἐνγὺς [τρισχείλια] καὶ πεντακόσια. |

c. 23.

ναυμαχίας θέαν τῶι δήμ[ωι ἔδω]κα πέ[ρ]αν τοῦ Τι|[βέριδος, ἐν ὧι τό]πω[ι] νῦν ἐστιν ἄλσος Καισάρων | ἐκκεχωσμ[ένης τῆς γῆς] ε[ἰ]ς μῆκ[ο]ς χειλίων ὀκτακο|σίων ποδῶν, εἰς πλάτος χειλίων διακο[σ]ίων. ἐν ἧι || τριάκο[ν]τα ναῦς ἔμβολα ἔχουσαι τριήρεις ἢ δί|κροτοι, αἱ δὲ XIII
ἥσσονες πλείους ἐναυμάχησαν. | ἐν τ[ούτωι] τῶι στόλωι ἠγωνίσαντο ἔξω τῶν ἐρετῶν | πρόσπου ἄνδρες τρ[ι]σχ[ε]ί[λ]ιοι. ||

c. 24.

[εἰς ν]αοὺς πασῶν πόλεων τῆς Ἀσίας νεικήσας τὰ ἀναθέ|[ματα ἀπ]οκατέστησα, [ἃ] κατεσχήκει ἱεροσυλήσας ὁ | ὑπ' ἐμοῦ καταγωνισθεὶς πολέ[μιος]. ἀνδριάντες πε|ζοὶ καὶ ἔφιπποί μου καὶ ἐφ' ἅρμασιν ἀργυροῖ εἱστήκει|σαν ἐν τῆι πόλει ἐνγὺς ὀγδοήκοντα, οὓς αὐτὸς ἦρα, || ἐκ τούτου τε τοῦ χρήματος ἀναθέματα χρυσᾶ ἐν | τῶι ναῶι τοῦ Ἀπόλλωνος τῶι τε ἐμῶι ὀνόματι καὶ | ἐκείνων, οἵτινές με [τ]ούτοις τοῖς ἀνδριᾶσιν ἐτείμη|σαν, ἀνέθηκα. |

c. 25.

θάλασσα[ν] πειρατευομένην ὑπὸ ἀποστατῶν δού||λων [εἰ]ρήνευσα· ἐξ ὧν τρεῖς που μυριάδας τοῖς | δε[σπόται]ς εἰς κόλασιν παρέδωκα.

dominis ad supplicium sumendum tradidi. **2** iuravit in mea ver[ba] tota Italia sponte sua, et me be[lli], quo vici ad Actium, ducem depoposcit. iuraverunt in eadem ver[ba provi]nciae Galliae, Hispaniae, Africa, Sicilia, Sardinia. **3** qui sub [signis meis tum] militaverint, fuerunt senatores plures quam DCC, in ii[s, qui vel antea vel pos]tea consules facti sunt ad eum diem, quo scripta su[nt haec, LXXXIII, sacerdo]tes ci[rc]iter CLXX.

c. 26.

omnium prov[inciarum populi Romani], quibus finitimae fuerunt gentes, quae non p[arerent imperio nos]tro, fines auxi. **2** Gallias et Hispanias provincias, i[tem Germaniam, qua inclu]dit Oceanus a Gadibus ad ostium Albis flumin[is pacavi. **3** Alpes a re]gione ea, quae proxima est Hadriano mari, [ad Tuscum pacificav]i nulli genti bello per iniuriam inlato. **4** cla[ssis m]ea p[er Oceanum] ab ostio Rheni ad solis orientis regionem usque ad fi[nes Cimbroru]m navigavit, quo neque terra neque mari quisquam Romanus ante id tempus adit, Cimbrique et Charydes et Semnones et eiusdem tractus alii Germanorum popu[l]i per legatos amicitiam meam et populi Romani petierunt. **5** meo iussu et auspicio ducti sunt [duo] exercitus eodem fere tempore in Aethiopiam et in Ar[a]biam, quae appel[latur] Eudaemon, [magn]aeque hos[t]ium gentis utr[iu]sque cop[iae] caesae sunt in acie et [c]om[plur]a oppida capta. in Aethiopiam usque ad oppi-

ὤμοσεν | εἰς τοὺς ἐμοὺς λόγους ἅπασα ἡ Ἰταλία ἑκοῦσα κά||[μὲ πολέμου], ὧι ἐπ' Ἀκτίωι ἐνείκησα, ἡγεμόνα ἐξη<ι>|[τήσατο. ὤ]μοσαν εἰς τοὺς [αὐτοῦ]ς λόγους ἐπαρ||χεῖαι Γαλατία, Ἱσπανία, Λιβύη, Σι[κελία, Σαρ]δώ. οἱ ὑπ' ἐ|μ[αῖς σημέαις τό]τε στρατευ[σάμε]νοι ἦσαν συνκλητι|κοὶ πλε[ίους ἑπτ]α[κοσί]ων· [ἐ]ν [αὐτοῖς οἳ ἢ πρότερον ἢ | μετέπει]τα ἐγένοντο ὕπατοι ἄχρι ἐ[κ]ε[ί]ν[ης τῆς ἡ]μέ||[ρας, ἐν ἧι ταῦτα γέγραπτα]ι, ὀ[γδοή]κοντα τρεῖς, ἱερεῖς || πρόσπου ἑκατὸν XIV ἑβδομή[κ]οντα. |

c. 26.

πασῶν ἐπαρχειῶν δήμο[υ Ῥω]μαίων, αἷς ὅμορα | ἦν ἔθνη τὰ μὴ ὑποτασσ[όμ]ενα τῆι ἡμετέραι ἡ|γεμονία<ι>, τοὺς ὅρους ἐπεύξ[ησ]α. Γαλατίας καὶ Ἰσ||πανίας, ὁμοίως δὲ καὶ Γερμανίαν, καθὼς Ὠκεα|νὸς περικλείει ἀπ[ὸ] Γαδε[ίρ]ων μέχρι στόματος | Ἄλβιος ποταμο[ῦ ἐν] εἰρήνη<ι> κατέστησα. Ἄλπης ἀπὸ | κλίματος τοῦ πλησίον Εἰονίου κόλπου μέχρι Τυρ|ρηνικῆς θαλάσσης εἰρηνεύσθαι πεπόηκα, οὐδενὶ || ἔθνει ἀδίκως ἐπενεχθέντος πολέμου. στόλος | ἐμὸς διὰ Ὠκεανοῦ ἀπὸ στόματος Ῥήνου ὡς πρὸς | ἀνατολὰς μέχρι ἔθνους Κίμβρων διέπλευσεν, οὗ οὔ|τε κατὰ γῆν οὔτε κατὰ θάλασσαν Ῥωμαίων τις πρὸ | τούτου τοῦ χρόνου προσῆλθεν· καὶ Κίμβροι καὶ Χάλυ||βες καὶ Σέμνονες ἄλλα τε πολλὰ ἔθνη Γερμανῶν | διὰ πρεσβειῶν τὴν ἐμὴν φιλίαν καὶ τὴν δήμου Ῥω|μαίων ἠ<ι>τήσαντο. ἐμῆι ἐπιταγῆι καὶ οἰωνοῖς αἰσί|οις δύο στρατεύματα ἐπέβη Αἰθιοπίαι καὶ Ἀραβίαι | τῆι Εὐδαίμονι καλουμένηι, μεγάλας τε τῶν πο||λεμίων δυνάμεις κατέκοψεν ἐν παρατάξει καὶ | πλείστας πόλεις δοριαλώτους ἔλαβεν καὶ προ|έβη ἐν Αἰθιοπίαι

dum Nabata pervent[um] est, cui proxima est Meroe. in Arabiam usque
in fines Sabaeorum pro[cess]it exercitus ad oppidum Mariba.

c. 27.

Aegyptum imperio populi [Ro]mani adieci. 2 Armeniam maiorem interfecto rege eius Artaxe c[u]m possem facere provinciam, malui maiorum
nostrorum exemplo regn[u]m id Tigrani regis Artavasdis filio, nepoti autem Tigranis regis, per T[i. Ne]ronem trad[er]e, qui tum mihi priv[ig]nus erat.
et eandem gentem postea d[e]sciscentem et rebellantem domit[a]m per Gaium
filium meum regi Ariobarzani regis Medorum Artaba[zi] filio regen-
dam tradidi et post eius mortem filio eius Artavasdi. quo interfecto Tig[ra]-
ne⟨m⟩, qui erat ex regio genere Armeniorum oriundus, in id regnum misi. 3 provincias omnis, quae trans Hadrianum mare vergunt ad orien[te]m, Cyre-
nasque, iam ex parte magna regibus ea possidentibus, et antea Siciliam et
Sardiniam occupatas bello servili reciperavi.

c. 28.

colonias in Africa, Sicilia, [M]acedonia, utraque Hispania, Achai[a], Asia, S[y]ria,
Gallia Narbonensi, Pi[si]dia militum deduxi. 2 Italia autem XXVIII [colo]ni-
as, quae vivo me celeberrimae et frequentissimae fuerunt, me[a auctoritate]
deductas habet.

c. 29.

signa militaria complur[a per] alios d[u]ces am[issa] devicti[s hostibu]s re[cepi]
ex Hispania et [Gallia et a Dalm]ateis. 2 Parthos trium exercitum Romano-

μέχρι πόλεως Ναβάτης, ἥτις | ἐστὶν ἔνγιστα Μερόη<ι>, ἐν Ἀραβίαι δὲ μέχρι πόλε|ως Μαρίβας. ||

c. 27.

Αἴγυπτον δήμου Ῥωμαίων ἡγεμονίαι προσέθηκα. | Ἀρμενίαν τὴν XV
μ[εί]ζονα ἀναιρεθέντος τοῦ βασιλέ|ως δυνάμενος ἐπαρχείαν ποῆσαι μᾶλλον ἐβου|λήθην κατὰ τὰ πάτρια ἡμῶν ἔθη βασιλείαν Τιγρά||νηι Ἀρταουάσδου υἱῶι, υἱωνῶι δὲ Τιγράνου βασι|λέως, δ[ο]ῦν[α]ι διὰ Τιβερίου Νέρωνος, ὃς τότε μου | πρόγονος ἦν· καὶ τὸ αὐτὸ ἔθνος ἀφιστάμενον καὶ | ἀναπολεμοῦν δαμασθὲν ὑπὸ Γαΐου τοῦ υἱοῦ | μου βασιλεῖ Ἀριοβαρζάνει, βασιλέως Μήδων Ἀρτα||βάζου υἱῶι, παρέδωκα, καὶ μετὰ τὸν ἐκείνου θάνα|τον τῶι υἱῶι αὐτοῦ Ἀρταουάσδη<ι>· οὗ ἀναιρεθέντος | Τιγράνην, ὃς ἦν ἐκ γένους Ἀρμενίου βασιλικοῦ, εἰς | τὴν βασιλείαν ἔπεμψα. ἐπαρχείας ἁπάσας, ὅσαι | πέραν τοῦ Εἰονίου κόλπου διατείνουσι πρὸς ἀνα||τολάς, καὶ Κυρήνην ἐκ μείσζονος μέρους ὑπὸ βασι|λέων κατεσχημένας καὶ ἔμπροσθεν Σικελίαν καὶ Σαρ|δὼ{ι} προκατειλημ<μ>ένας πολέμωι δουλικῶι ἀνέλαβον. |

c. 28.

ἀποικίας ἐν Λιβύηι, Σικελίαι, Μακεδονίαι, ἐν ἑκατέ|ρα<ι> τε Ἱσπανίαι, Ἀχαίαι, Ἀσίαι, Συρία<ι>, Γαλατίαι τῆι πε||ρὶ Νάρβωνα, Πισιδίαι στρατιωτῶν κατήγαγον. Ἰτα|λία δὲ εἴκοσι ὀκτὼ ἀποικίας ἔχει ὑπ' ἐμοῦ καταχθεί|σας, αἳ ἐμοῦ περιόντος πληθύουσαι ἐτύνχανον. |

c. 29.

σημέας στρατιωτικὰς [πλείστας ὑ]πὸ ἄλλων ἡγεμό|νων ἀποβεβλημένας [νικῶν τοὺ]ς πολεμίους || ἀπέλαβον ἐξ Ἱσπανίας καὶ Γαλατίας XVI
καὶ παρὰ | Δαλματῶν. Πάρθους τριῶν στρατευμάτων Ῥωμαί|ων

rum spolia et signa re[ddere] mihi supplicesque amicitiam populi Romani
petere coegi. ea autem si[gn]a in penetrali, quod e[s]t in templo Martis Ultoris,
reposui.

c. 30.

Pannoniorum gentes, qua[s a]nte me principem populi Romani exercitus nunquam adit, devictas per Ti. [Ne]ronem, qui tum erat privignus et legatus meus,
imperio populi Romani s[ubie]ci protulique fines Illyrici ad r[ip]am fluminis
Dan[u]i. **2** citr[a] quod [D]a[cor]u[m tr]an[s]gressus exercitus meis a[u]sp[icis vict]us profliga-
tusque [es]t, et pos[tea tran]s Dan[u]vium ductus ex[ercitus me]u[s] Da[cor]um
gentes im[peri]a p[opuli]R[omani perferre coegit].

c. 31.

ad me ex In[dia regum legationes saepe missae sunt non visae ante id t]em[pus]
apud qu[em]q[uam] R[omanorum du]cem. **2** nostram amic[itiam appetive]run[t]
per legat[os] B[a]starn[ae Scythae]que et Sarmatarum qui su[nt citra fl]umen
Tanaim [et] ultra reg[es, Alba]norumque rex et Hiberorum e[t Medorum].

c. 32.

ad me supplices confug[erunt] reges Parthorum Tirida[te]s et post[ea] Phrat[es]
regis Phrati[s] filiu[s], Medorum Ar[tavasdes, Adiabenorum A]rtaxa- VI
res, Britann[o]rum Dumnobellaunus et Tin[commius, Sugambr]orum
Maelo, Mar[c]omanorum Sueborum [. . . rus]. **2** ad [me re]x Parthorum
Phrates Orod[i]s filius filios suos nepot[esque omnes] misit in Italiam non

σκῦλα καὶ σημέας ἀποδοῦναι ἐμοὶ ἱκέτας τε φι|λίαν δήμου Ῥωμαίων ἀξιῶσαι ἠνάγκασα. ταύτας || δὲ τὰς σημέας ἐν τῶι Ἄρεως τοῦ Ἀμύντορος ναοῦ ἀ|δύτωι ἀπεθέμην. |

c. 30.

Παννονίων ἔθνη, οἷς πρὸ ἐμοῦ ἡγεμόνος στράτευ|μα Ῥωμαίων οὐκ ἤνγισεν, ἡσσηθέντα ὑπὸ Τιβερίου | Νέρωνος, ὃς τότε μου ἦν πρόγονος καὶ πρεσβευτής, || ἡγεμονίαι δήμου Ῥωμαίων ὑπέταξα τά τε Ἰλλυρι-|κοῦ ὅρια μέχρι Ἴστρου ποταμοῦ προήγαγον. οὗ ἐπει|τάδε Δάκων διαβᾶσα πολλὴ δύναμις ἐμοῖς αἰσίοις οἰω|νοῖς κατεκόπη, καὶ ὕστερον μεταχθὲν τὸ ἐμὸν στρά|τευμα πέραν Ἴστρου τὰ Δάκων ἔθνη προστάγματα || δήμου Ῥωμαίων ὑπομένειν ἠνάγκασεν. |

c. 31.

πρὸς ἐμὲ ἐξ Ἰνδίας βασιλέων πρεσβεῖαι πολλάκις ἀπε|στάλησαν, οὐδέποτε πρὸ τούτου χρόνου ὀφθεῖσαι παρὰ | Ῥωμαίων ἡγεμόνι. τὴν ἡμετέραν φιλίαν ἠξίωσαν | διὰ πρέσβεων Βαστάρναι καὶ Σκύθαι καὶ Σαρμα||τῶν οἱ ἐπιτάδε ὄντες τοῦ Τανάιδος ποταμοῦ καὶ | οἱ πέραν δὲ βασιλεῖς, καὶ Ἀλβανῶν δὲ καὶ Ἰβήρων | καὶ Μήδων βασιλέες. |

c. 32.

πρὸς ἐμὲ ἱκέται κατέφυγον βασιλεῖς Πάρθων μὲν | Τειριδάτης καὶ μετέπειτα Φραάτης, βασιλέως || Φράτου [υἱός, Μ]ήδ[ων] δὲ Ἀρτα- XVII
ο[υάσδ]ης, Ἀδιαβ[η]|νῶν [Ἀ]ρτα[ξάρης, Βριτ]ανῶν Δομνοελλαῦνος | καὶ Τ[ινκόμμιος, Σο]υ[γ]άμβρων [Μ]αίλων, Μαρκο|μάνων [Σουήβων . . .]ρος. [πρὸ]ς ἐμὲ βασιλε<ὺ>ς || Πάρθων Φρα[άτης Ὠρώδο]υ υἱὸ[ς υ]ἱοὺς [αὐτοῦ] υἱω|νούς τε πάντας ἔπεμψεν εἰς Ἰταλίαν, οὐ πολέμωι |

bello superatu[s], sed amicitiam nostram per [libe]ror[um] suorum pignora petens 3 plurimaeque aliae gentes exper[tae sunt p. R.] fidem me principe, quibus antea cum populo Roman[o nullum extitera]t legationum et amicitiae [c]ommercium.

c. 33.

a me gentes Parthorum et Medoru[m per legatos] principes earum gentium reges pet[i]tos acceperunt: Par[thi Vononem, regis Phr]atis filium, regis Orodis nepotem, Medi Arioba[rzanem], regis Artavazdis filium, regis Ariobarzanis nepotem.

c. 34.

in consulatu sexto et septimo, po[stquam b]ella [civil]ia exstinxeram, per consensum universorum [potitus reru]m om[n]ium, rem publicam ex mea potestate in senat[us populique Rom]ani [a]rbitrium transtuli. 2 quo pro merito meo senatu[s consulto Au]gust[us appe]llatus sum et laureis postes aedium mearum v[estiti] publ[ice coronaq]ue civica super ianuam meam fixa est [et clu]peus [aureu]s in [c]uria Iulia positus, quem mihi senatum pop[ulumq]ue Rom[anu]m dare virtutis clement[iaeque e]t iustitiae et pieta[tis caus]sa testatu[m] est pe[r e]ius clupei [inscription]em. 3 post id tem[pus a]uctoritate [omnibus praestiti, potes][t]atis au[tem n]ihilo ampliu[s habu]i quam cet[eri, qui m]ihi quoque in ma[gis]tra[t]u conlegae f[uerunt].

c. 35.

tertium dec[i]mum consulatu[m cum gereba]m, sena[tus et e]quester ordo

λειφθείς, ἀλλὰ τὴν ἡμ[ε]τέραν φιλίαν ἀξιῶν ἐπὶ τέ|κνων ἐνεχύροις. πλεῖστά τε ἄλλα ἔθνη πεῖραν ἔλ[α]||βεν δήμου Ῥωμαίων πίστεως ἐπ' ἐμοῦ ἡγεμόνος, || οἷς τὸ πρὶν οὐδεμία ἦν πρὸς δῆμον Ῥωμαίων π[ρε]σ-|βειῶν καὶ φιλίας κοινωνία. |

c. 33.

παρ' ἐμοῦ ἔθνη Πάρθων καὶ Μήδων διὰ πρέσβεων τῶν | παρ' αὐτοῖς πρώτων βασιλεῖς αἰτησάμενοι ἔλαβ[ον]· | Πάρθοι Οὐονώνην, βασιλέως Φράτου υ[ἱ]όν, βασιλ[έω]ς || Ὠρώδου υἱωνόν, Μῆδοι Ἀριοβαρζάνην, βα[σ]ιλέως | Ἀρταβάζου υἱόν, βασιλέως Ἀριοβαρζάν[ου υἱω]νόν. |

c. 34.

ἐν ὑπατείαι ἕκτηι καὶ ἑβδόμηι μετὰ τὸ τοὺς ἐνφυ|λίους ζβέσαι με πολέμους, [κ]ατὰ τὰς εὐχὰς τῶν ἐ|μῶν πολε[ι]τῶν ἐνκρατὴς γενόμενος πάντων τῶν || πραγμάτων, ἐκ τῆς ἐμῆς ἐξουσίας εἰς τὴν τῆς συν|κλήτου καὶ τοῦ δήμου τῶν Ῥωμαίων μετήνεγκα | κυριήαν. ἐξ ἧς αἰτίας δόγματι συνκλήτου Σεβαστὸς | προσ[ηγορε]ύθην καὶ δάφναις δημοσίαι τὰ πρόπυ|λ[ά μου ἐστέφθ]η, ὅ τε δρύινος στέφανος ὁ διδόμενος || ἐπὶ XVIII
σωτηρία<ι> τῶν πολειτῶν ὑπερά[ν]ω τοῦ πυλῶ|νος τῆς ἐμῆς οἰκίας ἀνετέθη ὅπ[λ]ον τε χρυ|σοῦν ἐν τῶι βο[υ]λευτηρίωι ἀνατεθ[έ]ν ὑπό τε τῆς | συνκλήτου καὶ τοῦ δήμου τῶν Ῥω[μα]ίων διὰ τῆς || ἐπιγραφῆς ἀρετὴν καὶ ἐπείκειαν κα[ὶ δ]ικαιοσύνην | καὶ εὐσέβειαν ἐμοὶ μαρτυρεῖ. ἀξιώμ[α]τι πάντων | διήνεγκα, ἐξουσίας δὲ οὐδέν τι πλεῖον ἔσχον | τῶν συναρξάντων μοι. |

c. 35.

τρισκαιδεκάτην ὑπατείαν ἄγοντός μου ἥ τε σύν||κλητος καὶ τὸ

populusq[ue] Romanus universus [appell]av[it me pat]re[m p]atriae idque
in vestibu[lo a]edium mearum inscribendum et in c[u]ria [Iulia e]t in foro Aug.
sub quadrig[i]s, quae mihi ex s. c. pos[it]ae [sunt, censuit. **2** cum scri]psi haec,
annum agebam septuagensu[mum sextum].

app. **1.**
summa pecun[i]ae, quam ded[it vel in aera]rium [vel plebei Romanae vel di]mis-
sis militibus: denarium sexien[s milliens].

app. 2.
opera fecit nova aedem Martis, [Iovis] Ton[antis et Feretri, Apollinis],
divi Iuli, Quirini, Minervae, [Iunonis Reginae, Iovis Libertatis],
Larum, deum Penatium, Iuv[entatis, Matris Magnae, Lupercal, pulvina]r
ad circum, curiam cum Ch[alcidico, forum Augustum, basilica]m
Iuliam, theatrum Marcelli, [p]or[ticum Octaviam, nemus trans T]iberim
Caesarum.

app. 3.
refecit Capito[lium sacra]sque aedes [nu]m[ero octoginta] duas, thea[t]rum Pom-
pei, aqu[arum r]iv[os, vi]am Flamin[iam].

app. 4.
impensa p[raestita in spec]tacul[a] sca[enica et munera] gladiatorum at-
[que athletas et venationes et] naumachi[am] et donata pe[c]unia [colo]-
[nis, municipiis, oppidis] terrae motu incendioque consum-
pt[is] a[ut viritim] a[micis senat]oribusque, quorum census explevit,
in[n]umera[bilis].

ἱππικὸν τάγμα ὅ τε σύνπας δῆμος τῶν | Ῥωμαίων προσηγόρευσέ με πατέρα πατρίδος καὶ τοῦτο | ἐπὶ τοῦ προπύλου τῆς οἰκίας μου καὶ ἐν τῶι βουλευτη|ρίωι καὶ ἐν τῆι ἀγορᾶι τῆι Σεβαστῆι ὑπὸ τῶι ἅρματι, ὅ μοι | δόγματι συνκλήτου ἀνετέθη, ἐπιγραφῆναι ἐψηφίσα||το. ὅτε ἔγραφον ταῦτα, ἦγον ἔτος ἑβδομηκοστὸν | ἕκτον. |

app. 1.

συνκεφαλαίωσις ἠριθμημένου χρήματος εἰς τὸ αἰρά|ριον ἢ εἰς τὸν δῆμον τὸν Ῥω[μαί]ων ἢ εἰς τοὺς ἀπολε|λυμένους στρατιώτας· ἓξ μυριάδες μυριάδων. ||

app. 2.

ἔργα καινὰ ἐγένετο ὑπ' αὐτοῦ ναοὶ μὲν Ἄρεως, Διὸς | Βροντησίου καὶ Τροπαιοφόρου, Πανός, Ἀπόλλω|νος, θεοῦ Ἰουλίου, Κυρείνου, Ἀ[θη]νᾶς, Ἥρας βασιλί|δος, Διὸς Ἐλευθερίου, ἡρώ[ων, θεῶν π]α-τρίων, Νε|ότητος, Μητρὸς θεῶν, β[ουλευτήριον] σὺν Χαλκι||δικῶι, XIX ἀγορὰ{ι} Σεβαστὴ{ι}, θέατρον Μαρκέλλου, β[α]σι|λικὴ Ἰουλία, ἄλσος Καισάρων, στοαὶ ἐ[ν] Παλατ[ί]ωι, | στοὰ ἐν ἱπποδρόμωι Φλαμινίωι.

app. 3.

ἐπεσκευάσθ[η τὸ Κα]|πιτώλιον, ναοὶ ὀγδοήκοντα δύο, θέ[ατ]ρον Π[ομ]||πηΐου, ὁδὸς Φλαμινία, ἀγωγοὶ ὑδάτων.

app. 4.

[δαπ]άναι δὲ | εἰς θέας καὶ μονομάχους καὶ ἀθλητὰς καὶ ναυμα|χίαν καὶ θηρομαχίαν δωρεαί [τε] ἀποικίαις πόλεσιν | ἐν Ἰταλίαι, πόλεσιν ἐν ἐπαρχείαις σεισμῶι κα[ὶ] ἐνπυ|ρισμοῖς πεπονηκυίαις ἢ κατ' ἄνδρα φίλοις καὶ συν||κλητικοῖς, ὧν τὰς τειμήσεις προσεξεπλήρωσεν, ἄ|πειρον πλῆθος.

II

FASTI. CALENDARS

THE FASTI

THE list of consuls has been conflated from all the epigraphic *fasti*, now published together by A. Degrassi in *Inscriptiones Italiae*, vol. xiii, fasc. I (Rome, 1947). Names or portions of names surviving in any of the *fasti* are printed in ordinary type, portions of names which have perished in square brackets. In round brackets we have added any names or portions of names, known from other sources, which do not appear in the existing *fasti*. The note 'no *suffecti*' has been added under any year in which *fasti* normally including *suffecti* survive, but do not record any *suffecti* for that year. For convenience of reference we have appended to the dates the numbers of the *tribunicia potestas* of Augustus, Agrippa, Tiberius, Drusus, and Gaius. The number recorded is that upon which the person concerned entered during the year in question, e.g. 20 B.C. (Aug. IV) means that in 20 B.C. Augustus completed his third and entered his fourth year of tribunician power.

The following abbreviations are used:

Amit. = fasti Amiternini
Ant. Min. = fasti Antiates minores
Arv. = fasti Arvalium
Cap. = fasti Capitolini consulares
Col. = fasti Colotiani
Cupr. = fasti Cuprenses
Gab. = fasti Gabini
Lat. = fasti feriarum Latinarum
Mag. = fasti magistrorum vici
Ost. = fasti Ostienses
Tr. Barb. = fasti triumphales Barberini
Tr. Cap. = fasti triumphales Capitolini
Ven. = fasti Venusini (*our no.* 323)

43 B.C. C. Vibius C. f. Pansa (Caetronianus): A. Hirtius A. f.
suf. C. Iulius C. f. Caesar
Q. Pedius Q. f.
C. Carrinas C. f.
P. Ventidius P. f.

Col. [M. A]emilius, M. Antonius, imp. Caesar IIIvir. r. p. c. ex a. d. V k. Dec. ad pr. k. Ian. sext.
Amit. bellum in cam[p]is Ph[ilippicis cum] M. Brut[o] e[t C. C]a[ssio]
Tr. Cap. L. Munatius L. f. L. n. Plancus procos. ex Gallia IIII k. Ian. M. Aimilius M. f. Q. n. Lepidus II, IIIvir r. p. [c.] procos. ex Hispania pridie k. [Ian.]

42 B.C. M. Aemilius M. f. [L]epidus II: [L.] Munatius L. f. (Plancus)

no *suffecti*

Col. [C. A]ntonius P. Sulpicius cens. lustr. n. f.
Amit. bellum Perusinu[m cum] L. Ant[o]nio
Tr. Cap. P. Vatinius P. f. procos. de Illurico pr. [k. Sex.]

41 B.C. L. Antonius (M. f. Pietas): P. Servilius P. f. (Vatia Isauricus II)

no *suffecti*

Tr. Cap. L. Antonius M. f. M. n. cos. ex Alpibus [k. Ian.]

40 B.C. Cn. Domitius M. f. (Calvinus II): C. Asinius Cn. f. (Pollio)

suf. L. Cornelius L. f. (Balbus)
P. Canidius P. f. (Crassus)

Tr. Cap. imp. Caesar divi f. ☐C. f.☐ IIIvir r. p. c. ov[ans] quod pacem cum M. Antonio fecit
M. Antonius M. f. M. n. IIIvir r. p. c. ovan[s] quod pacem cum imp. Caesare feci[t]
☐ *engraved after deletion.*

39 B.C. L. Marcius (L. f. Censorinus): C. Calvisius (C. f. Sabinus)

suf. C. Cocceius (Balbus)
P. Alfenus (P. f. Varus)

Tr. Cap. L. Marcius L. f. C. n. Censorinus cos. ex Macedonia k. Ian.
C. Asinius Cn. f. Pollio procos. ex Parthineis VIII k. Novem.
The second item perhaps belongs to 38 B.C.

38 B.C. Ap. Claudius (C. f. Pulcher): C. Norbanus (C. f. Flaccus)

suf. L. Cornelius (Lentulus)
L. Marcius (L. f. Philippus)

Tr. Cap. P. Ventidius P. f. procos. ex Tauro monte et Partheis V k. Decem.

37 B.C. M. Agrippa L. f.: L. Ca[niniu]s (L. f. Gallus)

suf. T. Statilius (T. f. Taurus)

Cap. M. Aimilius M. f. [Q. n. Lepidus II] M. Antonius M. f. [M. n. II] imp. Caesar divi [f. C. n. II IIIviri reipubl. constit. caussa]

36 B.C. L. Gellius L. f. (Poplicola): M. Cocceiu[s] (Nerva)
suf. L. Nonius L. f. (Asprenas)
[?. M]arcius

Tr. Cap. Cn. Domitius M. f. M. n. Calvinus procos. ex Hispania XVI k. Sextil.
imp. Caesar divi f. [C. f.] II, IIIvir r. p. c. II, ovans ex Sicilia idibus Novembr.
□ *engraved after deletion.*

35 B.C. Sex. Pomp(eius Sex. f.): L. Cornifi(cius L. f.)
suf. P. Cornelius (P. f. Scipio)
T. Peducaeus

34 B.C. M. Anton(ius M. f.) II: L. Scribonius (L. f. Libo)
suf. L. Sempronius (L. f. Atratinus)
Paul(lus) Aemilius (L. f. Lepidus)
C. Memmius (C. f.)
M. Herennius

Mag. gives this, the correct version. *Ven.* omits M. Antonius, making L. Sempronius *consul ordinarius.*
Ven. bellum Hiluricum
Tr. Cap. T. Statilius T. f. Taurus procos. ex Africa pridie k. Iul.
C. Sosius C. f. T. n. procos. ex Iudaea III nonas Septembr.
C. Norbanus C. f. Flaccus procos. ex Hispania IIII id[us Oc]tobr.

33 B.C. imp. Caesar (divi f.) II: L. Volcacius (L. f. Tullus)
suf. L. Autronius (P. f. Paetus)
L. Flavius
C. Fonteius (C. f. Capito)
M. Acilius (Glabrio)
L. Vinicius (M. f.)
Q. Laronius

Tr. Barb. L. Marcius Philipus ex Hispania V k. Mai. triumphavit palmam dedit
Ap. Claudius Pulcer ex Hispania k. Iun. triumphavit palmam dedit
L. Cornificius ex Africa III non. Dec. triumphavit palmam dedit

32 B.C. Cn. Domitius (L. f. Ahenobarbus): C. Sossius (C. f.)
suf. L. Cornelius (Cinna ?)
M. Valerius Messal(la)

Amit. bellum Acties. class[iar.] cum M. Antonio (*misplaced*)

31 B.C. imp. Caesar divi f. III: M. Valerius (M. f.) Messal(la) Corvinus
suf. M. Titius L. f.
Cn. Pompeius Q. f.

Ven. bellum Acti.

30 B.C. imp. Caesar (divi f.) IV: M. Licinius (M. f.) Crassus
suf. C. Antistius (C. f.) Vetus
M. Tullius (M. f.) Cicero
L. Saenius L. f.

Amit. bell[um classia]r. confect.
Ven. bellum Alexandreae

29 B.C. imp. Caesar (divi f.) V: Sex. Appuleius (Sex. f.)
suf. Potit(us) Valeri(us) (M. f. Messalla)

Tr. Barb. imp. Caesar de Dalmatis eid. Sext. triumph. palmam dedit
imp. Caesar ex A[egy]pto XIIX k. Sept. triumpavit

28 B.C. imp. Caesar (divi f.) VI: M. Agrippa (L. f.) II
no *suffecti*

Ven. idem censoria potest. lustrum fecer.
Tr. Barb. [C. C]alv[is]ius [S]abinus ex Hispania VII k. Iun. triumphavit palmam dedit
[C. Carr]inas ex [G]al[l]is prid. eid. Iu[l.] triumph. palmam dedit
Tr. Cap. L. Autronius P. f. L. n. Paetus procos. ex Africa XVII k. Septemb[r.]

27 B.C. imp. Caesar (divi f.) VII: M. Agrippa (L. f.) III
no *suffecti*

Tr. Cap. M. Licinius M. f. M. n. Crassus procos. ex Thraecia et Geteis IV non. Iul.
M. Valerius M. f. M. n. Messalla Corvinus procos. ex Gallia VII k. Oct.
Lat. [imp. Caesar vale]tudin. inpeditus fuit

26 B.C. imp. Caesar (divi f.) VIII: T. Statilius (T. f.) Taurus II
no *suffecti*

Tr. Cap. Sex. Appuleius Sex. f. Sex. n. procos. ex Hispania VII k. Febr.
Lat. [imp. Caesar in] Hispania fuit

25 B.C. imp. Caesar di[vi f.] VIIII: M. Iunius (M. f.) Silanus
no *suffecti*

Lat. [imp. Caes]ar in Hispan. fuit

24 B.C. imp. Caesar divi f. X: C. Norbanus (C. f.) Flaccus
no *suffecti*

Lat. [imp.] Caesar valetud. [impedit. fuit]

23 B.C. (Aug. I) [imp.] Caesar divi f. C. n. Augustus XI abd. in eius loc. factus est [L. Sestius P. f. L. n.] Quirin. [Albin.]
A. T[erentius A. f. ?. n. Var]ro Murena [in mag. damn.] est, in e. l. f. e. [Cn. Calpurn]ius Cn. f. Cn. n. Pis[o]
[imp. Caesar divi f. C. n. Augustus posteaquam consu]latu se abdicavit, tri[b. pot. accepit]

This is the version of *Cap.* The other surviving *fasti* all ignore Varro Murena, making Piso *consul ordinarius.*

Lat. [imp. Cae]sar in monte fuit. [. . . . imp. Ca]esar cos. abdicavit

22 B.C. (Aug. II) M. Claudius M. f. Mar[cellus] (Aeserninus): L. Arruntius L. f.
no *suffecti*

Col. L. Munatius Paul. Aemilius [cens. lustr. n. f.]

21 B.C. (Aug. III) Q. Aemilius (M'. f.) Lepid(us): M. Lolliu[s] (M. f.)
no *suffecti*

Tr. Cap. L. Sempronius L. f. L. n. Atratinus procos. ex Africa IIII idus Oct.

20 B.C. (Aug. IV) M. Appuleius Sex. f.: P. Silius (P. f. Nerva)
no *suffecti*

19 B.C. (Aug. V) C. Sentius (C. f.) Saturn(inus): Q. Lucreti(us Q. f. Vespillo)
suf. M. Vinicius P. f.

Tr. Cap. L. Cornelius P. f. Balbus procos. ex Africa VI k. April.

18 B.C. (Aug. VI, Agr. I) P. Cornelius P. f. (Lentulus Marcellinus): Cn. C[ornelius] (L. f.) Lentul(us)
no *suffecti*

17 B.C. (Aug. VII, Agr. II) C. Furnius C. f.: C. Iun[ius] (C. f.) Silanus
no *suffecti*

16 B.C. (Aug. VIII, Agr. III) L. Domitius Cn. f. (Ahenobarbus): P. Corne[lius] (P. f.) Scipio
suf. L. Tarius (Rufus)

15 B.C. (Aug. IX, Agr. IV) M. (Livius) Drusus L. f. (Libo): L. (Calpurnius L. f.) Piso (Frugi)
no *suffecti*

14 B.C. (Aug. X, Agr. V) M. Licinius M. f. (Crassus Frugi): Cn. (Cornelius Cn. f. Lentulus) Augu[r]
no *suffecti*

13 B.C. (Aug. XI, Agr. VI) Ti. Claudius Ti. f. (Nero): P. Quinctil(ius Sex. f. Varus)
no *suffecti*

12 B.C. (Aug. XII) M. Valerius M. f. (Messalla Barbatus) Appian(us): P. Sulpic(ius P. f. Quirinius)
suf. C. Valgius C. f. Ruf(us)
C. Caninius (C. f.) Rebil(us)
L. Volusius (Q. f.) Sa[turninus]

Cupr. [Caes]ar pontif. maxim. cre[atus est; ide]m congiarium populo [dedit]

11 B.C. (Aug. XIII) (Paulus) [Fa]bi[us] (Q. f. Maximus): (Q.) Aelius (Q. f. Tubero)
no *suffecti*

10 B.C. (Aug. XIV) (Iullus Antonius M. f.): (Africanus) [F]ab(ius Q. f. Maximus)
no *suffecti*

9 B.C. (Aug. XV) (Nero Claudius Ti. f. Drusus): (T. Quinctius T. f. Crispinus)
no *suffecti*

8 B.C. (Aug. XVI) (C. Marcius L. f. Censorinus): (C. Asinius C. f. Gallus)
no *suffecti*

7 B.C. (Aug. XVII) Ti. Claudius (Ti. f.) Nero iter.: Cn. Calpurnius (Cn. f.) Piso

no *suffecti*

Mag. imp. Caesar August[us pontif. maxim.] cos. XI tribun. potes[t. X]VII Lares Aug. mag. vici dedit

6 B.C. (Aug. XVIII, Tib. I) C. Antistius (C. f. Vetus): D. Laelius (D. f. Balbus)

no *suffecti*

5 B.C. (Aug. XIX, Tib. II) imp. Caesar (divi f.) August(us) XII: L. (Cornelius P. f.) Sulla

suf. L. Vinicius L. f.
Q. Haterius
C. Sulpicius C. f. Galba

4 B.C. (Aug. XX, Tib. III) C. Calvisius C. f. Sabinus: L. Passien(us Rufus)

suf. C. Caelius
Galus Sulpic(ius)

3 B.C. (Aug. XXI, Tib. IV) L. (Cornelius L. f.) Lentulus: M. (Valerius M. f.) Messal(la Messallinus)

no *suffecti*

2 B.C. (Aug. XXII, Tib. V) imp. Caesar (divi f. Augustus) XIII: M. Plaut(ius M. f. Silvanus)

suf. L. Caninius (L. f. Gallus)
C. Fufius (Geminus)
Q. Fabricius

1 B.C. (Aug. XXIII) Cossus Cornelius (Cn. f. Lentulus): L. (Calpurnius Cn. f.) Piso

suf. A. Plautius
A. Caecina (Severus)

A.D. 1. (Aug. XXIV) C. Caesar August[i f.]: L. (Aemilius Paulli f.) Paullus

suf. M. Herennius M. f. Picens

A.D. 2. (Aug. XXV) P. Vinicius M. f.: P. Alfenus P. f. Varus
suf. P. Cornelius Cn. f. (Lentulus) Scipio
T. Quinctius T. f. [Crispi]nus Val[erianus]

Gab. [L. Caesar] decessit XIII k. Oct. (*read:* Sept., *cf.* Calendars, *p.* 51)

A.D. 3. (Aug. XXVI) L. Aelius L. f. Lamia: M. Servilius (M. f.)
suf. P. Silius P. f.
L. Volusius L. f. [Saturni]n(us)

A.D. 4. (Aug. XXVII, Tib. VI) Sex. Aelius Q. f. Catus: C. Sentius (C. f.) Saturn(inus)
suf. Cn. Sentius C. f. Saturnin(us)
C. Clodius C. f. Licinus

Gab. C. Caesar decessit VIIII k. M[art.]
Cupr. [VIIII k. Mart. C. Caesar] Aug. f. dec[essit in Lycia annum agens XXI]II. Romae iustit[ium indictum est] donec ossa eius in [ma]esol[aeum inlata sunt.] V eid. Sept. bellum cum [hostibus p. R. gerens] in Armenia percuss[us est dum obsidet Ar]ta[g]iram Ar-[meniae oppidum]

A.D. 5. (Aug. XXVIII, Tib. VII) L. Valerius Potiti f. Messalla Volesus: Cn. Cornelius L. f. Cinna Mag(nus)
suf. C. Vibius C. f. Postumus
C. Ateius L. f. Capito

A.D. 6. (Aug. XXIX, Tib. VIII) M. Aemilius Paulli f. Lepidus: L. Arruntius L. f.
suf. L. Nonius L. f. Asprenas

A.D. 7. (Aug. XXX, Tib. IX) Q. Caecilius Q. f. Metellus Creticus Silan(us): A. Licinius A. f. Nerva Silianus

A *cos. suffectus*, named (Lucilius) Long(us), is recorded as colleague of Creticus in *Amit.* under August 10th (*see* Calendars, *p.* 50).

A.D. 8. (Aug. XXXI, Tib. X) M. Furius P. f. Camill(us): Sex. Nonius L. f. Quinctilian(us)
suf. L. Apronius C. f.
A. Vibius C. f. Habitus

A.D. 9. (Aug. XXXII, Tib. XI) C. Poppaeus Q. f. Sabinus: Q. Sulpicius Q. f. Camerinus
suf. M. Papius M. f. Mutilus
Q. Poppaeus Q. f. Secund(us)

A.D. 10. (Aug. XXXIII, Tib. XII) P. Cornelius P. f. Dolabella: C. Iunius C. f. Silanus flam. Mart.

suf. Ser. Cornelius Cn. f. Lentulus Malug(inensis) flam. Dial.

Q. Iunius Blaesus

A.D. 11. (Aug. XXXIV, Tib. XIII) M'. Aemilius Q. f. Lepidus: T. Statilius (T. f.) Taurus

suf. L. Cassius L. f. Longinus

A.D. 12. (Aug. XXXV, Tib. XIV) Germanicus Caesar Ti. f.: C. Fonteius C. f. Capito

suf. C. Visellius C. f. Varro

A.D. 13. (Aug. XXXVI, Tib. XV) C. Silius P. f. Caecina Largus: L. Munatius L. f. Plancus

In *Cap.* and *Ant. Min.* no *suffectus* recorded; *Arv.* appears to give a *suffectus* whose name ends in *-gus*. Degrassi, *Epigraphica* viii (1946), 34 ff., would place as *suffecti* in this year Favonius (*see our no. 209*) and M. Lollius, M. f.

A.D. 14. (Aug. XXXVII, Tib. XVI) Sex. Pompeius (Sex. f.): Sex. Appuleius (Sex. f.)

no *suffecti*

Ost. [August. I]II Ti. Caesar cens. [egerun]t. c. s. c. R. k.[1] |XXXXI|DCCCC [. . . . XI]V k. Sept. Augustus [excessit]

Cupr. [Caesar Aug. elatu]s funere pub[lico et crematus in Campo Ma]rtio. Caesar A[ug. . . . .

[1] c(ensa) s(unt) c(ivium) R(omanorum) k(apita)

A.D. 15. (Tib. XVII) Drusus Caesar Ti. f.: C. Norbanus (C. f.) Flaccus

suf. M. [Iu]nius (C. f.) Silanus

A.D. 16. (Tib. XVIII) Sisenna Statilius (T. f.) Taurus: L. Scribonius (L. f.) Libo

suf. (C. Vibius) Rufinus

(C. Pomponius L. f.) Graecinus

Ant. Min. wrongly gives: C. Vibius Libo, C. Pompeius Graecina

Ost. [. . . . .] populo patuit

A.D. 17. (Tib. XIX) L. Pomponius (L. f.) Flaccus: C. Caelius (C. f.) Rufu[s]

suf. C. Vibius Marsu[s]
L. Voluseius Procul(us)

Ost. [VII k. Iun. Germ]anic. Caes[a]r [triumphavi]t ex German.

A.D. 18. (Tib. XX) Ti. Caesar August(us) III: Germanicus (Ti Aug. f.) Caesar II

suf. L. Seius Tubero
[Livi]neius Regulus
C. Ru[be]llius (C. f.) Blandus
[M. Vip]stanus Gallus

A.D. 19. (Tib. XXI) M. Iunius (M. f.) Silanus (Torquatus): L. Norbanus (C. f.) Balbus

suf. P. Petronius (P. f.)

Ost. VI idus Dec. iustitium ob excessum G[er]manici (*read:* Oct., *cf.* Calendars, *p.* 53)

A.D. 20. (Tib. XXII) M. Valerius (M. f.) Messalla Messallinus: M. Aurelius (M. f. ?) Cotta (Maximus Messallinus ?)

no *suffecti*

Ost. V k. Iun. Drusus [Caesar] triumphavit ex Ill[yrico.] VII idus Iun. Nero to[g. vir.] sumpsit. cong. di[visum]

A.D. 21. (Tib. XXIII) Ti. Caesar (Augustus) IV: Drusus (Ti. Aug. f.) Caesar II

PIR.[2] i, no. 404, places here as *suffecti* (cf. *CIL.* vi. 2023 b, iv. 1553; Tac. *Ann.* iii. 66):

Mamercus Aemilius Scaurus
Cn. Tremellius

A.D. 22. (Tib. XXIV, Drusus I) D. Haterius (Q. f.) Agrippa: C. Sul[pici]us (C. f.) Galb[a]

A.D. 23. (Tib. XXV, Drusus II) (C. Asinius C. f.) [P]ollio: (C. Antistius C. f.) [V]etus

suf. (C. Stertinius M. f.) [M]axim(us)

A.D. 24. (Tib. XXVI) (Ser.) [Co]rnelius (Ser. f.) Cethegus: (L.) [Vis]ellius (C. f.) Varro

suf. C. Calpurn(ius) Aviola
P. (Cornelius P. f. Lentulus) Scipio

A.D. 25. (Tib. XXVII) Cossus Cornelius (Cossi f.) Lentulus: M. A[s]inius (C. f.) Ag[r]ippa

CIL. i. 766 gives C. Pet(ronius) as *suffectus* this year.

A.D. 26. (Tib. XXVIII) Cn. (Cornelius Cossi f. Lentulus Gaetulicus): C. Ca[lvisius] (C. f. Sabinus)

Degrassi places here as *suffecti* (cf. *ILS.* 7918):

Q. Iunius Q. f. Blaesus
L. Antistius C. f. Vetus

A.D. 27. (Tib. XXIX) L. Calpur[nius] (Cn. f. Piso): M. (Licinius M. f.) Crassus Frugi

suf. P. (Cornelius ?) Le[ntulus ?]
C. Sall[ustius] (Passienus Crispus)

A.D. 28. (Tib. XXX) (C. Appius) Iunius (C. f.) S[ilanus]: P. Silius Nerva

Degrassi places here as *suffecti* (*cf. ILS. 6099, our no. 354*):

L. Iunius Silanus
C. Vellaeus Tutor

A.D. 29. (Tib. XXXI) L. Rubell(ius Geminus): C. Fufius (C. f.) G[eminus]

suf. A. Plautius (A. f.)
L. Nonius (L. f.) Aspr[enas]

A.D. 30. (Tib. XXXII) L. Cassius (L. f.) Longinus: M. Vinicius (P. f.)

suf. L. Naevius (L. f.) Surdinus
C. Cassius (L. f.) Longinus

Ost. IIII idus Mart. arcus Dru[si] dedicatus

A.D. 31. (Tib. XXXIII) Ti. Caesar Aug[us]tus V

suf. Faustus Cornelius Sulla
Sex. Tedius (L. f. Valerius) Catullu[s]
L. Fulcinius Trio
P. Memmius (P. f.) Regulus

The name of the second *cos. ord.*, L. Aelius L. f. Seianus, is omitted (cf. our nos. 50a and 53).

Ost. XV k. Nov. Seianus s[trang.] VIIII k. Nov. Strabo [Seiani] f. strang. VII k. No[v. Apicata] Seiani se occidi[t . . . . . .] Dec. Capito Aelia[nus et] Iunilla Seiani [in Gem.] iacuerunt

A.D. 32. (Tib. XXXIV) Cn. Domitius (L. f.) Ahenobarbus: (L.) Arrunt(ius) Camillus (L. f. Scribonianus)
suf. A. Vitellius (P. f.)

A.D. 33. (Tib. XXXV) L. Livius Ocella Ser. Sulpicius (C. f.) Galba: L. [C]ornelius Sulla Felix
suf. L. Salvius (M. f.) Otho
C. Octaviu[s] (Laenas)

Ost. [. . . .] Aug. coniur. Seian[i exstincta e]t compl[ures in s]calis [Gemon. iacuer. . . .] Dec. Lami[a praef. urb. exc.]

A.D. 34. (Tib. XXXVI) [Pa]ullus Fabius Persic(us): L. Vi[tellius] (P. f.)
suf. Q. Marc(ius) Barea Sor[anus]
T. Rustius (Nummius) Gallu[s]

A.D. 35. (Tib. XXXVII) (C. Cestius Gallus): M. Servilius (M. f. ?) Noni[anus]
suf. [D. V]alerius As[iaticus]
[P. Gab]inius S[ecundus]

A.D. 36. (Tib. XXXVIII) (Sex. Papinius Q. f. Allenius): (Q. Plautius A. ? f.)
suf. M. Porcius (M. f. ?) Cato

Degrassi puts here an additional *suffectus* (Frontin. *de aqu.* 102): A. Didius Gallus

Ost. k. Nov. pars circa inter vitores arsit, ad quod T[i.] Caesar HS ∞ public. [d.]

A.D. 37. (Gaius I) Cn. Acerronius (Proculus): C. (Petronius) Pontius Ni[grinus]
suf. C. Caesar Aug(ustus) Germ[anicus]
Ti. Claudius Nero Ger[manicus]
A. Caecina Paetu[s]
C. Caninius (C. f.) Rebilu[s]

Ost. XVII k. Apr. Ti. Caesar Misen[i] excessit. IIII k. Apr. corpus in urbe perlatum per mili[t.] III non. Apr. f(unere) p(ublico) e(latus) e(st). k. Mais Antonia diem suum obit. k. Iun. cong. d. ✳ LXXV. XIIII [k.] Aug. alteri ✳ LXXV

THE CALENDARS

(*Fasti Anni Iuliani*)

THE following calendar has been conflated from the epigraphic calendars and similar documents quoted below. They will be collected in the forthcoming vol. xiii, fasc. 2, of the *Inscriptiones Italiae*. For earlier reconstructions cf. Mommsen, *CIL*. i², pp. 205–339, and J. Gagé, *Res Gestae Divi Augusti* (1935), pp. 155–85.

The following abbreviations are used (f.a. = fasti anni):

All. = f.a. Allifani, *CIL*. i, p. 217.
Amit. = f.a. Amiternini, *CIL*. i, p. 243.
Ant. = f.a. Antiates, *CIL*. i, p. 247; *Inscr. Ital.* xiii. 1, p. 328.
Arv. = acta Arvalium, *CIL*. i, p. 214.
*Arv.*² = ,, ,, *CIL*. vi, pp. 460 ff., nos. 2023 ff.; p. 3312.
Cae. = f.a. Caeretani, *CIL*. i, p. 212.
Cum. = feriale Cumanum, *ILS*. 108.
Maf. = f.a. Maffeiani, *CIL*. i, p. 222.
Opp. = f.a. Oppiani, *CIL*. vi, p. 3315.
Phil. = Philocalus, *CIL*. i, p. 254.
Pigh. = f.a. Pighiani, *CIL*. i, p. 246.
Pinc. = f.a. Pinciani, *CIL*. i, p. 219; *Inscr. Ital.* xiii. 1, p. 277.
Prae. = f.a. Praenestini, *CIL*. i, p. 230.
*Prae.*² = ,, ,, *Ann. ép.* 1898, no. 14.
*Prae.*³ = ,, ,, *Ann. ép.* 1922, no. 96.
*Prae.*⁴ = ,, ,, *Ann. ép.* 1937, no. 4.
Silv. = Polemius Silvius, *CIL*. i, p. 254.
Val. = f.a. Vallenses, *CIL*. i, p. 240; *Inscr. Ital.* xiii. 1, p. 316.
Vat. = f.a. Vaticani, *CIL*. i, p. 242.
Ver. = f.a. Verulani, *Ann. ép.* 1937, no. 5.

January 7 (vii id. Ian.)

43 B.C.

Cum. e[o die Caesar] primum fasces sumpsit. supp[l]icatio Iovi sempi[terno]

Prae. imp. Caesar Augustu[s primum fasces sumpsit] Hirtio et Pansa [cos. . . . . .]

Cf. our no. 100, A 23: . . . . . VII quoq. idus Ianuar. qua die primum imperium orbis terrarum auspicatus est . . .

Year?

Prae. VIIvir epul. creatus [est . . . . cos.]

January 8 (vi id. Ian.)

A.D. 13.

Prae. signum Iustitiae Augus[tae dedicatum Planco] et Silio cos.

January 11 (iii id. Ian.)

29 B.C.

Prae. . . . . . d[ebellavit imp. Caesar Augustus tertium] ab Romulo et Ianum c[lausit se V et Appuleio cos.]

January 12 (pr. id. Ian.)

Year?

Prae. Augustus Ti. Caesarem es[. . . . .?]

January 13 (id. Ian.)

27 B.C.

Prae. corona quern[a uti super ianuam domus imp. Caesaris] Augusti poner[etur senatus decrevit quod rem publicam] p. R. rest[i]tui[t]

Cf. Ovid, *Fasti* i. 589.

January 14 (xix k. Febr.)

82 B.C.

Ver. [dies vi]tiosus [ex s.]c. Ań(tonii) natal.
Opp. vitiosus

Cf. Suet. *Claud.* 11. 6: Drusi natalis (*38 B.C.*)

January 16 (xvii k. Febr.)

27 B.C.

Cum. eo di[e Caesar Augustu]s appellatus est. supplicatio Augusto
Prae. imp. Caesar [Augustus est a]ppellatus ipso VII et Agrip-[pa III cos.]

Cf. Ovid, *Fasti* i. 590; Censorinus, *de die natali* 21. 8.

9 B.C.

Prae.[4] Ti. Caesar ex Pan[nonia ovans urbem intr]avit

Hohl, *Sitzungsb. Deutsch. Ak.* 1952, restores: Ti. Caesar ex Pan[nonia rediens p. R. salut]avit, and refers it to A.D. 10.

A.D. 10

Ver. fer. ex s.c. quod eo die aedis [Con]cordiae in foro dedic. est
Prae. Concordiae Au[gustae aedis dedicat]a est P. Dolabella C. Silano co[s].

Cf. Ovid, *Fasti* i. 639 f.

January 17 (xvi k. Febr.)

38 B.C.

Ver. feriae ex s.c. quod eo die Augusta nupsit divo Aug[us]t[o]

Probably A.D. 5 or 9

Prae.[4] pontifices a[ugures XVviri s. f. VII]vir. epulonum victumas inm[ol]ant n[umini Augusti ad aram q]uam dedicavit Ti. Caesar. fe[riae ex s.c. q]u[od e. d. Ti. Caesar aram divo] Aug. patri dedicavit

A.D. 41 (?)

Arv.[2] (no. 2032) [ob consecr?]ationem divae Aug. in tem[plo novo?] divo Augusto bovem mar[em, divae Augustae] vaccam

January 17–22 (xvi–xi k. Febr.)

From A.D. 14 annually

Phil. Silv. ludi Palatini

January 27 (vi k. Febr.)

A.D. 6

Prae. aed[is Castoris et Po]llucis dedicat[a est]

Cf. Ovid, *Fasti* i. 705 f.

January 29 (iiii k. Febr.)

Year? (after 12 B.C.)

Prae. feriae ex [s.c. quod eo die] ab imp. Caes. [Augusto pont.] maxi[mo . . . .] marina [. . . . . . .]

January 30 (iii k. Febr.)

58 B.C.

Arv.[2] (no. 2028) . . . natali Iuliae Augustae . .

9 B.C.

Cum. [eo die ara Pacis Aug. dedicata] est. supplicatio imperio Caesaris Augusti cust[odis civium Romanorum orbisque terrar?]um

Cae. fer. ex s.c. q. e. d. ara Pacis Aug. d.

Prae. feriae ex s.c. quo[d eo] die ara Pacis Augusta[e in campo] Martio dedicata [e]st Druso et Crispino c[os.]

Cf. Ovid, *Fasti* i. 709 ff.

January 31 (pr. k. Febr.)

36 B.C.

Arv.[2] (no. 2028) . . . natali Antoniae Augustae . . . .

February 5 (non. Febr.)

2 B.C.

Prae. feriae ex s.c. quod eo die imperator Caesar Augustus pontifex maximus trib. potest. XXI cos. XIII a senatu populoque Romano pater patriae appelatus

Cf. Ovid, *Fasti* ii. 127 ff.

February 21 or 22 (viiii or viii k. Mart.)

A.D. 4

Our no. 69, 25: . . . di[em]que eum quo die C. Caesar obit, qui dies est a.d. VIIII k. Martias, pro Alliensi lu[gub]rem memoriae prodi . . .

Ver. (VIII k. Mart.) [inferiae C.] Caesaris

Cf. Fasti p. 39.

March 6 (pr. non. Mart.)

12 B.C.

Maf. hoc die Caesar pontif. maxim. fact. est

Cum. [eo die Caesar pontifex ma]ximus creatus est. supplicat[i]o Vestae, dis publ. P(enatibus) p. R. q(uiritium)

Prae. fe[riae ex s.c. quod eo die i]mp. Caesar August. pont. m[ax. factus est Quir]inio et Valgio cos. IIviri ob [eam rem inmolant, p]opulus coronatus feriatus [agit]

Cf. Ovid, *Fasti* iii. 419 ff., and Fasti, p. 37.

March 10 (vi id. Mart.)

A.D. 15

Our no. 101, 20 f.: qua die Ti. Caesar pontif. maximus felicissiṃe est creatus

Prae. feriae ex s.c. q. [e. d.] Ti. Caesar pontifex max. fac. est Druso et Norbano [cos.]

Vat. [fer. ex s.c. q.e.d. Ti. Caes. pont.] maxim. est factus [Drus]o et Norbano cos.

March 16 (xvii k. Apr.)

A.D. 37

See Fasti, p. 43 (Tiberius' death and funeral).

April 14 (xviii k. Mai.)

43 B.C.

Cum. [eo die Caesar primum vicit. supplica]tio Victoriae Augustae

Cf. Ovid, *Fasti* iv. 627.

April 16 (xvi k. Mai.)

43 B.C.

Cum. [eo die Caesar primum imperator app]ellatus est. supplicatio Felicitati imperi

Cf. Ovid, *Fasti* iv. 673 ff.

April 23 (viiii k. Mai.)

A.D. 22

Prae. sig. divo Augusto patri ad theatrum Marc[ell.] Iulia Augusta et Ti. Augustus dedicaverunt

April 24 (viii k. Mai.)

27 B.C.

Prae. Ti. Caesar togam virilem sumpsit imp. Caesare VII M. Agrippa III cos.

April 28 (iiii k. Mai.)

12 B.C.

Cae. fer. q. e. d. sig. Vest. in domo P(alatina) dedic.

Prae. feriae ex s.c. quod eo di[e aedicul]a et [ara] Vestae in domu imp. Caesaris Augu[sti po]ntif. ma[x.] dedicatast Quirinio et Valgio cos.

Cf. Ovid, *Fasti* iv. 949 ff.

May 1 (k. Mai.)

A.D. 37

See Fasti, p. 43 (death of Antonia).

May 12 (iiii id. Mai.)

From 19 B.C. annually

Cum. [eo die aedes Martis dedicatast. supplica]tio Molibus Martis

Maf. lud. Mart. in circ.

Phil. Martialici

Cf. Ovid, *Fasti* v. 595 ff.

May 24 (viiii k. Iun.)

15 B.C.

Cum. [Germanici Caesaris natalis. supp]licatio Vestae

Arv.[2] (no. 2030) . . . ob natalem Germanici [Caesaris] . . .

May 26 (vii k. Iun.)

A.D. 17

Amit. [fer. ex s.c. quo]d eo die [Germanicus C]aesar [triumphans] invictus (*sic*) est [in urbem]

May 28 (v k. Iun.)

A.D. 20

Amit. [fer. ex s.c. qu]od eo die [Drusus Caesar triumphans invectus est in urbem]

Cf. Fasti, p. 41.

June 7 (vii id. Iun.)

A.D. 20

See Fasti, p. 41 (Nero's *toga virilis*).

June 26 or 27 (vi or v k. Iul.)

A.D. 4

Amit. (VI. k. Iul.) fer. ex s.[c. q]uod eo die [imp.] Augus[tus ado]p[tav]it [sibi] filiu[m Ti. Caesarem] Aelio [et Sentio cos.]

Cf. Vell. Pat. ii. 103 (V k. Iul.)

July 4 (iiii non. Iul.)

13 B.C.

Amit. fer. ex s.c. q. e. d. ara Pacis Aug. in camp. Mar. constituta est Nerone et Varo cos.

Ant. [ara P]acis August. [c]onstitut.

August 1 (k. Aug.)

30 B.C.

Prae.[2] [Aegypt]us in potestatem po[puli Romani redacta.] Victoriae Virgini in Palatio. Spei in foro holitorio. fer. [ex. s.c.] q. e. d. imp. Caes[ar Aug. rem publicam tristissimo periculo liberavit]

Arv. [Spei] in foro holit. f. ex s.c. [q. e. d. imp. Caesar rem pu]blic. tristiss. periculo [libera]vit

Amit. feriae ex s.c. q. e. d. imp. Caesar divi f. rem public. tristissimo periculo liberat (*sic*)

Ant. Spei. Aug. Alexan(driam) recepit

10 B.C.

Val. natal. Ti. Claudii Germanici
Ant. Ti. Clau[di Caes. Aug. nat.]

Cf. Suet. *Claud.* 2.

2 B.C.

Vell. Pat. ii. 100: dedicato Martis templo

Cf. Dio 60. 5. 3.

August 3 (iii non. Aug.)

Probably A.D. 8

Ant. Ti. Aug. ⟨in⟩ Inlyrico vic(it)

August 10 (iiii id. Aug.)

Probably A.D. 7

Val. feriae. arae Opis et Cereris in vico Iugario constitutae sunt
Amit. feriae quod eo die arai Cereri Matri et Opi Augustae ex voto suscepto constituta[e] sunt Cretico et Long. c[os.]
Ant. feriae Cereri et Opi Aug.

August 13–15 (id. Aug., xix, xviii k. Sept.)

29 B.C.

Ant. (xix k. Sept.) August. triump(havit)

Cf. Fasti, p. 35, and Dio 51. 21. 5 ff.

August 18 (xv k. Sept.)

29 B.C.

Amit. All. divo Iulio ad forum
Ant. aedis divi Iul. ded.

Cf. also *frag. min.* 8, *CIL.* i^2, p. 252; *CIL.* vi, p. 3317, no. 32499.

August 19 (xiiii k. Sept.)

43 B.C.

Cum. [eo die Caesar pri]mum consulatum in[iit. supplicatio ....]

Cf. Tac. *Ann.* i. 9, Dio 56. 30. 5.

A.D. 14

Amit. dies tristissi(mus)
Ant. Augustus excess(it)

Cf. Suet. *Aug.* 100. 1, Tac. Dio *ll. cc.*, and Fasti, p. 40.

August 20 (xiii k. Sept.)

A.D. 2

Ant. infer(iae) L. Caesaris

Our no. 68, 17: . . . quodannis a.d. X[III K. Sept. p]ublice manibus eius . . .

Cf. Fasti, p. 39.

August 28 (v k. Sept.)

29 B.C.

Maf. h. d. ara Victoriae in curia dedic. est

Vat. feria[e h. d.] q. de[ae Vict. ara] de[d]icata est

August 31 (pr. k. Sept.)

A.D. 12

Val. nat. C. Caesaris Germanici

Pigh. nat. Germanic(i)

September 1 (k. Sept.)

22 B.C.

Arv. Iovi Tonanti in Capitolio. Iovi Libero, Iunoni Reginae in Aventino

Amit. Iovi Tonanti in Capitolio

Ant. feriae Iovi

Cf. Dio 54. 4. 2.

September 2 (iiii non. Sept.)

31 B.C.

Arv. feriae ex s.c. imp. Caesaris h(onoris) c(ausa) quod eo die vicit ⟨apud⟩ Actium

Amit. fer. ex s.c. quod eo die imp. Caes. divi f. Augustus apud Actium vicit se et Titio cos.

Ant. [Aug. ad Ac]ti[um vic.]

Val. Act[i. . . . .]

Cf. Dio 51. 1. 1; Lydus, *de mensibus* 4. 80.

September 3 (iii non. Sept.)

36 B.C.

Arv. feriae et supplicationes ad omnia pulvinaria q. e. d. Caesar August. in Sicilia vicit

Amit. fer. et supplicationes aput omnia pulvinaria quod eo die Caes. divi f. vicit in Sicilia Censorin. et Calvis. cos. (*wrong date*)

Between September 4 and 22 (pr. non. Sept.–x k. Oct.)

36 B.C.

Cum. [. . . . . eo die exer]citus Lepidi tradidit se Caesari. suppli[c]a[tio . . . . .]

September 9 (v id. Sept.)

A.D. 3

See Fasti, p. 39 (A.D. 4) (wounding of C. Caesar).

September 13 (id. Sept.)

A.D. 16

Amit. fer. ex s.c. q. e. d. nefaria consilia quae de salute Ti. Caes. liberorumque eius et aliorum principum civitatis deq(ue) r.p. inita ab M. Libone erant in senatu convicta sunt

September 14 (xviii k. Oct.)

A.D. 23

Opp. inferiae Drusi Caesaris

Ant. infer(iae) Dr[usi Caesaris]

September 17 (xv k. Oct.)

A.D. 14

Opp. feriae ex s.c. [quo]d eo die honores caelestes divo Augusto [a se]natu decreti sunt Pompeio et Appuleio cos.

Amit. fer. ex s.c. q. e. d. divo Augusto honores caelestes a senatu decreti Sex. Appul. Sex. Pomp. cos.

Ant. [Aug. hon.] cael. d[ecreti]

September 23 and 24 (viiii et viii k. Oct.)

63 B.C.

Cum. [n]atalis Caesaris. immolatio Caesari hostia, supp[l]icatio

Pinc. fer. ex s.c. quod is dies imp. Caesar. natalis est

Arv. f. ex s.c. q. e. d. imp. Caesar Aug. pont. ma[x.] natus est. Marti Neptuno in campo, Apollini ad theatrum Marcelli

Arv.[2] (no. 2028) . . . natali divi Augusti divo Augusto [bovem marem inmola]vit . . .

Maf. h. d. Augusti natalis. lud. circ.

Our no. 100, A 14: . . . . VIIII k. Octobr. qua die eum saeculi felicitas orbi terrarum rectorem edidit . . . et VIII k. Octob. . . .

Our no. 101, 4: victimae natali Aug. VIII k. Octobr. duae . . . VIIII et VIII k. Octobr. inmolentur . . .

Val. nata[lis imp. Caesaris]
Pigh. nat. Aug., epul(um)
Phil. n. divi Augusti

Cf. Suet. *Aug.* 5; *our no.* 98, 51 f.

October 5 (iii non. Oct.)
From A.D. 14 annually

Amit. ludi divo Augusto et Fort. Reduci committ(untur)

See also Oct. 12.

October 7 (non. Oct.)
Between 15 and 11 B.C.

Cum. Drusi Caesaris natalis. supplicatio Vestae

October 9 (vii id. Oct.)
28 B.C.

Arv. geni. publico, faustae Felicitat., V.V. in Capit., Apollin. in Palat.
Amit. genio public., faustae Felicitati, Vener(i) Victr(ici) in Capitol., Apol. in Pal. ludi
Ant. ludi. Aug. aed. Apol. dedicavit

October 10 (vi id. Oct.)
A.D. 19

Ant. infer(iae) Germanic(i)

October 12 (iiii id. Oct.)
19 B.C.

Amit. fer. ex s.c. q. e. d. imp. Caes. Aug. ex transmarin. provinc. urbem intravit araq. Fort. Reduci constit(uta)
Opp. feriae ex s.c. divu[s Aug. ex transmarinis provinciis redit et aram Fortunae Reduci dicavit]
Maf. August(ales)
Phil. Augustales. c[ircenses]) m(issus) XXIV

See also Oct. 5.

October 18 or 19 (xv or xiv k. Nov.)
Probably 48 B.C.

Cum. eo die Caesar togam virilem sumpsit. supplicatio Spei et Iuve[ntuti]
Ant. (XIV k. Nov.) divus Aug. tog. [v]irilem sum(psit)

October 18 (xv k. Nov.)

A.D. 31

See Fasti, p. 42 (death of Seianus and family); cf. *our nos. 51 and 52.*

A.D. 33

Tac. *Ann.* vi. 25 (death of Agrippina).

October 23 (x k. Nov.)

42 B.C.

Prae.[3] [imp. Caesa]r Augustus vicit Philippis posteriore proelio Bruto occiso

A.D. 12 (or possibly A.D. 11 or 13)

Prae.[3] Ti. Caesar curru triumphavit ex Ilurico

On or before October 26 (vii k. Nov.)

After 17 B.C.

Arv.[2] (no. 2029) . . . nata[li Agrippinae Germanici Caes]aris matris [C. Caesaris Augusti Ger]manici

End of October or beginning of November

40 B.C.

See Fasti, p. 33 (Octavian's first *ovatio*).

November 6 (viii id. Nov.)

A.D. 16

Ant. Agripp(inae) Iul(iae) nat.

Arv.[2] (no. 2041, cf. 2039) . . . ob natalem Agrippinae Aug. matris . . .

November 13 (id. Nov.)

36 B.C.

See Fasti, p. 34 (Octavian's second *ovatio*).

November 16 (xvi k. Dec.)

42 B.C.

Cum. natalis Ti. Caesaris. supplicatio Vestae

Ant. Aug. natal.

Arv.[2] (no. 2025, cf. 2028) . . . [ob natalem] Ti. Caesaris divi August[i f. Augusti pontificis maximi] tribunic. potestate XXXV[II] . . .

December 15 (xviii k. Ian.)

19 B.C.

Cum. eo die a[r]a Fortunae Reducis dedicatast quae Caesarem A[ugustum ex transmari]nis provincis red[uxit]. supplicatio Fortunae Reduci

Amit. (xvii k. Ian.) ara Fortunae Reduci dedic. est

III

HISTORICAL EVENTS

See also nos. 94a, 231, 363a

1. Denarius, 45–44 B.C., Spain. Sydenham, 1041 ff.

Obv. Head of Pompey. SEX. MAG. PIVS IMP.
Rev. Pietas. PIETAS

2. As, 45–44 B.C., Spain. Sydenham, 1045.

Obv. Head of Janus. MAGNVS PIVS IMP. F
Rev. Prow. EPPIVS LEG.

2a. Bronze coin, 43 B.C., Lugdunum. Grant, *FITA*. 206.

Obv. Bust of city-goddess. COPIA FELIX
Rev. Hercules with bull. MVNATIA

3. Denarius, 43–42 B.C., East. Sydenham, 1287 ff.

Obv. Head of Libertas. LEIBERTAS
Rev. CAEPIO BRVTVS PRO COS.

4. Denarius, 43–42 B.C., East. Sydenham, 1301.

Obv. Head of Brutus. L. PLAET. CEST. BRVT. IMP.
Rev. Cap of Liberty between two daggers. EID. MAR.

5. Denarius, *c.* 42–38 B.C., Sicily. Sydenham, 1344 f.

Obv. Head of Pompey. MAG. PIVS IMP. ITER.
Rev. Neptune. PRAEF. CLAS. ET ORAE MARIT. EX S.C.

6. Denarius, 18–17 B.C., Spain (?). Mattingly, p. 59, nos. 323 ff.; cf. 357.

Obv. Head of Augustus. CAESAR AVGVSTVS
Rev. Comet. DIVVS IVLIVS

7. Denarius, 41 B.C., issue by L. Antonius, Gaul. Sydenham, 1171 ff.

Obv. Head of Antony. M. ANTONIVS IMP. IIIVIR R.P.C.
Rev. Pietas (? more likely Fortuna), with lighted censer (? or *sors*) and cornucopiae on which two storks. PIETAS COS.

8. Aureus, *c.* 39 B.C., East. Sydenham, 1356 f.

Obv. Head of Labienus. Q. LABIENVS PARTHICVS IMP.
Rev. Parthian horse with bridle, saddle, and bow-case

9. Probably 36 B.C., Narona (Dalmatia). *ILS.* 8893.

imp. Caesari divi f. Sicilia recepta C. Papius Celsus, M. Papius Kanus fratres

10. Denarius, *c.* 32–31 B.C., East. Sydenham, 1210.

Obv. Head of Antony. ANTONI ARMENIA DEVICTA
Rev. Bust of Cleopatra. CLEOPATRAE REGINAE REGVM FILIORVM REGVM

11. Forum Livii. *ILS.* 2672.

C. Baebius T. f. Clu. tr. mi[l. leg.] XX, praef. ora[e marit. His]pan. citer[ioris b]ello Actiensi IIIIvir i. d. arb.[1] M. Sappini L. f. et Gallae l.

[1] arb(itratu)

12. Dedication after Actium. 29 B.C., Nicopolis. *Mél. d'archéol. et d'hist.* (*École franç. de Rome*), 1936, 98.

[Nep]tuno [Marti] [Apollini Actio ?] . . . [imp. Caesa]r div[i f.] . . . [cons]ul . . . [i]mperat[or se]ptimum . . . pac[e] parta terra [marique q]uod in hac regio[ne c]astra [posuit] . . . . . . [e] quibu[s egr]essu[s] vict[oriam con]sec[utus est] . . .

Reconstruction from many small pieces and uncertain in parts.

13. Silver quinarius, 29–27 B.C., East (?). Mattingly, p. 105, nos. 647 ff.

Obv. Head of Augustus. CAESAR IMP. VII
Rev. Victory on *cista mystica.* ASIA RECEPTA

14. Bases of obelisks, 10–9 B.C., Rome. *ILS.* 91.

imp. Caesar divi f. Augustus pontifex maximus imp. XII cos. XI trib. pot. XIV Aegupto in potestatem populi Romani redacta Soli donum dedit

15. Denarius, 28 B.C., East. Mattingly, p. 106, nos. 650 ff.; cf. 655 ff.

Obv. Head of Augustus. CAESAR COS. VI
Rev. Crocodile. AEGVPTO CAPTA

16. Denarius, 29–27 B.C., East. Mattingly, p. 101, nos. 617 ff.; cf. 616.

Obv. Victory on ship's prow, with wreath and palm.
Rev. Octavian in quadriga. IMP. CAESAR

17. 29 B.C., Rome, Forum. *ILS.* 81.

senatus populusque Romanus imp. Caesari divi Iuli f. cos. quinct. cos. design. sext. imp. sept. re publica conservata

18. Tetradrachm, 28 B.C., Asia Minor. Mattingly, p. 112, nos. 691 ff.

Obv. Head of Augustus. IMP. CAESAR DIVI F. COS. VI LIBERTATIS P. R. VINDEX

Rev. Pax with *cista mystica*. PAX

19. Sestertius, 23–22 B.C. (?), Rome. Mattingly, p. 29, nos. 134 ff.; cf. 139 ff., 147 ff., &c., also 5 f., 51, 314, 317, 330 f., &c.

Obv. Oak-wreath. OB CIVIS SERVATOS

Rev. S. C. CN. PISO CN. F. IIIVIR A. A. A. F. F.[1]

[1] a(uro) a(rgento) a(eri) f(lando) f(eriundo)

20. Mylasa (Asia). Abbott and Johnson, *Municipal Administration in the Roman Empire*, no. 32 (Le Bas–Waddington, nos. 442–3).

. . . . . . τῆς πόλεως οὐδ[ὲ τὴν]|| ἐπανόρθωσιν τῶν ἐκ τῆς Λαβιήνο[υ] λῃστήας ἐρειπίων ἑτοίμως ἀ[ν]|αφερούσης, ὃ δὴ καὶ αὐτοὶ προϊδόμε[νοι] προδανεισμοῖς ἰδιωτῶν [εἰς]| χρέα δημόσια τὴν πόλιν ὑπηγάγο[ν]το, οὐ διὰ τὸ καθ' ὑπαλλαγὴ[ν ἀνα|λ]ωμάτων τὴν Καίσαρος ὑπὲρ Μυλασέ[ων . . . . .]|

Part of what seems to be a letter of a proconsul to Mylasa, concerning the financial difficulties of the city; it is very obscure, and we omit ll. 1–9. For the reference to Labienus cf. our no. 8.

21. April 15, 29 B.C., Philae. *ILS*. 8995.

C. Cornelius Cn. f. Gallu[s eq]ues Romanus pos[t] rege[s] | a Caesare deivi f. devictos praefect[us Alex]andreae et Aegypti primus, defection[is] | Thebaidis intra dies XV quibus hostem v[icit, bis a]cie victor, V urbium expugnator Bore[se]|os Copti Ceramices Diospoleos meg[ales Op]hieu, ducibus earum defectionum inter[ce]||ptis exercitu ultra Nili catarhacte[n transd]ucto, in quem locum neque populo | Romano neque regibus Aegypti [arma ante s]unt prolata, Thebaide, communi omn[i]|um regum formidine, subact[a] leg[atisque re]gis Aethiopum ad Philas auditis eoq[ue] | rege in tutelam recepto, tyrann[o] Tr[iacontas]choenundi Aethiopiae constituto, die[is] | patrieis et Nil[o adiu]tori d. d. ||

[Γ]άϊος Κορνήλιος Γναΐου υἱὸς Γάλλ[ος ἱππεὺ]ς Ῥωμαίων, μετὰ τὴν κατάλυσιν τῶν | ἐν Αἰγύπτωι βασιλέων πρῶτος ὑπὸ Καίσ[αρος ἐπὶ] τῆς Αἰγύπτου κατασταθείς, τὴν Θηβαΐδα ἀ|ποστᾶσαν ἐν πεντεκαίδεκα ἡμέραις δὶς [ἐν παρ]ατάξει κατὰ κράτος νικήσας, σὺν τῶι τοὺς ἡ|γεμόνας τῶν ἀντιταξαμένων ἑλεῖν πέν[τε τε πό]λεις τὰς μὲν ἐξ ἐφόδου, τὰς δὲ ἐκ πολιορκί[ας] | καταλαβόμενος, Βόρησιν Κόπτον Κεραμικὴ[ν

Διόσπ]ολιν μεγάλην Ὀφιῆον, καὶ σὺν τῆι στρατιᾶι ὑ||περάρας τὸν καταράκτην, ἀβάτου στρατια[ῖς τῆς χώρ]ας πρὸ αὐτοῦ γενομένης, καὶ σύμπασαν τὴ[ν] | Θηβαΐδα μὴ ὑποταγεῖσαν τοῖς βασιλεῦσιν [ὑποτάξ]ας, δεξάμενός τε πρέσβεις Αἰθιόπων ἐν Φί|λαις καὶ προξενίαν παρὰ τοῦ βασιλέως λ[αβὼν τύ]ραννόν τε τῆς Τριακοντασχοίνου τοπαρχία[ς] | μιᾶς ἐν Αἰθιοπίαι καταστήσας, θεοῖς πατ[ρώοις καὶ Ν]είλῳ συνλήπτορι χαριστήρια

22. 27 B.C., Arelate. *RA.* 1952, 48. Cf. *ILS.* 82.

senatus populusque Romanus imp. Caesari divi f. Augusto cos. VIII dedit clupeum virtutis clementiae iustitiae pietatis erga deos patriamque

23. Altar, with Victory holding shield, Rome. *ILS.* 83.

senatus populusq. Romanus imp. Caesari divi f. Augusto pontif. maxum. imp. (*vac.*) cos. (*vac.*) trib. potestat. (*vac.*)

24. Denarius, 18–17 B.C., Spain. Mattingly, p. 59, no. 322; cf. 333 ff., 353 ff., &c.

Obv. Head of Augustus.

Rev. Shield inscribed: CL. V.[1] S.P.Q.R. CAESAR AVGVSTVS

[1] cl(ipeus) v(irtutis)

25. Denarius, 12 B.C., Rome. Mattingly, p. 26, no. 124 f.

Obv. Head of Augustus. AVGVSTVS

Rev. Augustus, with shield inscribed C.V.,[1] placing star on statue of Agrippa. L. LENTVLVS FLAMEN MARTIALIS

[1] c(lipeus) v(irtutis)

26. Denarius, 18 B.C., Rome. Mattingly, p. 3, no. 10 ff.; cf. 40 f., 56 ff.

Obv. Head of Liber. TVRPILIANVS IIIVIR

Rev. Kneeling Parthian, extending standard. CAESAR AVGVSTVS SIGN. RECE.

27. Aureus, 18–17 B.C., Spain (?). Mattingly, p. 73, nos. 427 ff.

Obv. Head of Augustus. S.P.Q.R. IMP. CAESARI AVG. COS. XI TR. POT. VI

Rev. Triumphal arch. CIVIB. ET SIGN. MILIT. A PART. RECVP.

28. Denarius, 18 B.C., Rome. Mattingly, p. 4, nos. 18 ff.; cf. 43 f.

Obv. Head of Liber. TVRPILIANVS IIIVIR

Rev. Armenian king kneeling. CAESAR DIVI F. ARME. CAPT.

29. Denarius, 19 B.C., Rome. Mattingly, p. 1, nos. 2 ff.; cf. 358 ff.

Obv. Busts of Fortuna Victrix and Fortuna Felix. Q. RVSTIVS FORTVNAE ANTIAT.

Rev. Altar inscribed: FOR. RE.[1] CAESARI AVGVSTO EX S.C.

[1] For(tunae) Re(duci)

30. SCC. de ludis saecularibus, 17 B.C., Rome. *FIR.* no. 40.

A

a. d. X k. Iun. in saeptis [Iulis . . . . scribundo adfuerunt . . . .] | Aemilius Lep[id]us L. Cestius L. Petronius Rufus [. . . . .] |

quod C. Silanus [co]s. v. f.[1] ludos saecularis post complur[es annos eo qui nunc est facientibus (?) imp. Caesare] | August. et M. Agrippa tribunic. potestate futuros, quos [quod spectare quam plurimos convenit] | propter re[ligione]m atque etiam quod tali spectaculo [nemo iterum intererit, permittendum videri . . . lu]||dorum eo[ru]m [diebu]s qui nondum sunt maritati, sin[e fraude sua ut adsint, q. d. e. r. f. p., d. e. r. i. c.,[2] ut quoniam ludi iei] | religio[nis] causa sun[t in]stituti neque ultra quam semel ulli mo[rtalium eos spectare licet . . . . ludos] | quos [m]ag. XVvir. s. f.[3] [ed]ent, s. f. s.[4] spectare liceat ieis qui lege de marita[ndis ordinibus tenentur] |

B

eodemque die ibidem sc.[5] [id]em adfuer. et senatusconsultum factum est |

quod C. Silanus cos. v. f.[1] pe[rti]nere ad conservandam memoriam tantae b[enevolentiae deorum commentarium ludorum] || saecularium in colum[n]am aheneam et marmoream inscribi s[tatuique ad futuram rei memoriam utramque] | eo loco, ubi ludi futu[ri s]int, q. d. e. r. f. p., d. e. r. i. c.:[2] uti cos. a. a.ve[6] ad f[uturam rei memoriam columnam] | aheneam et alteram [m]armoream, in quibus commentari[um ludorum eorum inscriptum sit, eo loco statuant et id opus eidem] | locent praetoribusque q. a. p.[7] inperent, uti redemptoribus ea[m summam qua locaverint solvant]

[1] v(erba) f(ecit) [2] q(uid) d(e) e(a) r(e) f(ieri) p(laceret), d(e) e(a) r(e) i(ta) c(ensuerunt) [3] mag(istri) XVvir(um) s(acris) f(aciundis) [4] s(ine) f(raude) s(ua) [5] sc(ribundo) [6] co(n)s(ules) a(lter) a(mbo)ve [7] q(ui) a(erario) p(raesunt)

31. Edictum XVvirum s. f. de luctu feminarum minuendo per ludos saeculares, 17 B.C., Rome. *ILS.* 5050, l. 110 ff., *FIR.* no. 57.

XVvir. s. f. dic.[1] | cum bono more et proind[e c]elebrato frequentibus exsemplis, quandocumq[ue i]usta laetitiae publicae caussa fuit, | minui luctus matrona[r]um placuerit, idque tam sollemnium sacroru[m l]udorumque tempore referri | diligenterque opserva[r]i pertinere videatur et ad honorem deorum et ad [m]emoriam cultus eorum, statuimus | offici nostri esse per edictum denuntiare feminis, uti luctum minuant ||

[1] XVvir(i) s(acris) f(aciundis) dic(unt)

32. From the Acta sacrorum saecularium, 17 B.C., Rome. *ILS.* 5050, ll. 147 ff.

sacrificioque perfecto puer. [X]XVII quibus denuntiatum erat patrimi et matrimi et puellae totidem | carmen cecinerunt eo[de]mque modo in Capitolio. | carmen composuit Q. Hor[at]ius Flaccus ||

33. Aureus, 17 B.C., Rome. Mattingly, p. 13, nos. 69 ff.; cf. 85, 431.

Obv. Herald. AVGVST. DIVI F. LVDOS SAE.

Rev. Head of Iulus (?). M. SANQVINIVS IIIVIR

34. Denarius, 16 B.C., Rome. Mattingly, p. 17, no. 90; cf. 86 ff., 437 ff.

Obv. Bust of Augustus on round shield. S. C. OB R. P. CVM SALVT. IMP. CAESAR. AVGVS. CONS.

Rev. Mars. S. P. Q. R. V. P. S. PR. S. ET RED. AVG.

Obv. s(enatus) c(onsulto) ob r(em)p(ublicam) cum salut(e) imp(eratoris) Caesar(is) Augus(ti) cons(ervatam)

Rev. s(enatus) p(opulus)q(ue) R(omanus) v(ota) p(ublica) s(uscepta) pr(o) s(alute) et red(itu) Aug(usti)

35. Denarius, 16 B.C., Rome. Mattingly, p. 17, nos. 91 ff.

Obv. Oak-wreath. I. O. M. S. P. Q. R. V. S. PR. S. IMP. CAE. QVOD PER EV. R. P. IN AMP. ATQ. TRAN. S. E.'

Rev. Cippus with inscription: IMP. CAES. AVGV. COMM. CONS. Outside of cippus: S. C. L. MESCINIVS RVFVS IIIVIR

Obv. I(ovi) o(ptimo) m(aximo) s(enatus) p(opulus)q(ue) R(omanus) v(ota) s(uscepta) pr(o) s(alute) imp(eratoris) Cae(saris) quod per eu(m) r(es)p(ublica) in amp(liore) atq(ue) tran(quilliore) s(tatu) e(st)

Rev. imp. Caes(ari) Augu(sto) comm(uni) cons(ensu). s(enatus) c(onsulto)

36. 13 B.C., Rome. *ILS.* 88; cf. 95 (*our no. 39*).

[P. Quinctilius S]ex. f. Varus [pontifex ?] cos. [ludos votivos pr]o reditu [imp. Caesaris div]i f. Augusti [Iovi optimo m]aximo fecit [cum Ti. Claudio Ner]one conlega [ex s.]c.

37. SC. de mense Augusto, 8 B.C. Macrobius, *Sat.* I. 12. 35; *FIR.* no. 42.

cum imperator Caesar Augustus mense Sextili et primum consulatum inierit et triumphos tres in urbem intulerit et ex Ianiculo legiones deductae secutaeque sint eius auspicia ac fidem, sed et Aegyptus hoc mense in potestatem populi Romani redacta sit finisque hoc mense bellis civilibus inpositus sit, atque ob has causas hic mensis huic imperio felicissimus sit ac fuerit, placere senatui ut hic mensis Augustus appelletur

38. 8 B.C., Rome. *ILS.* 8894.

[C. Marcius] L. f. Censo[rinus augu]r [cos. lu]dos votivos pro [reditu imp. Ca]esaris divi f. Aug[usti pont.] maximi [Iovi opti]mo maximo [fecit cum C. Asi]nio Gallo [conlega] ex s.c.

39. 7 B.C., Rome. *ILS.* 95; cf. 88 (*our no. 36*).

Ti. Claudius Ti. f. Nero pontifex cos. iterum imp. iterum ludos votivos pro reditu imp. Caesaris divi f. Augusti pontificis maximi Iovi optimo maximo fecit ex s.c. /[1]

[1] *Erased:* cum Cn. Calpurnio Pisone conlega

40. 7–6 B.C., Tropaea Augusti (Alpes maritimae). Plin. *nat. hist.* iii. 136–7; cf. *CIL.* v. 7817. See A. Stein, *Röm. Inschr. in d. ant. Lit.* (1930), 34.

imp. Caesari divi filio Aug. pont. max. imp. XIIII tr. pot. XVII s.p.q.R., quod eius ductu auspiciisque gentes Alpinae omnes quae a mari supero ad inferum pertinebant sub imperium p. R. sunt redactae. gentes Alpinae devictae Tr{i}umpilini Camunni Venostes Vennonetes Isarci Breuni Genaunes Focunates Vindelicorum gentes quattuor Consuanetes Rucinates Licates Catenates Ambisontes Rugusci Suanetes Calucones Brixenetes Leponti Uberi Nantuates Seduni Varagri Salassi Acitavones Medulli Ucenni Caturiges Brigiani Sogionti(i) Brodionti(i) Nemaloni Edenates ⟨V⟩esubiani Veamini Galli taetri Ulatti Ecdini Vergunni Egui Turi Nematuri Oratelli Nerusi Velauni Suetri

41. 4 B.C., Rome, Forum. *ILS.* 99.

Laribus publicis sacrum imp. Caesar Augustus pontifex maximus tribunic. potestat. XVIIII ex stipe quam populus ei contulit k. Ianuar. apsenti C. Calvisio Sabino L. Passieno Rufo cos.

42. Basis of golden statue of Augustus, Rome, Forum Augusti. *ILS.* 103.

imp. Caesari Augusto p. p. Hispania ulterior Baetica quod beneficio eius et perpetua cura provincia pacata est. auri p. C.[1]

[1] p(ondo) c(entum)

43. A.D. 6–7, Lepcis Magna. *CRAcInscr.* 1939, 99.

Marti Augusto sacrum auspiciis imp. Caesaris Aug. pontificis maxumi patris patriae ductu Cossi Lentuli cos. XVviri sacris faciundis procos. provincia Africa bello Gaetulico liberata civitas Lepcitana

43a. Near Tusculum. *ILS.* 8965.

[. . . M. Vini?]cius [. . . | cos. xv]vir s. f. [. . | legatus pro] pr. Augusti Caesaris in [Illyrico | primus? t]rans flumen Danivium [. . . || . . .]m et Basternarum exer[citum . . .| . . . fu]gavitque Cotinos [. . . | . . .]s et Anartio[s . . . | . . . A]ugusti [. . .

43b. Dalmatia. *ILS.* 3320.

Iano patri Aug. sacrum C. Iulius C. f. Ser. Aetor aed. donatus ab Ti. Caes. Aug. f. Augusto torq. maiore bello Delmatico ob honorem IIviratus cum liberis suis posuit

44. Between A.D. 4 and 14, Bagacum Nerviorum. *ILS.* 8898.

Ti. Caesari Augusti f. divi nepoti. adventui eius sacrum. Cn. Licinius C. f. Vol. Navos

45. Castra Vetera (Germania Inferior). *ILS.* 2244; cf. *RhM.* 1952, 95. 97.

(*Relief of soldier*) M. Caelio T. f. Lem. Bon.[1] t.o.[2] leg. XIIX ann. LIII [ce]cidit bello Variano, ossa [l.?[3] i]nferre licebit. P. Caelius T. f. Lem. frater fecit

(*Bust*) M. Caelius M. l. Privatus

(*Bust*) M. Caelius M. l. Thiaminus

[1] Bon(onia) [2] t(riario) o(rdini)? [3] l(ibertorum)

46. Beneath the relief of a reclining banqueter, A.D. 2, Cyrene. *SEG.* ix. 63 and p. 121.

Lλγʹ. *ἐπὶ ἱερέως Πανσανία Φιλίσκω φύσει δὲ Εὐφάνευς, πανσαμένων πάντων τῆς ἀνείας. Λούκιος Ὄρβιος Λουκίου πυλοκλειστὴς τὸν λυσιπόλεμον.*

ἡνίκα Μαρμαρικοῦ λῆξεν πολέμοιο κυδοιμός,
γήθησεν Βάττου πολλὰ πόλις μερόπων·
τῆμος ἀναγλύψας κατακείμενον ἡδυπο{πο}τοῦντα
Λεύκιος εἰνοδίωι θῆκε παρὰ προθύρωι,
κλεῖ[δ]α πύλης διέπων· ὧραι φίλαι, οὗ χάλις ἔσχεν
Πανσανίαν ἱερῆ καιρ[ῶν](?) πανσάμενον.

Photos: Arch. Anz. *1941, fig. 160–1; cf. Robert,* Hellenica *ii. 142.*

47. Cyrene, *OGIS.* 767; *SEG.* ix. 6.

(*a*) . . . .] *αυτ[. . . . . | τὰν ἐ]π̣ι̣μ̣ε̣λ̣ειαν ταύ[ταν καὶ ἀ|ξία]ν κα[ὶ τ]ῶν προγόνω̣[ν καὶ τᾶς | πα]τρίδος ποιησάμεν[ος, ἱερα||τε]ύσας τε δὶς Καίσαρος τ[οῦ θε|οῦ] ἐκτενῶς καὶ φιλοτείμως | [καὶ] πρεσβεύσας ἐν τῷ Μαρμα|ρικῶι πολέμῳ ἐν χειμῶσι ἑαυ|τὸν ἐς τὸς κινδύνος ἐπιδὸς || καὶ τὰν ἐπικαιροτάταν συμμα||[χ]ίαν καὶ πρὸς σωτηρίαν τ̇[ᾶ]ς πό̣||[λι]ος ἀνήκοισαν ἀγαγών· παρλ<α>|βών τε τὸν τῶ κτίστα τᾶς πό|λιος ἁμῶν Ἀπόλλωνος σ{π}τέ||φανον καὶ τὰ πρὸς θεὸς ἐκτε|νῶς καὶ εὐσεβῶ{ι}ς ἐτέλ[ε]σεν κ<αὶ> | τὰ ποτὶ τὸς ἀνθρώπος μεγαλ[ο]||ψύχως καὶ πλουσίως ὑπὲρ δύ|ναμιν· δεδόχθαι, ποτὶ τα[ῖς] || προγεγονοίσαις αὐτῶι τειμαῖ[ς] | ἐπαινέσαι τε αὐτὸν τὰν πόλι[ν] | δαμοσίαι καὶ παρκαλέ[σαι. . . .]||*

(*b*) . . . .]*χοντα, ἀνθέμε[ν εἰκόνας ἐς] | ὅς κα δήληται δαμ[οσίος ἢ ἱερὸς τό]||πος, καὶ ἐς τὸ τ[ῶ] Ἀ[πόλλωνος] | ἱαρὸν ἄγα[λ]μα Πάριν̣[ον καὶ ὅ]|πλον ἐπίχρυσον, ἔ[χοντα τὰς ἐπι]|γρα[φὰ]ς Φάον Κλεά[νδρω τῶ Φι]|λοπάτριδος ἀρετᾶς [καὶ τᾶς] || ποτὶ τὰν πόλιν ε̣ὔν[οιας ἕνε]|κε Κυραναῖοι*

48. Bizye (Thrace). *OGIS.* 378.

θεῷ ἁγίῳ ὑψίστῳ ὑπὲρ τῆς Ῥοιμητάλκου καὶ Πυθοδωρίδος ἐκ τοῦ κατὰ τὸν Κοιλα<λ>ητικὸν πόλεμον κινδύνου σωτηρίας εὐξάμενος καὶ ἐπιτυχὼν Γάϊος Ἰούλιος Πρόκ<λ>ος χαριστήριον

49. Sestertius, A.D. 22–3, Rome. Mattingly, p. 129, nos. 70 ff.

Obv. S. C. TI. CAESAR DIVI AVG. F. AVGVST. P. M. TR. POT. XXIIII

Rev. Tiberius on curule chair. CIVITATIBVS ASIAE RESTITVTIS

50. A.D. 30, later restored, Puteoli. *ILS.* 156 and iii. 2, p. clxx.

Ti. Caesari divi Augusti f. divi Iuli n. Augusto pontif. maximo cos. IIII imp. VIII trib. potestat. XXXII Augustales. res publica restituit. henia[1] Sa[rde]s ulloron[1] [Magnes]ia Philadelphia Tmolus Cyme Temnos Cibyra Myrina Ephesos Apollonidea Hyrca[nia] Mostene [Aeg]ae [Hieroc]aesarea

[1] *Unintelligible.*

50a. Bronze coin, A.D. 31, Bilbilis (Spain). Heiss, p. 183, no. 21; Vives, p. 56, no. 17..

Obv. Head of Tiberius. TI. CAESAR DIVI AVGVST. F. AVGVSTVS

Rev. Wreath. MVN. AVGVSTA BILBILIS TI. CAESARE V. L. AELIO SEIANO COS.

51. A.D. 32, Interamna (Umbria). *ILS.* 157.

saluti perpetuae Augustae | libertatique publicae | populi Romani |

genio municipi anno post | Interamnam conditam | DCCIIII ad Cn. Domitium | Ahenobarbum ////////|////////////////[1] cos. |

providentiae Ti. Caesaris Augusti nati ad aeternitatem | Romani nominis sublato hoste perniciosissimo p. R.[2] | Faustus Titius Liberalis VIvir Aug. iter. | p. s. f. c.|

[1] *Name of* L. Arruntius Camillus Scribonianus (*cos.* A.D. *32*) *erased after his revolt in* A.D. *42*.

[2] *Refers to Seianus* (*executed* A.D. *31*).

52. Gortyn (Crete). *ILS.* 158.

[num]ini ac providentiae [Ti. Ca]esar. Aug. et senatus [in mem.] eius die(i) qui fuit XV k. Novembr.[1] [P.] Viriasius Naso pro cos. tertio sua pecunia consecravit

[1] *Day of Seianus' death.*

53. Rome. *ILS.* 6044.

. . . . | n]unc quoniam n[. . . . . . | a]nnorum LX, Seiani sce[lerati | . . . . .]itatio et inprobae comitiae || [q]uae fuerunt in Aventino, ubi | [Sei]anus cos. factus est, et ego | [de]bilis inutilis baculi comes, | ut supplex fierem omni nunc | vos rogo,[1]

boni contri||[bu]les, si semper apparui | [v]obis bonus et utilis tri|[bul]is, si nunquam offic[ii mei | immemor f]ui nec rei [. . . . . | . . . . .]m co[. . . . . || . . . .]rif[. . . . .

1 *Perhaps* omni nunc ⟨vi⟩|vos rogo (*Hirschfeld*).

54. As, later years of Tiberius, Rome. Mattingly, p. 141, nos. 146 ff.

Obv. Head of Augustus. DIVVS AVGVSTVS PATER

Rev. Altar. S.C. PROVIDENT.

IV

THE IMPERIAL FAMILY

Other examples of the imperial titulature are nos. 14, 17, 23, 40–1, 49, 50, 50a, 104, 134, 148, 166, 209a, 218a, 225, 232a, 265, 267, 281, 284, 286, 288–90, 292–4, 301–3, 311–12, 318, 338, 344–6, 363a. Members of the imperial family are also recorded in Chapters V and VI, and in nos. 130a, 165, 177, 227, 299–30, 237, 244, 269, 308, 320, 347, 365.

55. 43–40 B.C., Samnium. *ILS.* 76.

C. Iulio C. f. Caesari imp. triumviro r. p. c. patrono d. d.

56. Aureus, 38 B.C., Gaul. Sydenham, 1329.

Obv. Head of deified Julius Caesar with star. IMP. DIVI IVLI F. TER. IIIVIR R. P. C.

Rev. M. AGRIPPA COS. DESIG.

57. Tergeste. *ILS.* 77.

imp. Caesar cos. desig. tert. IIIvir r. p. c. iter. murum turresque fecit

58. 23–22 B.C. (?), Tridentum. *ILS.* 86.

imp. Caesar divi f. Augustus cos. XI trib. potestate dedit, M. Appuleius Sex. f. leg. iussu eius fac. curavit

58a. Copper as, Emerita. Mattingly, p. 54, nos. 298 ff.

Obv. Head of Augustus. CAESAR AVG. TRIB. POTEST.

Rev. P. CARISIVS LEG. AVGVSTI

59. Various coins, various eastern mints. Mattingly, p. 115, nos. 707 ff.; cf. 713 ff., 739 ff.

Obv. Head of Augustus. CAESAR (or AVGVSTVS)

Rev. In laurel wreath: C. A.[1]

[1] C(aesar) A(ugustus)? C(aesaris) A(uctoritate)?

60. 6–5 B.C., Urgavo (Baetica). *ILS.* 96.

imp. Caesari Augusto divi f. pontufici max. trib. potest. XIIX cos. XI patri patriae d. d.

61. A.D. 7–8, Pavia or Ticinum (extant in *Codex Einsidlensis*). *ILS.* 107.

(5) imp. Caesari divi f. Augusto pontific. maximo patri

patriae aug. XVvir. s. f. VIIvir. epulon. cos. XIII imp. XVII tribunic. potest. XXX

(6) Livia[e] Drusi f. uxori Caesaris Aug.

(7) [C.] Caesari Augusti f. divi nepot. pontific. cos. imperatori

(8) [L.] Caesari Augusti f. divi nepot. auguri cos. design. principi iuventutis

(4) Ti. Caesari Augusti f. divi nepot. pont. cos. [i]ter. imp. ter. augurique tribuniciae pot. VIII[I]

(3) Germanico Iulio [T]i. f. Augusti nepot. divi pron. Caesari

(2) D[ruso Iulio Ti.] f. Augusti nepoti divi pron. Caesari pontifici

(1) Neroni Iulio Germanici [f.] Aug. pronepot. Caesari

(9) Druso Iulio Germanici f. Aug. pronepot. Germanico

(10) Ti. Claudio Drusi Germanici f. Neroni Germanico

62. 4 B.C., Pelusium (Egypt). *CRAcInscr.* 1903, 608.

ὑπὲρ αὐτοκράτορος Καίσαρος θεοῦ υἱοῦ Σεβαστοῦ καὶ Λειουίας Σεβαστοῦ καὶ Γαΐου Καίσαρος καὶ Λευκίου Καίσαρος τῶν υἱῶν τοῦ αὐτοκράτορος καὶ Ἰουλίας τῆς θυγατρὸς τοῦ αὐτοκράτορος καὶ Γαΐου Τουρρανίου ἐπάρχου τῆς Αἰγύπτου Κοΐντος Κόρουιος Κοΐντου υἱὸς Φλάκκος ἐπιστρατηγήσας Θηβαΐδος δικαιοδοτῶν Πηλουσίωι τ[ὸ]ν θρόνον καὶ τὸν βωμὸν ἀνέθηκε ἔτους κς΄ Καίσαρος Τῦβι ιγ΄

63. Eresus (Lesbos). *CIL.* iii. 7156–7. *IG.* xii. 2, 537.

Iuliae Caesaris f. Veneri Genetrici

Ἰουλίᾳ Καίσαρος θύγατρι Ἀφροδίτᾳ Γενετείρᾳ

63a. Rome. *CIL.* vi. 899 and 39207; cf. Degrassi, *Doxa* 1949 (= *Epigrafia Romana*, i), 79.

[pl]eps urbana quae hab[itat] in regione urbis X[III . . .]i vicorum [. . . C.] Caesari [Augusti f.] principi [iu]ventutis pontif. cos. [designato] aere c[onlato]

64. Athens, Theatre of Dionysus. *IG.*[2] ii. 3, 3250; cf. *Hesperia*, xvi (1947), 68.

ὁ δῆμος Γάϊον Καίσαρα Σεβαστοῦ υἱὸν νέον Ἄρη

65. 3 B.C., Rome. *Bull. Comm.* 1899, 141.

L. Caesari Augusti f. divi n. principi iuventutis cos. desig. [c]um esset ann. nat. XIIII, aug., senatus

66. Aureus, 2 B.C.–A.D. 11, Lugdunum. Mattingly, p. 88, nos. 513 ff.

Obv. Head of Augustus. CAESAR AVGVSTVS DIVI F. PATER PATRIAE

Rev. C. and L. Caesar standing. C. L. CAESARES AVGVSTI F. COS. DESIGN. PRINC. IVVENT.

67. Mytilene. *IG.* xii. 2, 168.

Γαΐῳ Καίσαρι καὶ Λευκίῳ Καίσαρι το[ῖς] παίδεσσι τῶ Σεβάστω θέω Καίσαρος ἀγιμόνεσσι τ[ᾶ]ς νεότατος

Μάρκῳ Ἀγρίππᾳ θέῳ [σ]ώτηρι καὶ κτίστᾳ τᾶς πόλι{λι}ος καὶ τῷ παῖδι αὔτω Μάρκῳ Ἀγρίππᾳ παιδόπαιδι δὲ τῶ Σεβάστω

68. Cenotaph for L. Caesar, A.D. 2–3, Pisa. *ILS.* 139.

[a.] d. XIII k. Octobr. Pisis in foro in Augusteo scrib.[1] adfuer[e] | Q. Petillius Q. f., P. Rasinius L. f. Bassus, M. Puppius M. [f.], | Q. Sertorius Q. f. Pica, Cn. Octavius Cn. f. Rufus, A. Albiu[s] | A. f. Gutta ||

quod C. Canius C. f. Saturninus IIvir v. f. de augendis honoribus | L. Caesaris, Augusti Caesaris patris patriae pontificis maximi | tribuniciae potestatis XXV fili, auguris consulis designati princip[is] | iuventutis patroni coloniae nostrae, q. d. e. r. f. p., d. e. r. i. c.[2] |

cum senatus populi Romani inter ceteros plurimos ac maxsimos || honores L. Caesaris (*sic*), Augusti Caesaris patris patriae pontificis maximi tribu|niciae potestatis XXV filio, auguri consuli designato, per | consensum omnium ordinum studio [. . . . | . . . . | . . . .]tetur, data cura C. Canio Saturnino IIvir. et decem primis elig[endi] || aspiciendique, uter eorum locus magis idoneus videatur, emendi[que] | publica pecunia a privatis eius loci qu[em] magis probaverint; utique | apud eam aram quodannis a. d. X[III k. Sept. p]ublice manibus eius per magis|tratus eosve, qui ibi iuri dicendo pr[ae]runt, togis pullis amictos, | quibus eorum ius fasque erit eo die [eiu]s vestis habendae, inferiae mit||tantur, bosque et ovis atri infulis caerulis infulati diis manibus eiu[s] | mactentur eaeque hostiae eo loco adoleantur superque eas | singulae urnae lactis mellis olei fundantur, ac tum demum fact[am] | c[eteris p]otestatem, si qui privatim velint manibus eius inferias mitter[e | nive quis] amplius uno cereo unave face coronave mittat, dum ii qui im||[molaver]int cincti Cabino[3] ritu struem lignorum succendant adque | [peri]nde habeant; | [utique] locus ante eam aram, quo ea strues congerantur conponantur, pate[at | q]uoque versus pedes XL stipitibusque robustis saepiatur lignorumque | acervos eius rei gratia quodannis ibi constituatur cippoque grandi || secundum aram defixso hoc decretum cum superioribus decretis ad ei[us] | honores pertinentibus incidatur insculpaturve; nam quod ad cetera | solemnia quae eodem illo die vitari caverive placuissent placerent|que, id sequendum quod de iis senatus p. R. censuisset; utique prim[o] | quoque tempore legati ex nostro ordine imp. Caesare⟨m⟩ Augustum || patrem patriae pontificem maximum tribuniciae potestatis XXV | adeant petantque ab eo, uti colonis Iuliensibus coloniae Opsequenti | [Iu]liae Pisanae ex hoc decreto ea om[n]ia facere exsequique permittat

[1] scrib(endo) [2] q(uid) d(e) e(a) r(e) f(ieri) p(laceret), d(e) e(a r(e) i(ta) c(ensuerunt) [3] *Read:* Gabino

69. Cenotaph for C. Caesar, A.D. 4, Pisa. *ILS.* 140.

[. . . . Pisis in foro in Augusteo (?) scrib. ad]fu[e]r. Q. Sertorius Q. f. Atilius Tacitus, P. Rasinius L. f. Bassus, L. Lappius | [L. f. G]allus, Q. Sertorius Q. f. Alpius Pica, C. Vettius L. f. Virgula, M. Herius | M. [f. P]riscus, A. Albius A. f. Gutta, Ti. Petronius Ti. f. Pollio, L. Fabius L. f. Bassus, | Sex. [A]ponius Sex. f. Creticus, C. Canius C. [f.] Saturninus, L. Otacilius Q. f. Panthera ||

quod [v. f.][1] sunt, cum in colonia nostra propter contentiones candidato|ru[m m]agistratuus non essent et ea acta essent quae infra scripta sunt: | cum a. [d. II]II nonas Apriles allatus esset nuntius C. Caesarem, Augusti patris patri|ae [po]ntif. maxsumi custodis imperi Romani totiusque orbis terrarum prae|si[dis f]ilium, divi nepotem, post consulatum quem ultra finis extremas popu||li [Ro]mani bellum gerens feliciter peregerat, bene gesta re publica, devicteis aut | in [fid]em receptis bellicosissimis ac maxsimis gentibus, ipsum volneribus pro re | pu[bli]ca exceptis ex eo casu crudelibus fatis ereptum populo Romano, iam designa|tu[m i]ustissumum ac simillumum parentis sui virtutibus principem coloniaeque | no[st]rae unicum praesidium, eaque res nondum quieto luctu, quem ex deces||su [L. C]aesaris fratris eius, consulis designati auguris patroni nostri princ[i]|pis [iu]ventutis, colonia universa susceperat, renovasset multiplicassetque | ma[er]orem omnium singulorum universorumque, ob eas res universi decu|rio[ne]s colonique, quando eo casu in colonia neque IIvir. neque praefecti | er[ant] neque quisquam iure dicundo praerat, inter sese consenserunt, pro || ma[g]nitudine tantae ac tam inprovisae calamitatis oportere ex ea die, | qu[a ei]us deces⟨s⟩us nuntiatus esset usqu[e] ad eam diem qua ossa relata atque | co[nd]ita iustaque eius manibus perfecta essent, cunctos veste mutata, templis|qu[e d]eorum immortalium balneisque publicis et tabernis omnibus clausis, | co[nv]ictibus sese apstinere, matronas quae in colonia nostra sunt sublugere || di[em]que eum quo die C. Caesar obit, qui dies est a. d. VIIII k. Martias, pro Alliensi | lu[gub]rem memoriae prodi, notarique in praesentia omnium iussu ac | vo[lun]tate caverique, ne quod sacrificium publicum neve quae suppli|ca[tio]nes nive sponsalia nive convivia publica postea in eum diem | eo[ve d]ie qui dies erit a. d. VIIII k. Mart. fiant concipiantur indican||tu[rve], nive qui ludi scaenici circiensesve eo die fiant spectenturve; | ut[ique] eo die quodannis publice manibus eius per magistratus eosve, | qu[i Pi]sis iure dicundo praerunt, eodem loco eodemque modo, quo | L. C[aes]ari parentari institutum est, parentetur; | utique [arc]us celeberrimo coloniae nostrae loco constituatur orna||tu[s sp]oleis devictarum aut in fidem receptarum ab eo gentium, super | eu[m st]atua pedestris ipsius triumphali ornatu circaque eam duae | eq[uest]res inauratae Gai et Luci Caesarum statuae ponantur: uti|que [cu]m primum per legem coloniae duoviros creare et habere po|tu[eri]mus, ii duo viri qui primi creati erunt hoc quod decurionibus || et [uni]versis colonis placuit, ad decuriones referant, eorum pu|bl[ica] auctoritate adhibita legitume id caveatur auctoribusque | iis [in t]abulas publicas referatur; interea T. Statulenus Iuncus | fla[me]n Augustalis pontif. minor publicorum p. R. sacrorum rogare|tu[r, uti] cum legatis excusata praesenti coloniae necessitate hoc || of[ficiu]m publicum et voluntatem universorum libello reddito | im[p. Ca]esari Augusto patri patriae pontif. maxsimo tribuniciae | po[test]. XXVI indicet; idqu[e T. St]atulenus Iuncus princeps coloniae nostrae flamen August. | po[ntif.] minor publicorum p. R. sacrorum, libello ita uti supra scriptum | es[t imp]eratori Caesari Augusto pontif. maximo tribun. potest. XXVI pat[ri] || pat[riae] reddito, fecerit |

placere conscriptis quae a. d. IIII nonas Apriles, | qu[ae Sex.] Aelio Cato C. Sentio Saturnino cos. fuerunt, facta acta con|st[ituta] sunt per consensum omnium ordinum, ea omnia ita fieri agi ha|be[ri opse]rvarique ab L. Titio A. f. et T. Allio T. f. Rufo IIviris et ab eis quicum||qu[e post]ea in colonia nostra IIvir. praefecti sive qui ali magistratus | er[unt], omnia in perpetuom ita fieri agi haberi opservarique, utiq. L. Titius | A. [f. T. A]llius T. f. Rufus IIviri ea omnia quae supra scripta sunt ex decreto | nos[tro] coram proquaestoribus primo quoque tempore per scribam pu|bl[i]c[um i]n tabulas publicas referenda curent. || censuere |

1 v(erba) f(acta)

70. Denarius, 13 B.C., Rome. Mattingly, p. 23, nos. 112 ff.; cf. 103, 107 ff., 121 ff.

Obv. Head of Augustus. CAESAR AVGVSTVS

Rev. Head of Agrippa. M. AGRIPPA. PLATORINVS IIIVIR

71. 4–3 B.C., Ephesus. *ILS.* 8897; cf. *Forschungen in Ephesos*, iii. 52.

imp. Caesari divi f. Augusto pontifici maximo cos. XII tribunic. potest. XX et Liviae Caesaris Augusti

M. Agrippae L. f. cos. tert. imb. (*sic*) tribunic. potest. VI et Iuliae Caesaris Augusti fil.

Mazaeus et Mithridates patronis

Μαζ[αῖ]ος καὶ Μιθριδάτης τ[οῖς] πά[τ]ρωσι καὶ τῶι δή[μωι]

72. Myra (Lycia). Petersen u. Luschan, *Reisen in Lykien*, 43.

θεὸν Σεβαστὸν θεοῦ υἱὸ[ν] Καίσαρα αὐτοκράτορα γῆς καὶ θαλάσσης, τὸν εὐεργέτ[ην] καὶ σωτῆρα τοῦ σύνπαντος κόσμου, Μυρέων ὁ δῆμος. [Μᾶρκ]ον Ἀγρίππαν τὸν εὐεργέτην καὶ σωτῆρα τοῦ ἔθνους, Μυρέων ὁ δῆμος

73. Between 18 and 12 B.C., Corinth. *Corinth*, viii. 2, no. 16.

M. Agrippae cos. tert. trib. poṭest. d. d. tribus Vinicia patrono

74. 16–15 B.C., Emerita, theatre. *ILS.* 130.

M. Agrippa L. f. cos. III trib. pot. III

75. 16–15 B.C., Nemausus, 'Maison carrée'. *CRAcInscr.* 1919, 332. *Earliest inscription:*

M. Agrippa L. f. cos. III imp. tribun. potest. III col. Aug. Nem. dat.

Later replaced by:

C. Caesari Augusti f. cos. L. Caesari Augusti f. cos. designato principibus iuventutis

76. Between 17 and 12 B.C., Thespiae. *BCH.* 1926, 447.

(*a*) ὁ δῆμος Ἀγριππῖναν Μάρκου Ἀγρίππα θυγατέρα

ὁ δῆμος Μᾶρκον Ἀγρίππαν Λευκίου υἱὸν Μούσαις

(*b*) ὁ δῆμος Λούκιον Καίσαρα

ὁ δῆμος Γάϊον Καίσαρα

ὁ δῆμος Ἰουλίαν αὐτοκράτορος Καίσαρος Σεβαστοῦ θυγατέρα γυναῖκα Μάρκου Ἀγρίππα Μούσαις

ὁ δῆμος [Λιβίαν αὐτοκράτορος] Καίσαρος [Σεβαστοῦ] γυν[αῖκα Μούσαις]

77. Thasos. *ILS.* 8784.

ὁ δῆμος Λειβίαν Δρουσίλλαν τὴν τοῦ Σεβαστοῦ Καίσαρος γυναῖκα θεὰν εὐεργέτιν

ὁ δῆμος Ἰουλίαν Καίσαρος Σεβαστοῦ θυγατέρα τὴν ἀ[πὸ] προγόνων εὐεργέτιν

Ἰουλίαν Μάρκου Ἀγ[ρ]ίππου θυγατέρα ὁ δῆμος

77a. Bronze coin, Asia Minor. Grant, *FITA.* 362.

Obv. Head of Augustus. ΣΕΒΑΣΤΟΥ ΘΕ.

Rev. Agrippa Postumus, standing. ΑΓΡΙΠΠΑΣ ΑΓΡΙΠΠΟΥ ΚΑΙ ΤΗΣ ΙΟΥΛΙΑΣ ΥΙΟΣ

77b. Between 6 B.C. and A.D. 2, Pythion (Rhodes). *Studi offerti a E. Ciaceri* (1940), 254.

ὁ δᾶμος ὁ Ῥοδίων ὑπὲρ Τεβερίου Κλαυδίου Νέρωνος

78. A.D. 1 or earlier, Olympia. *Syll.*³ 782.

Τιβέριον Κλαύδιον Τιβερίου υἱὸν Νέρωνα νικήσαντα Ὀλύμπια τεθρίππωι τελείωι [. . . .]ο[. .] Ἀπολλ[ώ]νιος Ἀπολλωνίου ὑὸς Ἠλεῖος ὁ καὶ Τιβέριος [Κλ]αύδιος τὸν ἑαυτοῦ πάτρωνα καὶ εὐεργέ{τη}την Διὶ Ὀλυμπίωι

79. A.D. 2–4, Saepinum. *ILS.* 147.

Ti. Claudius Ti. f. Nero pont. cos. II [imp. I]I trib. potest. V, Nero Claudius Ti. f. Drusus Germa[nicus] augur c[os.] imp. [. . .] murum portas turris d. [s. p.] f. c.

80. Rome, Forum Augusti. *NdS.* 1933, 460.

[Nero] Cl[aud]ius Ti. f. [Drus]us Ge[r]mani[c]us [cos. p]r. urb. q. aug. imp. [est appellat]us [i]n Germania

81. Aureus, A.D. 13–14, Lugdunum. Mattingly, p. 87, nos. 506 ff.

Obv. Head of Augustus. CAESAR AVGVSTVS DIVI F. PATER PATRIAE

Rev. Head of Tiberius. TI. CAESAR AVG. F. TR. POT. XV

81a. Athens. *IG.*² ii. 3233 and *Hesperia*, xvii (1948), p. 41, no. 30 (cf. J. H. Oliver, *A. J. P.* lxix, 1948, 436, also *Studies presented to D. M. Robinson*, ii. 330, 938).

. . . . *πρεσ]βευτὴν αὐτοκρά[τορος Καίσαρος Σεβαστοῦ] καὶ Τιβερίου Καίσα[ρος* . . . . . .

82. A.D. 21, bridge near Ariminum. *ILS.* 113.

imp. Ca[e]sar divi f. Augustus pontifex maxim. cos. XIII imp. XX tribunic. potest. XXXVII p.p., Ti. Caesar divi Augusti f. divi Iuli n. August. pontif. maxim. cos. IIII imp. VIII trib. potest. XXII dedere

83. Dupondius, A.D. 22–23, Rome. Mattingly, p. 131, nos. 79 ff.

Obv. S.C. TI. CAESAR DIVI AVG. F. AVG. P. M. TR. POT. XXIII

Rev. Female head. IVSTITIA

84. Dupondius, A.D. 22–23, Rome. Mattingly, p. 131, nos. 81 ff.

Obv. S.C. TI. CAESAR DIVI AVG. F. AVG. P. M. TR. POT. XXIII

Rev. Female head. SALVS AVGVSTA

85. A.D. 32–33, Via Flaminia, near Capena. *ILS.* 159.

Ti. Caesari divi Augusṭi f. Augusto pontif. maximo cos. V trib. potest. XXXIIII principi optumo ac iustissimo conservatori patriae pro salute et incolumitate eius A. Fabius Fortunatus viator [cos.] et pr[aet.] Augustalis prim[us] voto suscepto p.

86. A.D. 33, Oneum (Dalmatia). *Boll. di arch. e di stor. dalmat.* 1914, 104.

[Ti. Cae]sari div[i Aug. f.] divi Iul[i nep. Augu]sto ponti[fici max. c]os. V imp. V[III trib.] pot. XXXV au[guri XVvir]o sacris fa[ciundis VIIviro] epu[lonum . . . . . .

87. Sestertius, A.D. 22–23, Rome. Mattingly, p. 130, nos. 76 ff.

Obv. S.C. TI. CAESAR DIVI AVG. F. AVGVST. P. M. TR. POT. XXIII

Rev. Coach (*carpentum*) with mules. S. P. Q. R. IVLIAE AVGVST.

88. Myra (Lycia). *IGRR.* iii. 721.

Τιβέριον Καίσαρα θεὸν Σεβαστὸν θεῶν Σεβαστῶν υἱὸν αὐτοκ[ρ]άτορα γῆς καὶ θαλάσσης, τὸν εὐεργέτην καὶ σωτῆρα τοῦ σύνπαντος [κ]όσμου, Μυρέων ὁ δῆμος

89. Athens, Agora, near Bouleuterion. *Hesperia* VI (1937), 464.

'Ιουλίαν Σεβαστὴν Βουλα[ί]αν Τιβερίου Σεβαστοῦ μητέρα ἡ βουλὴ ἡ ἐξ Ἀρείο[υ π]ά[γου]

90. A.D. 22–23, near Caudium. *NdS.* 1924, 514.

Druso Caesar[i] Ti. Augusti f. divi Aug. n. divi Iuli pron. cos. II trib. potest. II

91. As, A.D. 22–23, Rome. Mattingly, p. 133, nos. 95 ff.

Obv. S.C. DRVSVS CAESAR TI. AVG. F. DIVI AVG. N. PONT. TR. POT. $\overline{\text{II}}$.

Rev. Winged caduceus between two cornucopiae, each with bust of small boy

92. A.D. 23 or later, Rome. *ILS.* 168, 176.

(*a*) pleps urbana quinque et triginta tribuum Druso Caesari Ti. Aug. f. divi Augusti n. divi Iulii pronepoti pontifici auguri sodal. Augustal. cos. iterum tribunic. potest. iter. aere conlato

(*b*) pleps urbana quinque et triginta tribuum Germanico Caesari Ti. Augusti f. divi Augusti n. auguri flamini Augustali cos. iterum imp. iterum aere conlato

93. Ilium. *IGRR.* iv. 206 (Le Bas–Waddington, no. 1039).

Ἀντωνίαν τὴν ἀδελφιδῆν τὴν θεοῦ Σεβαστοῦ γυναῖκα δὲ γενομένην Δρούσου Κλαυδίου τοῦ ἀδελφοῦ τοῦ αὐτοκράτορος Τιβερίου Σεβαστοῦ υἱοῦ Σεβαστοῦ, μητέρα δὲ Γερμανικοῦ Καίσαρος καὶ Τιβερίου Κλαυδίου Γερμανικοῦ καὶ Λειβίας θεᾶς Ἀφροδείτης Ἀγχεισιάδος, πλείστας καὶ μεγίστας ἀρχὰς τοῦ θειοτάτου γένους παρασχοῦσαν, Φίλων Ἀπολλωνίου τὴν ἑαυτοῦ θεὰν καὶ εὐεργέτιν ἐκ τῶν ἰδίων

93a. Bronze coin, Romula (Spain). Heiss, p. 393, no. 4; Vives, p. 124, no. 4.

Obv. Head of Germanicus. GERMANICVS CAESAR TI. AVG. F

Rev. Shield. PERM. AVG. COL. ROM.

94. Eresos (Lesbos). *IG*. xii. 2, 540.

Γερμάνικον Κλα[ύδιον Καίσαρα α]ὐτοκράτορος [Τιβερίω Καίσαρος] Σεβάστω παῖδα, παιδόπ[αιδα δὲ αὐτοκράτορ]ος Καίσαρος Ὀλ[υ]μπίω [Σεβάστω τὸν] εὐεργέ[ταν] ὀ [ἀρχιέρευς] Δάμ[αρχος Λέο]ντος

The words underlined have been deleted.

94a. *Rogatio* in honour of Germanicus, A.D. 19–20, Heba (Etruria). *Notizie degli Scavi*, lxxii (ser. 8, vol. 1), 1947, 49 ff. (U. Coli); new fragments, *PdP*. 1951, 435; bibliography in G. Tibiletti, *Principi e magistrati repubblicani* (1953), 269–89, and (with revised text) J. H. Oliver and R. E. A. Palmer, *AJP*. 1954, 225 (*O.–P.*).

1 utique in Palatio in porticu quae est ad Apollinis in eo templo in quo senatus haberi solet, [inter ima]|gines virorum inlustris ingeni Germanici Caesaris et Drusi Germanici patris eius natural[is fratrisq.] | Ti. Caesaris Aug. qui ipse quoq. fecundi ingeni fuit imagines ponantur supra capita columna[rum eius fas]|tigi quo simulacrum Apollinis tegitur. 2 utiq. Sali carminibus suis nomen Germanici Caesa[ris pro ho]||norifica memoria interponant, qui honos C. quoq. et L. Caesarib. fratr. Ti. Caesaris Aug. habitus est. 3 [utiq. ad X]| centur. Caesarum quae de cos. pr. destinandis suffragium ferre solent adiciantur V centur[iae, et cum] | primae X citabuntur C. et L. Caesar., adpellentur insequentes V Germanici Caesaris, inq. is omnib[us centuris] | senatores et equites omnium decuriarum quae iudicior. publicor. caussa constitutae sunt erun[t suffragium] | ferant; quiq.cumq. magistratu⟨u⟩m destinationis faciendae caussa senatores quibusq. in ṣẹṇ[a]tu sen[tentiam] || dicere licebit, itemq. eq. in consaeptum ex lege quam L. Valerius Messalla Volesus Cn. Corn[el]ius Cin[na Magnus] | cos.[1] tulerunt suffragi ferendi caussa convocabit, is uti senatores itemq. equites omnium decuria[rum quae | iudiciorum publi]corum (*vacat*) gratia constitutae sunt erunt suffragium ferant, quod eius r[ei fieri poterit, | in XV centur. curet; qu]amq. ex ea lege nongentor., sive ii custodes adpellantur, sortitionem ad X centu[rias fieri | cautum perscr]ịptumvest uti fiat, eam is quem ex ea lege exve hac rogatione{m} nongentorum, siv[e ii custodes] || adpella[ntur, sort]itionem facere oportebit in XV centur. faciat, proinde ac si ea lege in XV centuria[s nongentor.] | sive custodum sortitionem fieri haberive oporteret.[2] 4 utiq. eo die in quem ex lege quam L. Valerius M[essalla Vole]|sus Cn. Cornelius Cinna

Magnus cos. tulerunt exve h. r.[3] senatores et eq. suffragi ferendi caussa adess[e debebunt, is] | adsidentibus pr. et tr. pl. cistas XV vimineas grandes poni iubeat ante tribunal suum, in quas tabeḷ[lae suffra]|giorum demittantur, itemq. tabellas ceratas secundum cistas poni iubeat tam multas quam [opus esse ei] || videbitur, item tabulas dealbatas in quib. nomina candidatorum scripta sint, quo loco commo[dissime legi] | possint, ponendas curet; deinde in conspectu omnium magistratuum et eorum qui suffrag[ium laturi] | erunt sedentium in subsellis, sicuti cum in X centurias Caesarum suffragium ferebatur se[debant, is] | trium et XXX trib. excepta Suc. et Esq.[4] pilas quam maxime aequatas in urnam versatilem coici e[t sortitio]|nem pronuntiari iubeat ⟨et⟩ sortiri qui senatores et eq. in quamq. cistam suffragium ferre debea⟨n⟩t; du[m in centur.] || primas quae C. et L. Caesar. adpellantur sortitio fiat ita uti in primam II III IIII cistas sortiatur b[inas trib., in] | V cistam tres, in VI VII VIII VIIII binas, in X tres, in eas quae Germanici Caesaris adpellantur so[rtitio fiat ita] | ut in XI XII XIII XIIII cistas sortiatur binas trib., in XV tres trib.; ita ut cum tribum unam cuius[cumq. sors e]|xierit citaverit, senatores quibusq. in senatu sententiam dicere licebit qui ex ea trib. erun[t ordine? vocet] | et ad primam cistam accedere et suffragium ferre iubeat, deinde cum itạ ṭ[uleri]ṇṭ suffra[gium ad subsellia] || redierint, ex eadem tribu vocet equites ẹ[osq. in] ẹạndem cistam suffragium fer[re iu]beat, dẹ[inde alteram et] | alteram tribum sortiatur et singularu[m omnium trib]⟨u⟩um senatores deinde eq. iṭ[a vocet ut in quam cistam suffra]|gium ferre debebunt suffragium fer[ant, dummodo quod a]d eorum suffragium perti[nebit si qui ex Suc. tribu] | Esq.ve erunt, item si qua [in] tribu senator [nem]o e[rit a]ut si nemo eq. erit et senatorụ[m . . . . .][5] | erunt, item quod ad cista[s suff]ragis latis signandas et pr. qui aer. praesunt praerint tr[adendas ut cum suffragis] || destinationis in saep[ta d]eferantur, deq. signis cognoscendis suffragis diribend[is, omnia quae . . . . .] | ṛ[e]ị caussa in ea lege quam Cinna et Volesus cos. de X centuris Caesar. tuler. scripta c[omprehensave sunt | servet,] eademq. omnia in XV centur. agat faciat agenda facienda curet uti eum ex ea l. qụ[am Cinna et Volesus | cos. tuler]unt [in X c]ent[uris Caes]ar. agere facere oporteret, quaeq. ita acta erunt ea iusta rạ[taq. sint; deinde diri|bitis cos. pr. destinationi]s suffragis ex XV centuris C. et L. Caesar. et

Germanici Cae[s. adductaq. tabella centur. || quaecumq. ducta eri]ṭ, is qui eam destinationem habebit eam tabellam ita r[ecitet uti eum ex lege | quam L. Valerius Messalla] Volesus Cn. Cornelius Cinna Magnus cos. tuler. X centur. [Caesar. eam tabellam quae | ex is centuris sorte ducta] esset recitare oporteret, dum quae tabula centuriae C. [et L. Caesar. cuiusq. sorte ex|ierit, eam sub nomine] C. et L. Caesarum recitandam quiq. ea centur. candidati dest[inati sint unumquemq. sub illo|rum nomine pronunti]andum[6] curet, quae tabula ex is centuris quae Germanici Cae[saris ex h. r. adpellantur sorte || exierit eam s]ub nomine Germanici Caesar. recitandam quiq. ea centuria candid[ati destinati sint, unumquemq. | item quoq. pr]ọnuntiandum[7] curet; isq. numerus centuriarum qui h. r. adicitur in nu[merum reliquarum centuriarum][8] | pẹrịnde cedat atq. eum numerum qui X centuriar. est cedere ex lege quam Cinna e[t Volesus cos. tulerunt cautum] | comprehensumve est uti cedat; itaq. qui cos. pr. creandorum caussa destinatione[m habuerit, uti eius numeri comitiis][9] | ratio habeatur itaq. suffragium feratur curet; cetera quae nominatim h. r. scrip[ta non sint ea omnia perinde atq.] || ex ea lege quam Cinna et Volesus cos. tuler. agantur fiant serventur. **5** utiq. ludis Augu[stalibus cum subsellia sodalium] | ponentur in theatris, sellae curules Germanici Caesaris inter ea ponantur cu[m querceis coronis in memoriam] | eius sacerdoti, quae sellae cum templum divi Aug. perfectum erit ex eo templo pr[oferantur et interea in templo] | Martis Ultoris reponantur et inde proferantur, quiq.cumq. eos ludos q. s. s. s. fac[iat, uti ex eo templo q. s. s. e. in the]|atris ponantur et cum reponendae erunt in eo templo reponantur curet. **6** uti[q. quo die cautum est ut ossa Germanici] || Caesaris in tumulum inferrentur templa deor. clauderentur, et qui ordini [equestri adscripti erunt neq. pub. eq]|uom[10] habebunt, qui eor. officio fungi volent et per valetudinem perq. domestic[um funus non impedientur, cum[11]] | clavo, ii qui equom pub. habebunt cum trabeis in campum veniant. **7** utiq. ad [memoriam Germanici Caes. quo die defun]|ctus est, templa deor. inmortalium quae in urbe Roma{m} prop{r}iusve urbem [Romam passus M sunt erunt, quotannis] | clausa sint, idque ut ita fiat ii qui eas aedes tuendas redemptas habent h[abebunt curent, et in memoriam eius magistri] || sodalium Augustalium qui quoq. anno erunt inferias ante tumulu[m eodem die dis manibus Germanici Cae]|saris mittendas curent, aut si magistri unus pluresve ad id sacrif[icium adesse non poterint, ii qui pro]|ximo anno magisterio fungi debebunt in locum eorum qui eo mun[ere fungi non poterint fungantur]

[1] A.D. 5.

[2] oportebit *inscr.*

[3] h(ac) r(ogatione)

[4] Suc(cusana) et Esq(uilina)

[5] senatorẹ[s equitesq. si minus quam V] *O.–P.*

[6] *rest. O.–P.* eorum priorem | ceteris renunti] *Coli.* eorum quemque | ordine renunti] *Nesselhauf.* eorum nomen ex ea le|ge exve h. r. pronunti] *Tibiletti.* eorum locum ex | ordine renunti] *Seston.*

[7] *rest. O.–P.* eor. | priorem re] *Coli.* eorum | quemque re] *Nesselhauf.* eorum no|men item pr]ọ *Tibiletti.* eor. | locum ex ordine re] *Seston.*

[8] *rest. Tibiletti.* omnium centuriarum *Coli.* ad quem creari oportebit *de Visscher.* omnium suffragiorum *Seston.* centur. C. et L. Caesarum *Nesselhauf.* centuriarum iure rogatarum *Piganiol.* centuriar. C. et L. Caesar. *O.–P.*

[9] *rest. Tibiletti.* habebit ut in alis centur. eadem *Coli.* habuerit uti eorum comitiis *de Visscher.* habuerit uti earum centuriar. *PdP. 1950, 104.* habebit uti eius l(egis) eiusve r(ogationis) *Seston.* habebit uti eorum quae s(upra) s(cripta) s(unt) *Nesselhauf.* habebit uti earum extra ordinem *Piganiol.* destinatione acta comitia habebit, uti eorum *O.–P.*

[10] adscripti privatum *Coli.* adscripti senator. fili *PdP. 1950, 106.* ordinis utrius erunt pompam irent qui latum clavom *O.–P.*

[11] lato *inserted in PdP. 1950, 106.* ii sine lato *O.–P.*

94b. *Rogatio* in honour of Drusus (?), A.D. 23–24 (?) Ilici (Spain). U. Coli, *NdS.* 1947, 66 f. A. d'Ors, *Iura* I (1950), 280. Further bibliography and text: Oliver and Palmer, *AJP.* 1954, 248. Cf. no. 94a, ll. 19–32.

. . . item]q. tabellas c[eratas secundum cistas poni iubeat tam multas | quam opus esse ei videbitur item t]abulas dealbatas in [quib. nomina candidatorum scripta | sint, quo loco commodissime legi p]ossint ponendas curet; [deinde in conspectu omnium | magistratuum et eorum qui suffragi]um laturi erunt sed[entium in subsellis, sicuti cum in || XV centurias Caesarum et Germani]ci Caesaris suffragi[um ferebatur sedebant, is trium | et XXX tribuum excepta Suc. et Esq. pila]s quam maxime a[equatas in urnam versatilem coici | et sortitionem pronuntiari iubeat et] sortiri qui sen[atores et equites in quamq. cistam | suffragium fere debeant, dum in centurias pri]mas qu[ae C. et L. Caesar. adpellantur, sortitio . . . (*ll. 9–11*) | . . .] c[istas sortiatur . . . . . ita ut cum tribum unam | cuiuscumq. s]ors [exierit citaverit, senatores quibusq. in senatu sententiam dice|re licebit q]ui ex ea [tribu erunt vocet . . . . . et ad primam cistam accedere et suf||fragium f]erre iube[at; deinde cum ita tulerint suffragium et ad subsellia redierint, | ex eadem t]ribu vocet eq[uites eosq. in eandem cistam suffragium ferre iubeat; deinde | alteram et] alteram tri[bum sortiatur et singularum omnium tribuum senatores, deinde eq. ita | vocet ut in c]istam in qu[am suffragium ferre debebunt suffragium ferant . . .

95. Mytilene. *IG.* xii. 2, 212.

ὁ δᾶμος Νέρωνα Ἰούλιον Καίσαρα παῖδα θέω νέω Γερμανίκω Καίσαρος καὶ θέας Αἰόλιδος καρποφόρω Ἀγριππίνας

96. A.D. 27–29, Rome. *ILS.* 182.

Neroni Caesari Germanici Caesaris f. Ti. Caesaris Augusti n. divi Augusti pron. flamini Augustali sodali Augustali sodali Titio fratri Arvali fetiali quaestori ex s. c.

96a. Bronze coin, Tingis (Mauretania). Boyce, *Numism. Notes and Monographs*, 109 (1947), 21, nos. 8, 9.

Obv. Head of Nero, son of Germanicus. NERO IVL. TIN.
Rev. Head of Drusus, son of Germanicus. DRVSVS

97. Between A.D. 33 and 37, Vienna Allobrogum. *ILS.* 189.

C. Caesari Germanici f. Ti. Aug. n. [d]ivi Augusti pronepoti Germanico [p]ontifici q.

V

IMPERIAL CULT

See also nos. 63, 64, 67, 88–89, 93, 95, 315, 316, 343a, 345, 352.

98. Letter of proconsul and decrees of the province of Asia on new calendar, probably 9 B.C. Copies from Priene, Apamea, Eumeneia, Dorylaeum. *OGIS.* 458 and *SEG.* iv. 490; ll.40–49 from unpublished stone from Apamea.

(*a*) . . . . | παρ]ὰ τῶν πρότ[ερ]ον παρειλ[ήφαμεν . . . . | . .] τῶν θεῶν [ε]ὐμενὲς κα[ὶ . . . . | πότ]ερον[1] ἡδείων ἢ ὠφελ[ιμωτέρα ἐ]στὶν ἡ τοῦ θειοτάτου Καίσαρος γενέ||θλιος ἡμέρα, ἣν τῆι τῶν πάντων ἀρχῆι ἴσην δικαίως ἂν εἶναι ὑπ[ολά]βοιμεν, | καὶ εἰ μὴ τῆι φύσει, τῶι γε χρησίμωι, εἴ γε οὐδὲ[ν ο]ὐχὶ διαπεῖπτον καὶ εἰς ἀτυ|χὲς μεταβεβηκὸς σχῆμα ἀνώρθωσεν, ἑτέραν τε ἔδωκεν παντὶ τῶι | κόσμωι ὄψιν, ἥδιστα ἂν δεξαμένωι φθοράν, εἰ μὴ τὸ κοινὸν πάντων εὐ|τύχημα ἐπεγεννήθη Καῖσαρ. διὸ[2] ἄν τις δικαίως ὑπολάβοι τοῦτο ἁτῶι || ἀρχὴν τοῦ βίου καὶ τῆς ζωῆς γεγονέναι, ὅ ἐστιν πέρας καὶ ὅρος τοῦ με|ταμέλεσθαι, ὅτι γεγέννηται. καὶ ἐπεὶ οὐδεμιᾶς ἂν ἀπὸ ἡμέρας εἴς | τε τὸ κοινὸν καὶ εἰς τὸ ἴδιον ἕκαστος ὄφελος εὐτυχεστέρας λάβοι | ἀφορμὰς ἢ τῆς πᾶσιν γενομένης εὐτυχοῦς, σχεδόν τε συμβαίνει | τὸν αὐτὸν ταῖς ἐν Ἀσίαι πόλεσιν καιρὸν εἶναι τῆς εἰς τὴν ἀρχὴν εἰσόδου, || δηλονότι κατά τινα θείαν βούλησιν οὕτως τῆς τάξεως προτετυπωμέ|νης, ἵνα ἀφορμὴ γένοιτο τῆς εἰς τὸν Σεβαστὸν τιμῆς, καὶ ἐπειδὴ δύσκο|λον μέν ἐστιν τοῖς τοσούτοις αὐτοῦ εὐεργετήμασιν κατ' ἴσον ε[ὐχαρισ]||τεῖν, εἰ μὴ παρ' ἕκαστα ἐπινοήσαιμεν τρόπον τινὰ τῆς ἀμείψε[ως καινόν,] | ἥδειον δ' ἂν ἄνθρωποι τὴν κοινὴν πᾶσιν ἡμέραν γενέθλιον ἀγά[γοιεν || ἐ]ὰν προσγένηται αὐτοῖς καὶ ἰδία τις διὰ τὴν ἀρχὴν ἡδονή, δοκεῖ μοι | πασῶν τῶν πολειτηῶν εἶναι μίαν καὶ τὴν αὐτὴν[3] νέαν νουμηνίαν | τὴν τοῦ θηοτάτου Καίσαρος γενέθλιον, ἐκείνῃ τε πάντας εἰς τὴν | ἀρχὴν ἐνβαίνειν, ἥτις ἐστὶν πρὸ ἐννέα καλανδῶν Ὀκτωβρίων, ὅπως | καὶ περισσότερον τιμηθῆι προσλαβομένη ἔξωθέν τινα θρησκήαν καὶ || μᾶλλον πᾶσιν γείνηται γνώριμος, ἣν οἴομαι καὶ πλείστην εὐχρηστίαν | τῆι ἐπαρχήᾳ παρέξεσθαι. ψήφισμα δὲ ὑπὸ τοῦ κοινοῦ τῆς Ἀσίας δεή|σει γραφῆναι πάσας ἐνπεριειληφὸς τὰς ἀρετὰς αὐτοῦ, ἵνα τὸ ἐπινοη|θὲν ὑφ' ἡμῶν εἰς τὴν τειμὴν τοῦ Σεβαστοῦ μείνῃ αἰώνιον. προστάξω | δὲ χαραχθὲν <ἐν> τῇ στήλῃ τὸ ψήφισμα ἐν τῷ ναῷ ἀνατεθῆναι, προτά||ξας τὸ διάταγμα ἑκατέρως γραφέν

(*b*) ἔδοξεν τοῖς ἐπὶ τῆς Ἀσίας | Ἕλλησιν, γνώμῃ τοῦ ἀρχιερέως Ἀπολλωνίου τοῦ Μηνοφίλου Ἀζανίτου· | ἐπε[ιδὴ ἡ θείως] διατάξασα τὸν βίον ἡμῶν πρόνοια σπουδὴν εἰσεν[ενκα|μ]ένη καὶ φιλοτιμίαν τὸ τεληότατον τῶι βίωι διεκόσμη[σεν ἀγαθὸν] | ἐνενκαμένη τὸν Σεβαστόν, ὃν εἰς εὐεργεσίαν ἀνθρώ[πων] ἐπλή||ρωσεν ἀρετῆς, ‹ὥ›σπερ ἡμεῖν καὶ τοῖς μεθ' ἡ[μᾶς σωτῆρα χαρισαμένη] | τὸν παύσαντα μὲν πόλεμον, κοσμήσοντα [δὲ εἰρήνην, ἐπιφανεὶς δὲ] | ὁ Καῖσαρ τὰς ἐλπίδας τῶν προλαβόντων [εὐανγέλια πάντων ὑπερ]|έθηκεν, οὐ μόνον τοὺς πρὸ αὐτοῦ γεγονότ[ας εὐεργέτας ὑπερβα]|λόμενος, ἀλλ' οὐδ' ἐν τοῖς ἐσομένοις ἐλπίδ[α ὑπολιπὼν ὑπερβολῆς], || ἦρξεν δὲ τῶι κόσμωι τῶν δι' αὐτὸν εὐανγελί[ων ἡ γενέθλιος ἡμέ]ρα | τοῦ θεοῦ, τῆς δὲ Ἀσίας ἐψηφισμένης ἐν Σμύρνῃ [ἐπὶ ἀνθυ]π̣άτου | Λευκίου Οὐολκακίου Τύλλου, γραμματεύοντος Παπ[ίωνος Διοσιεριτοῦ | τῶι μεγίστας γ' εἰς τὸν θεὸν καθευρόντι τειμὰς εἶναι στέφανον, | Παῦλλος Φάβιος Μάξιμος ὁ ἀνθύπατος τῆς ἐπαρχήας εὐεργέτης || ἀπὸ τῆς ἐκείνου δεξιᾶς καὶ [γ]νώμης ἀπεσταλμένος ξὺν τοῖς ἄλλοις | οἷς εὐεργέτησεν τὴν ἐπαρχήαν, ὧν εὐεργεσιῶν τὰ μεγέθη λόγος | εἰπεῖν οὐδεὶς ἂν ἐφίκοιτο, καὶ τὸ μέχρι νῦν ἀγνοηθὲν ὑπὸ τῶν Ἑλλή|νων εἰς τὴν τοῦ Σεβαστοῦ τειμὴν εὕρετο, τὸ ἀπὸ τῆς ἐκείνου γενέ|σεως ἄρχειν τῷ βίῳ τὸν χρόνον· διὸ τύχῃ ἀγαθῇ καὶ ἐπὶ σωτηρίᾳ δεδό||χθαι τοῖς ἐπὶ τῆς Ἀσίας Ἕλλησι, ἄρχειν τὴν νέαν νουμηνίαν πάσα[ις] | ταῖς πόλεσιν τῇ πρὸ ἐννέα καλανδῶν Ὀκτωβρίων, ἥτις ἐστὶν γενέ|θλιος ἡμέρα τοῦ Σεβαστοῦ. ὅπως δὲ ἀεὶ ἡ {τε} ἡμέρα στοιχῇ καθ' ἑκάσ|την πόλιν, συνχρηματίζειν τῇ Ῥωμαϊκῇ καὶ τὴν Ἑλληνικὴν ἡμέραν. | ἄγεσθαι δὲ τὸν πρῶτον μῆνα Καίσαρα, καθὰ καὶ προεψήφισται, ἀρχόμε||νον ἀπὸ πρὸ ἐννέα μὲν καλανδῶν Ὀκτωβρίων, γενεθλίου δὲ ἡμέρας | Καίσαρος, τὸν δὲ ἐψηφισμένον στέφανον τῷ τὰς μεγίστας εὑρόντι | τειμὰς ὑπὲρ Καίσαρος δεδόσθαι Μαξίμωι τῶι ἀνθυπάτωι, ὃν καὶ ἀεὶ | ἀναγορεύεσθαι ἐν τῷ γυμ[νι]κῷ ἀγῶνι τῶι ἐν Περγάμωι τῶν Ῥω[μα]ίων | Σεβαστῶν, ὅτι στεφανοῖ [ἡ Ἀσ]ία Παῦλον Φάβιον Μάξιμον εὐ[σεβ]έ[σ]||τατα παρευρόντα τὰς εἰς Καίσαρα τειμάς. ὡσαύτως δὲ ἀνα[γορεύ]εσ|θαι καὶ ἐν τοῖς ἀγομένοις κατὰ πόλιν ἀγῶσιν τῶν Καισαρήων. | ἀναγραφῆναι δὲ τὸ δελτογράφημα τοῦ ἀνθυπάτου καὶ τὸ ψήφισμα τῆς | Ἀσίας ἐν στήλῃ λευκολίθωι, ἣν καὶ τεθῆναι ἐν τῶι τῆς Ῥώμης καὶ τοῦ | Σεβαστοῦ τεμένει. προνοῆσαι δὲ καὶ τοὺς καθ' ἔτος ἐκδίκους ὅπως || ἐν ταῖς ἀφηγουμέναις τῶν διοικήσεων πόλεσιν ἐν στήλαις λευ|κολίθοις ἐνχαραχθῇ τό τε δελτογράφημα τοῦ Μαξίμου καὶ τὸ τῆς Ἀσίας | ψήφισμα, αὗταί τε αἱ στῆλαι τεθῶσιν ἐν τοῖς Καισαρήοις. ἀχθήσονται | οἱ μῆνες κατὰ τάδε· Καῖσαρ ἡμερῶν $\overline{\lambda\alpha}$· Ἀπελλαῖος ἡμερῶν λ· | Αὐδναῖος ἡμερῶν $\overline{\lambda\alpha}$· Περίτιος ἡμερῶν $\overline{\lambda\alpha}$· Δύστρος $\overline{\kappa\eta}$·

Ξανδικός λα· || Ἀρτεμισιὼν ἡμερῶν λ· Δαίσιος λα· Πάνημος λ· Λῶος λα· Γορπιαῖος λα· | Ὑπερβερεταῖος λ· ὁμοῦ ἡμέραι τξε. ἐφ' ἔτος δὲ διὰ τὴν ἰντερκαλάριον | ὁ Ξανδικὸς ἀχθήσεται ἡμερῶν λβ'. ἵνα δὲ ἀπὸ τοῦ νῦν στοιχήσωσιν οἱ | μῆνες καὶ αἱ ἡμέραι, ὁ μὲν νῦν ἐνεστὼς Περίτιος μὴν ἀχθήσεται μέχρι τῆς | ιδ, τῇ δὲ πρὸ ἐννέα καλανδῶν Φεβρουαρίων ἄξομεν νουμηνίαν μηνὸς || Δύστρου, καὶ καθ' ἕκαστον μῆνα ἀρχὴ{ι} ἔσται τῆς νουμηνίας ἡ πρὸ ἐννέα | καλανδῶν· ἡ δὲ ἐνβόλιμος ἡμέρα ἔσται πάντοτε τῶν ἰντερκαλαρίων κα|λανδῶν τοῦ Ξανδικοῦ μηνός, δύο ἐτῶν μέσων γεινομένων |

(c) ἔδοξεν τοῖς ἐπὶ τῆς Ἀσίας Ἕλλησιν, γνώμῃ τοῦ ἀρχιερέως Ἀπολλωνίου τοῦ | Μηνοφίλου Ἀζεανείτου· ἐπεὶ τὴν νέαν νουμηνίαν ἀεὶ δεῖ ἑστάναι τὴν αὐτὴ[ν] || ἅπασιν τῆς εἰς τὰς ἀρχὰς εἰσόδου κατά τε τὸ Παύλου Φαβίου Μαξίμου τοῦ ἀν|θυπάτου διάταγμα καὶ τὸ τῆς Ἀσία‹ς› ψήφισμα, ἐνποδίζεται δὲ ἡ τοῦ χρόνου | τάξις παρὰ τὰς ἐν τοῖς ἀρχαιρεσίοις ἐπικλήσεις, γείνεσθαι τὰ κατὰ τὰ | ἀρχαιρέσια μηνὶ δεκάτῳ, ὡς καὶ ἐν τῷ Κορνηλίωι νόμωι γέγραπται, ἐντὸς | δεκάτης ἱσταμένου

Extant fragments of the Latin version:

1. (*l. 4–5*): iucundior an salubrior natalis principis nost[ri . . .

2. (*ll. 9–19*): [propterea recte homines existimant hoc sibi principium | vitae,] quod paenitendi fuerit natos se esse [fi]nis. | cumque non ullo ex die feliciora et privatim singulis et uni|versis publice trahi possint aus[pici]a quam ex eo quem felicissi||mum communiter ⟨credunt⟩, fere autem omnium in Asia civitatium idem | tempus anni novi initiumque magistratuum sit, in quod [fort]ui|to, videlicet ut honoraretur, principis nostri natalis incidit, vel | quia tot erga divina merita gratum esse difficile est nisi omnis | pietatis temptetur materia, vel quia [dies est] pro[p]ria [cui]que || laetitia ingressui honoris [st]atu[t]us, publicum videtur m[ihi . . .

3. (*l. 21–22*): quem Graeci suo nomine diem nean numenian appellant eum clarissimi viri Caesaris . . .

98a. Halicarnassus. *IBM*. iv. 1, no. 894.

. . . | ἐ]πεὶ ἡ αἰώνιος καὶ ἀθάνατος τοῦ παντὸς φύσις τὸ [μέ|γ]ιστον ἀγαθὸν πρὸς ὑπερβαλλούσας εὐεργεσίας ἀνθρ[ώ]|ποις ἐχαρίσατο, Καίσαρα τὸν Σεβαστὸν ἐνεν[κ]αμένη [τ]ὸ[ν]|| τῷ καθ' ἡμᾶς εὐδαίμονι βίῳ πατέρα μὲν τῆς [ἑαυ]τοῦ πα|τ[ρ]ίδος θεᾶς Ῥώμης, Δία δὲ πατρῷον καὶ σωτῆρα τοῦ κο[ι|ν]οῦ τῶν ἀνθρώπων γένους, οὗ ἡ πρόνοια τὰς πάντων [εὐ|χ]ὰς οὐκ ἐπλήρωσε μόνον ἀλλὰ καὶ ὑπερῆρεν· εἰρηνεύο[υ|σ]ι μὲν γὰρ γῆ καὶ θάλαττα, πόλεις δὲ ἀνθοῦσιν εὐνομία[ι]|| ὁμονοίᾳ τε καὶ εὐετηρίᾳ, ἀκμή τε καὶ φορὰ παντός ἐστι[ν| ἀ]γαθοῦ, ἐλπίδων μὲν χρηστῶν πρὸς τὸ μέλλον, εὐθυμία[ς | δ]ὲ εἰς τ[ὸ] παρὸν τῶν ἀνθρώπων ἐνπεπλησμένων ἀγῶ|[σ]ιν κἀ[ναθή]μασιν θυσίαις τε καὶ ὕμνοις τὴν ἑαυτῶν |

(*ll. 14–39 are almost completely missing.*)

. . . . .] πολ[. .]σμ[. . ἀναγρα||φῆναι δὲ ἀντίγρα]φον [τ]οῦδε τοῦ ψηφίσματ[ος | καὶ τεθῆναι ἐν τῷ] τεμένει τῆς Ῥώμης καὶ τ[οῦ | Σεβαστοῦ ὑπ]ὸ [τοῦ] ἀρχιερέως Γαΐου Ἰουλίου Μ|[. .τ]ο[ῦ] φιλοκαίσαρος, ἐν δὲ ταῖς ἄλλαις πόλ[εσι | ὑπὸ τ]ῶν ἀρχόντων, καθιερωθῆναι δὲ τ[οὺς βωμούς? || ἐ]ν τῇ πρὸ ἑπτὰ καλανδῶν Δεκε[μβρίων ἡμε|ρ]ῶν [ὑ]πό τε ἱερέων καὶ ἀρχ[όντων . . . | ἑ]ορταζόντων τῶν ἀν[θρώπων . . .

(*ll. 48–55 are largely destroyed.*)

99. Honours for Menogenes, son of Isidoros, 5–2 B.C., Sardes. *Sardis*, vii. 1 (1932), no. 8.

τὸ κοινὸν | τῶν ἐπὶ τῆς Ἀσίας | Ἑλλήνων καὶ ὁ δῆμος ὁ Σαρδι|ανῶν καὶ ἡ γερουσία ἐτίμησαν Μηνογέ||νην Ἰσιδώρου τοῦ Μηνογένους τοῖς ὑπογεγραμμένοις· |

(I) εἰσανγειλάντων Μητροδώρου Κόνωνος καὶ Κλεινίου καὶ Μουσαίου καὶ Διονυσίου στρατηγῶν· | ἐπεὶ Γάϊος Ἰούλιος Καῖσαρ ὁ πρεσβύτατος τῶν τοῦ Σεβαστοῦ παίδων τὴν εὐκταιοτάτην | ἐκ περιπορφύρου λαμπρὰν τῷ παντὶ κό<σ>μῳ ἀνείληφε τήβεννον, ἥδονταί τε πάντες | ἄνθρωποι συνδιεγειρομένας ὁρῶντες τῷ Σεβαστῷ τὰς ὑπὲρ τῶν παίδων εὐχάς, ἥ τε ἡ||μετέρα πόλις ἐπὶ τῇ τοσαύτῃ εὐτυχίᾳ τὴν ἡμέραν τὴν ἐκ παιδὸς ἄνδρα τεληοῦσα[ν] | αὐτὸν ἱερὰν ἔκρινεν εἶναι, ἐν ᾗ κατ' ἐνιαυτὸν ἐν λαμπραῖς <ἐ>σθῆσιν στεφανηφορεῖν ἅπαντας, θ[υ]|σίας τε παριστάν<αι> τοῖς θεοῖς τοὺς κατ' ἐνιαυτὸν στρατηγοὺς καὶ κατευχὰς ποιεῖσθαι διὰ τῶν | ἱεροκηρύκων ὑπὲρ τῆς σωτηρίας αὐτοῦ, συνκαθιερῶσαί τε ἄγαλμα αὐτοῦ τῷ τοῦ πατρὸς ἐν|ιδρύοντας ναῶι, ἐν ᾗ τε εὐανγελίσθη ἡ πόλις ἡμέρᾳ καὶ τὸ ψήφισμα ἐκυρώθη καὶ ταύτην στε||φ<αν>ηφορῆσαι τὴν ἡμέραν καὶ θυσίας τοῖς θεοῖς ἐκπρεπεστάτας ἐπιτελέσαι, πρεσβήαν τε | ὑπὲρ τούτων στεῖλαι τὴν ἀφιξομένην εἰς Ῥώμην καὶ συνχαρησομένην αὐτῶι τε καὶ τῶι Σε|[β]αστῶι· δεδόχθαι τῇ βουλῆι καὶ τῶι δήμωι ἐξαποσταλῆναι πρέσβεις ἐκ τῶν ἀρίστων ἀν|δρῶν τοὺς ἀσπασομένους τε παρὰ τῆς πόλεως καὶ ἀναδώσοντας αὐτῶι τοῦδε τοῦ δό|γματος τὸ ἀντίγραφον ἐσφραγισμένον τῇ δημοσίᾳ σφραγῖδι, διαλεξομένους τε τῶι Σε||βαστῶι περὶ τῶν κοινῇ συμφερόντων τῇ τε Ἀσίαι καὶ τῆι πόλει καὶ ᾑρέθησαν πρέσβεις Ἰόλλας Μητροδώρο[υ] | καὶ Μηνογένη‹ς› Ἰσιδώρου τοῦ Μηνογ‹έ›νους |

(II) αὐτοκράτωρ Καῖσαρ θεοῦ υἱὸ‹ς› Σεβα‹σ›τὸς ἀρχιερεὺς δημαρχικῆς ἐκξουσίας ιθ', | Σαρδιανῶν ἄρχουσι βουλῆι χαίρειν· οἱ πρέσβεις ὑμῶν Ἰόλλας τε Μητροδώρου καὶ | Μηνογένης Ἰσιδώρου τοῦ Μηνογένους συνέτυχον ἐν Ῥώμῃ μοι καὶ τὸ παρ' ὑμῶν || ψήφισμα ἀπέδοσαν δι' οὗ τά τε δόξαντα ὑμεῖν περὶ ὑμῶν δηλοῦντες καὶ συνήδεσθε ἐπὶ τῆι τε-|λειώσει τοῦ πρεσβυτέρου μου τῶν παίδων· ἐπαινῶ οὖν ὑμᾶς φιλοτειμουμένους ἀνθ' ὧν εὐεργε|τῆσθε ὑπ' ἐμοῦ εὐχαρίστους ἁτοὺς εἴς τε ἐμὲ καὶ τοὺς ἐμοὺς πάντας ἐνδείκνυσθαι· ἔρρωσθε |

Sections III–VI (ll. 28–74) are decrees by the authorities of Sardes (βουλή, βουλὴ καὶ δῆμος, γερουσία) *in which Menogenes is honoured in similar terms.*

(VII) || Χαρῖνος Χαρίνου Περγαμηνὸς ὁ ἀρχιερεὺς θεᾶς Ῥώμης καὶ αὐτοκράτορος Καίσαρος θεοῦ υἱοῦ Σεβαστο[ῦ, Σαρδιανῶν] | ἄρχουσι βουλῇ δήμῳ χαίρειν· ἐ‹κ›κλησίας ἀρχαιρετικῆς συναχθείσης καὶ συνελθόντων τῶν ἀπὸ τῶν [πόλεων ἑ]|κατὸν κ‹αὶ› ν' ἀνδρῶν τιμᾶν ἐπηνέχθησαν ἄθροοι τὸν καθ' ἔτος ἔκδικον τοῦ κοινοῦ τῶν ἐπὶ τῆς Ἀσί[ας Ἑλ]|λήνων Μηνογένην Ἰσιδώρου τοῦ Μηνογένους τὸν πολείτην ‹ὑ›μῶν, διὰ τὴν ἐξ αὐτοῦ ἰς τὴν Ἀσίαν [εὔδη]|λον εὔνοιαν καὶ διὰ τὸ τὴν ἀρχὴν αὐτὸν τετελεκέναι καθαρῶς καὶ συνφερόντως, ἰκόνι γραπτῇ ἐνόπλῳ ‹ἐ›πιχρ[ύσῳ] || ἣν καὶ ἀνατεθῆναι ἐν ᾗ ἂν βούληται πόλει τῆς Ἀσίας, ἐφ' ἧς καὶ ἐπιγραφῆναι· οἱ ἐπὶ τῆς Ἀσίας Ἕλ‹λ›ηνες ἐτίμησ[αν] | Μηνογένην Ἰσιδώρου τοῦ Μηνογένους Σαρδιανὸν ἔκδικον τελέσαντα τὴν ἀρχὴν κα‹θ›αρῶς καὶ σ[υν]|φερόντως τῇ Ἀσίᾳ· δι' ὃ καὶ γεγράφαμεν ὑμεῖν περὶ τῶν τιμῶν αὐτοῦ ἵνα ἰδῆτε |

Section VIII (ll. 83–88) is a letter by Demetrios, another high priest of Roma et Augustus, sections IX and X (ll. 89–119) are decrees of οἱ ἐπὶ τῆς Ἀσίας Ἕλληνες, *sections XI and XII (ll. 120–39) two decrees by the* βουλή *of Sardes, all concerned with the same and similar honours for Menogenes.*

100. A.D. 12–13 (reingraved in second century), Narbo. *ILS.* 112.

A

T. Statilio Taur[o] | L. Cassio Longino | cos. X k. Octobr. | numini Augusti votum || susceptum a plebe Narbo|nensium inperpetuom: |

quod bonum faustum felixque sit imp. Caesari | divi f.

Augusto p.p. pontifici maximo trib. potest. | XXXIIII coniugi liberis gentique eius senatui || populoque Romano et colonis incolisque | c. I. P. N. M.,[1] qui se numini eius inperpetuum | colendo obligaverunt. pleps Narbonen|sium aram Narbone in foro posuit, ad | quam quot annis VIIII k. Octobr. qua die || eum saeculi felicitas orbi terrarum | rectorem edidit, tres equites Romani | a plebe et tres libertini hostias singu|las inmolent et colonis et incolis ad | supplicandum numini eius thus et vinum || de suo ea die praestent; et VIII k. Octob. | thus vinum colonis et incolis item prae|stent; k. quoque Ianuar. thus et vinum | colonis et incolis praestent; VII quoq. | idus Ianuar. qua die primum imperium || orbis terrarum auspicatus est, thure | vino supplicent et hostias singul. in|molent et colonis incolisque thus vi|num ea die praestent; | et pridie k. Iunias, quod ea die T. Statilio || Tauro M'. Aemilio Lepido cos. iudicia | plebis decurionibus coniunxit, hostias | singul. inmolent et thus et vinum ad | supplicandum numini eius colonis et | incolis praestent. || exque iis tribus equitibus Roman[is tribusve]| libertinis unu[s . . . .]

B

[plep]s Narbonesis a[ram] | numinis Augusti de[di]cavit / / / / / / / | / / / / / / / / / / / / | / / / / legibus iis q. i. s. s.[2] ||

numen Caesaris Aug. p. p., quando tibi | hodie hanc aram dabo dedicabo|que his legibus hisque regioni|bus dabo dedicaboque, quas hic | hodie palam dixero uti infimum || solum huiusque arae titulorum|que est: si quis tergere ornare | reficere volet, quod beneficii | causa fiat, ius fasque esto; sive | quis hostia sacrum faxit, qui || magmentum nec protollat, id|circo tamen probe factum esto; si | quis huic arae donum dare au|gereque volet, liceto eademq. | lex ei dono esto quae arae est; || ceterae leges huic arae titulisq. | eaedem sunto quae sunt arae | Dianae in Aventino. hisce legi|bus hisque regionibus, sicuti | dixi, hanc tibi aram pro imp. || Caesare Aug. p. p. pontifice maxi|mo tribunicia potestate XXXV coniuge liberis genteque eius | senatu populoque R. colonis | incolisque col. Iul. Patern. Narb. Mart.[3], qui se numini eius inper|petuum colendo obligaverunt, || doque dedicoque uti sies volens | propitium

[1] c(oloniae) I(uliae) P(aternae) N(arbonis) M(artii)

[2] q(uae) i(nfra) s(criptae) s(unt)

[3] *See note 1.*

101. Decree on worship of emperors, A.D. 18, Forum Clodii (Etruria). *ILS*. 154.

Ti. Caesare tert. Germanico Caesare iter. cos. | Cn. Acceio Cn. f. Arn. Rufo Lutatio, T. Petillio P. f. Qui. IIvir. | decreta: | aediculam et statuas has, hostiam dedicationi. victimae natali Aug. VIII k. Octobr. duae, quae p.p.[1] || inmolari adsueta[e] sunt ad aram, quae numini Augusto dedic. est, VIIII et VIII k. Octobr. | inmolentur; item natali Ti. Caesaris perpetue acturi decuriones | et populus cenarent—quam inpensam Q. Cascell[i]o Labeone | in perpetuo pollicenti, ut gratiae agerentur munificentiae eius—eoque | natali ut quotannis vitulus inmolaretur. || et ut natalibus Augusti et Ti. Caesarum, prius quam ad vescendum | decuriones irent, thure et vino genii eorum ad epulandum ara | numinis Augusti invitarentur. | ara(m) numini Augusto pecunia nostra faciendam curavimus; ludos | ex idibus Augustis diebus sex p. n. faciendos curavimus. || natali Augustae mulsum et crustlum mulieribus vicanis ad | Bonam Deam pecunia nostra dedimus. | item dedicatione statuarum Caesarum et Augustae mulsum et crustla | pecunia nostra decurionib. et populo dedimus, perpetuoque eius die | dedicationis daturo[s] nos testati sumus, quem diem quo frequentior quod||annis sit, servabimus VI idus Martias, qua die | Ti. Caesar pontif. maximus felicissime est creatus

[1] p(er)p(etuo)

102. Decree on Imperial cult and letter of Tiberius, Gytheion (Laconia). *SEG*. xi. 922–3.

(*a*) . . . . . ẹ̄π̣ι̣τ̣ιθέτ̣ῳ . . . . . | [ἐπὶ μὲν τὴν πρώτην θεοῦ Σεβαστοῦ Καίσα]ρος τοῦ πατρός, ἐπὶ δὲ τὴν ἐκ δẹξιῷ̣[ν | δευτέραν Ἰουλίας Σεβα]στῆς, ẹ̄π̣ὶ̣ δὲ τὴν τρίτην αὐτοκράτορος Τιβερίου Κα[ίσα|ρος τ]οῦ Σεβαστοῦ, [τὰς] εἰκόνας παρεχούσης αὐτῷ τῆς πόλεως. προτιθέσ̣[θω || δὲ κ]αὶ τράπεζα ὑπ' αὐτοῦ ἐν μέσῳ τῷ θεάτρῳ καὶ θυμιάτήριον ἐπικείσθω κα[ὶ | ἐπι]θυέτωσαν πρὶν εἰσιέναι τὰ ἀκροάματα ὑπὲρ τῆς τῶν ἡγεμόνων σωτηρία[s] | οἵ τε σύνεδροι καὶ αἱ συναρχίαι πᾶσαι. ἀγέτω δὲ τὴν μὲν πρώτην ἡμέραν θεοῦ Καίσ[α]|ρος θεοῦ υἱοῦ Σεβαστοῦ Σωτῆρος Ἐλευθερίου, τὴν δὲ δευτέραν αὐτοκράτορος [Τι]-|βερίου Καίσαρος Σεβαστοῦ καὶ πατρὸς τῆς πατρίδος, τὴν δὲ τρίτην Ἰουλίας Σεβαστῆ[s] || τῆς τοῦ ἔθνους καὶ πόλεως ἡμῶν Τύχης, τὴν δὲ τετάρτην Γερμανικοῦ Καίσαρος τῆς Ν[ί]|κ̣ης, τὴν δὲ πέμπτην Δρούσου Καίσαρος τῆς Ἀφροδείτης, τὴν δὲ ἕκτην Τίτου Κοϊνκτίο[υ]

| *Φλαμενίνου* καὶ ἐπιμελείσθω τῆς τῶν ἀγωνιζομένων εὐκοσμίας. φερέ{ρε}τω δὲ καὶ πά|σ̣ης τῆς μισθώσεως τῶν ἀκροαμάτων <καὶ> τῆς διοικήσεως τῶν ἱερῶν χρημάτων τὸν λόγον τῇ πόλ[ει] | μ̣ετὰ τὸν ἀγῶνα τῇ πρώτῃ ἐκκλησίᾳ κἂν εὑρηθῇ νενοσφισμένος ἢ ψευδῶς λογογραφῶν ἐξελε[ν]||χθείς, μηκέτι μηδεμίαν ἀρχὴν ἀρξάτω καὶ ἡ οὐσία αὐτοῦ δημευέσθω. ὧν δ' ἄν ποτε δημευθῇ τὰ ὄντα, | ταῦτα <τὰ> χρήματα ἱερὰ ἔστω καὶ ἐξ αὐτῶν προσκοσμήματα ὑπὸ τῶν κατ' ἔτος ἀρχόντων κατασκε[υ]|αζέσθω. ἐξέστω δὲ τῷ βουλομένῳ *Γυθεατῶν* παντὶ περὶ τῶν ἱερῶν ἐκδικεῖν χρημάτων ἀθῴῳ [ὄν]||τι. ἐπεισαγέτω δὲ ὁ̣ ἀ̣γο̣ρ̣α̣νόμος μετὰ τὸ τὰς τῶν θεῶν καὶ ἡγεμόνων ἡμέρας τελέσαι τῶν θυ̣|μελικῶν ἀγώνων ἄ̣λ̣λα[ς δύ]ο̣ ἡμέρας τὰ ἀκροάματα, μίαν μὲν εἰς μνήμην *Γαΐου Ἰουλίου Εὐρυκλέου*[ς] || εὐεργέτου τοῦ ἔθνου̣ς κ̣αὶ τῆς πόλεως ἐν πολλοῖς γενομένου, δευτέραν δὲ εἰς τειμὴν *Γ̣α̣|ΐου Ἰουλίου Λάκωνος* κηδεμόνος τῆς τοῦ ἔθνους καὶ τῆς πόλεως ἡμῶν φυλακῆς καὶ σωτηρία[ς] | ὄντος. ἀγέτω δὲ τοὺς ἀγῶνας ἀπὸ τῆς θεοῦ ἐν αἷς ἂν ᾖ̣ δυνατὸν ἡμέραις αὐτῶι· ὅταν δὲ τῆς ἀρχῆς | ἐξί̣ῃ παραδιδότω τῷ ἀντιτυγχάνοντι ἀγορανόμωι διὰ γραφῆς δημοσίας τὰ εἰς τοὺς ἀγῶνας χρη[στή]|ρ̣ια πάντα καὶ λαμβανέτω{ι} χειρόγραφον παρὰ τοῦ παραλαβόντος ἡ πόλις. ὅταν ὁ ἀγορανόμος τοὺ[ς || ἀγῶ]νας ἄγῃ τοὺς θυμελικούς, πομπὴν στελλέτω ἐκ τοῦ ἱεροῦ τοῦ *Ἀσκληπιοῦ* καὶ τῆς *Ὑγιεία*[ς] | πομπευόντων τῶν τε ἐφήβων καὶ τῶν νέων καὶ τῶν ἄλλων πολειτῶν ἐστεμμένων δάφ̣ν̣[ης] | σ̣τεφάνοις καὶ λευκὰ ἀ̣μπεχομέν<ω>ν. συμπομπευέτωσαν δὲ καὶ αἱ ἱεραὶ κόραι καὶ αἱ γυναῖκες ἐ̣ν̣ | [τ]αῖς ἱεραῖς ἐσθῆσιν. ὅταν δὲ ἐπὶ τὸ *Καισάρηον* ἡ πομπὴ παραγένηται, θυέτωσαν οἱ ἔφοροι ταῦ|[ρ]ο̣ν ὑπὲρ τῆς τῶν ἡγεμόνων καὶ θεῶν σωτηρίας καὶ ἀϊδίου τῆς ἡγεμονίας αὐτῶν διαμονῆς κα[ὶ || θ]ύσαντες ἐπαναγκ̣ασάτωσαν τά τε φιδείτια καὶ τὰς συναρχίας ἐν ἀγορᾷ θυσιάσαι. εἰ δὲ ἢ μὴ τε||[λ]ἐ̣σουσιν τὴν πομπὴν ἢ μὴ θύσουσιν ἢ θύσαντες μὴ ἐπαναγκάσουσι θυσιάζειν ἐν ἀγορᾷ τὰ | [φ]ιδείτια καὶ τὰς συναρχίας, ἐκτεισάτωσαν ἱερὰς τοῖς θεοῖς δραχμὰς δισχιλίας. ἐξέστω δὲ τῶι | βουλομένῳ *Γυθεατῶν* κατηγορεῖν αὐτῶν. οἱ ἔφοροι οἱ ἐπὶ *Χαίρωνος* στρατηγοῦ καὶ ἱερέως θε|οῦ *Σεβαστοῦ Καίσαρος* οἱ περὶ *Τερέντιον Βιάδαν* ἐγδότωσαν τρεῖς γραπτὰς εἰκόνας τοῦ θε||οῦ *Σεβαστοῦ* καὶ *Ἰουλίας* τῆς *Σεβαστῆς* καὶ *Τιβερίου Καίσαρος* τοῦ *Σεβαστοῦ* καὶ τὰ διὰ θέατρον | ἴκρια τῷ χορῷ καὶ θύρας μιμικὰς τέσσερας καὶ τῇ συνφωνίᾳ ὑποπόδια. στησάτωσαν δὲ καὶ στή|λην λιθίνην χαράξαντες εἰς αὐτὴν τὸν ἱερὸν νόμον καὶ εἰς τὰ δημόσια δὲ γραμματοφυλάκια θέτω|σαν ἀ̣ν̣τ̣ίγραφον τοῦ ἱεροῦ νόμου ἵνα καὶ ἐν δημοσίωι καὶ ἐν ὑπαίθρῳ καὶ πᾶσιν ἐν φανερῷ κείμενος ὁ νό|μος [διηνε]κ̣ῆ τὴν τοῦ δήμου τῶν *Γυθεατῶν* εὐχαριστίαν εἰς{ς} τοὺς ἡγεμόνας παρέχῃ πᾶσιν ἀνθρώ||ποις. εἰ δὲ ἢ μὴ ἐνχαράξουσι τοῦτον τὸν νόμον

ἢ μὴ ἀναθήσουσιν τὴν στήλην πρὸ τοῦ ναοῦ ἢ μὴ γρά|[*ψουσι τὸ ἀντί-γραφον* . . . . .]

(*b*) | . . | . . | . . *εἰ δέ τις* || . . . . . [*ἔ*]*σεσθαι κυρι*|. . . . *μήτε ψήφισμα* | . . . . . *ἔκσπονδος ἔστω* | . . . . [*ἡ οὐσία?*] *αὐτοῦ καθιερούσθω τοῖς ἡ*|[*γεμόσι* . . . . . *τ*]*ὰς τῶν θεῶν τειμὰς ἁλούς* || [*ἐναγὴς ἀπολλύσθω ἀκρίτου ὄ*]*ντος τοῦ κτείναντος αὐτόν* |

[*ἐπιστολὴ τοῦ Τιβερ*]*ίου.* | [*Τιβέριος Καῖσαρ θεοῦ Σεβ*]*ạσṭοῦ υἱὸ*[*ς Σ*]*ẹβαστὸς ἀρχιερεὺς δημαρχικῆς ἐξουσίας* | [*τὸ ἑκκαιδέκατο*]*ν Γ̣ṿθεα-τῶν ἐφόροις καὶ τῇ πόλει χαίρειν. ὁ πεμφθεὶς ὑφ' ὑμῶν* | [*πρός τ*]*ε ἐμὲ καὶ τὴν ἐμὴν μητέρα πρεσβευτὴς Δέκμος Τυρράνιος Νεικάνωρ* || [*ἀνέδ*]*ωκέν μοι τὴν ὑμετέραν ἐπιστολὴν ᾗ προσεγέγραπτο τὰ νομο-θετηθέν*|[*τα ὑφ' ὑ*]*μῶν εἰς εὐσέβειαν μὲν τοῦ ἐμοῦ πατρός, τιμὴν δὲ ἡμετέραν.* | [*ἐ*]*φ' οἷς ὑμᾶς ἐπαινῶν προσήκειν ὑπ‹ο›λαμβάνω*{*ι*} *καὶ κοινῇ πάντας ἀνθρώ*|*πους καὶ ἰδίᾳ τὴν ὑμετέραν πόλιν ἐξαιρέτους φυλάσσειν τῶι μεγέθει τῶν τοῦ* | *ἐμοῦ πατρὸς εἰς ἅπαντα τὸν κόσμον εὐεργεσιῶν τὰς θεοῖς πρέπουσας* || *τιμάς, αὐτὸς δὲ ἀρκοῦμαι ταῖς μετριωτέραις τε καὶ ἀνθρωπείοις· ἡ μέντοι ἐμὴ μή*|*τηρ τόθ' ὑμῖν ἀποκρινεῖται ὅταν αἴσθηται παρ' ὑμῶν ἣν ἔχετε περὶ τῶν εἰς αὐτὴν* | *τιμῶν κρίσιν*

103. Altar with Lar, near Cosa (Etruria). *NdS.* 1938, 5.

[imp. Caes.] divi f. Augusto pont. max. Q. Lucretius Eros Murdianus L. Volumnius Eros mag. Aug.[1]

[1] mag(istri) Aug(ustales)

104. 13–12 B.C., Nepet (Etruria). *ILS.* 89.

imp. Caesari divi f. Augusto pontif. maxim. cos. XI tribunic. potestat. XI magistri Augustal. prim. Philippus Augusti l. M. Aebutius Secundus M. Gallius Anchia[l]us P. Fidustius Antigonus

105. Lex de flamonio provinciae, Narbo. *ILS.* 6964; *FIR.* 22. Omitted from this reprint (see now McCrum and Woodhead, *Select Documents of the Principates of the Flavian Emperors*, no. 128). In its place is here printed:

105*. Nikoklia (near Palaipaphos). *JRS.* l (1960), 75 ff.

[*Νὴ τ*]*ὴν ἡμετέραν Ἀκραίαν Ἀφροδίτην κα*[*ὶ*] | *τὴ*[*ν ἡμ*]*ετέραν Κόρην* v *καὶ τὸν ἡμέτερον* '*γλά-*|*τη*[*ν Ἀπόλλ*]*ω καὶ τὸν ἡμέτερον*

Κε[ρ]υṇήτην | Ἀπόλλω v καὶ τοὺς ἡμετέρους σωτῆρας | Διοσκούρους v καὶ τὴν κοινὴν τῆς νήσ̣ου || βουλαίαν Ἑστίαν v καὶ Θεοὺς Θεάς τε τού[ς] | κοινοὺς τῆς νήσου πατρώους vv καὶ τὸν | ἔκγονον τῆς Ἀφροδίτης Σεβαστὸν Θεὸν | Καίσαρα vv καὶ τὴν ἀέναον Ῥώμην v καὶ τού[ς] | ἄλλους Θεοὺς πάντας τε καὶ πάσας v αὐτο[ί] || τε καὶ οἱ ἔκγονοι ἡμῶν ὑπακ̣ούσεσθαι | πειθαρχήσειν v κατά τε γῆν καὶ κατὰ θάλαττ[αν] | εὐνοήσειν v σεβάσεσθαι – v 12 – | Τιβέριον Καίσαρα Σεβαστοῦ ὑὸν (*sic*) Σεβασ-|τὸν σὺν τῶι ἅπαντι αὐτοῦ οἴκωι vv καὶ vv || τὸν αὐτὸν ἐκείνοις φίλον τε καὶ ἐχθρὸν v | ἕξειν v μετά τε τῶν ἄλλων θεῶν μ̣όνοις | Ῥώμη (*sic*) καὶ Τιβερίωι Καίσαρι v Σεβ̣α̣στοῦ υἱῶι̣ | Σεβαστῶι – v 12 – ὑοῖ̣ς̣ (*sic*) τε τοῦ | αἵματος αὐτοῦ v καὶ οὐδενὶ ἄ̣λ̣λω τῶν || πάντων v εἰσηγήσεσθαι ψηφι̣σ̣[α]σ̣[θαι]? | [ἱερά ....].

Cf. no 315. And, for another oath taken to Augustus at Samos in 6/5 B.C. (?), see P. Herrmann, *Athenische Mitteilungen* 75 (1960) 70 ff. = *Der Röm. Kaisereid*, 1969, 125 ff.

105a. A.D. 11–12, Lepcis Magna. *ITrip.*, no. 324 (a).

numini imp. Caesaris divi f. Aug. pont. m[ax. imp. XX cos. XII]I tr. pot. XXXIIII calchidicum et porticus et porta et via ab XVvir. sac. [. . . . . dedica]ta est

105b. 9–8 B.C., Lepcis Magna. Bilingual (Latin and Neopunic). *ITrip.*, no. 319.

[imp. Caesar divi f. Augustus] cos. XI imp. XIIII trib. pot. XV pont. m[axi]mus M. Licinio M. f. Crasso Frugi cos. augure procos. patrono flaminib. August. Caesaris Iddib[a]le Arinis f. [. . .]one [. . . . . A]nnobalis [f. . . .]on[. . . su]fetib. M[uttun Ammonis f. . . .]

Annobal Imilchonis f. Tapapius Rufus sufes flamen praefectus sacrorum de sua pequ[nia] faciun[dum coe]ravit idem[que] de[d]icavit

106. Thinissut (Africa). *ILS.* 9495.

Augusto deo cives Romani qui Thinissut negotiantur curatore L. Fabricio

107. Theatre, Stobi. *Arch. Anz.* 1938, 106.

deo Caes. Aug. p. p. et munic. Stob. Vltricem[1] Augustam Sex. Cornelius Audoleo et C. Fulcinius Epictetus et L. Mettius Epictetus Augustales f.

[1] *Nemesis.*

107a. Bronze coin, Tarraco. Heiss, p. 124, no. 56; Vives, p. 131, no. 12.

Obv. Augustus on curule chair. DEO AVGVSTO

Rev. Temple. AETERNITATIS AVGVSTAE. C.V.T.T.[1]

[1] C(olonia) V(ictrix) T(riumphalis) T(arraco).

108. Acanthus (Macedonia). *BSA.* 1918–19, 35.

[αὐτοκράτορι Καίσ]α[ρι θ]εῶι θεοῦ [υἱῶι] Σεβαστῷ ἡ πόλις καὶ οἱ συνπραγματευόμενοι Ῥωμαῖοι καὶ οἱ παροικοῦντες

109. Ancyra, Augusteum. *OGIS.* 533. New readings: Rostovtzeff, *Mél. Boissier* (1903), 419. Krenker and Schede, *Tempel in Ankara* (1936), 52. Robert, *Les gladiateurs dans l'orient grec* (1940), 135.

(*a*) [Γα]λατῶν ο[ἱ | ἱε]ρασάμενοι| θεῶι Σεβαστῶι | καὶ θεᾷ Ῥώμηι. |

(*b*) . . . . .]τω[.] βασ̣ι̣λ̣έ̣[ω]ς Βριγάτο[υ] | υἱὸ[ς] δημ[οθ]οινίαν ἔδω||κε[ν] ἔλαιον ἔθηκεν | μῆν̣α̣ς τ̣έ̣σ̣σ̣α̣ρ̣α̣ς̣ θέ|ας ἔδωκεν καὶ μον[ο]|μάχω[ν] ζεύγη τριάκο[ντα] | καὶ κυνήγιον ἔδωκ̣[εν] || ταύρων καὶ θηρίων. | [Ῥ]οῦφος δημοθοινίαν | ἔδωκεν, θέας καὶ | κυνήγιον ἔδωκεν |

ἐπὶ Μετειλίου· || [Πυ]λαιμένης βασιλέως Ἀμύ|[ν]του υἱὸς δημοθοιν̣ί̣[αν]| δὶς ἔδωκεν, θέας δὶς | ἔδωκεν, ἀγῶνα γυμνικὸν | καὶ ἁρμάτων καὶ κελήτων ἔ||δωκεν· ὁμοίως δὲ ταυρομα|χίαν καὶ κυνήγιον· ἤλιψεν τὴν | πόλιν· τόκους ἀνῆκε ὅπου | τὸ Σεβαστῆόν ἐστιν καὶ ἡ πανήγυ|ρις γείνεται καὶ ὁ ἱπποδρόμος. || Ἀλβιόριξ Ἀτεπόρειγος δημο[θ]οι|νίαν ἔδωκεν, ἀνδριάντας ἀνέ|θηκε Καίσαρος καὶ Ἰουλίας | Σεβαστῆς· | [Ἀ]μύντας Γαιζατοδιάστου δημοθοινίαν || δὶς ἔδωκε, ἑκαθόνβην ἔθυσεν, θέα[ς] | ἔδωκεν. σειτομετρίαν ἔδωκ[εν] | ἀνὰ πέντε μοδίους | [. . .]είας Διογνήτου. | Ἀλβιόριξ Ἀτεπόρειγος τὸ δεύτ[ερον] || δημοθοινίαν ἔδωκεν |

ἐπὶ Φρόντωνος·| [Μ]ητρόδωρος Μενεμάχου φύσει δὲ | [Δο]ρυλάου δημοθοινίαν ἔδωκε, [ἔλαιον] | ἔθηκεν μῆνας τέτταρας. || [Μ]ουσαῖος Ἀρτίκνου δημοθοινίαν ἔδω[κεν, | . . .] Σελεύκου δημοθοινίαν ἔδω[κεν], | ἤλιψεν μῆνας τέσσαρας. | [Π]υλαιμένης β[ασ]ιλέως Ἀμύντου υἱὸς | δη[μοθοινίαν ἔδ]ωκεν [το]ῖ̣ς τρισὶ[ν] || ἔθνε[σιν, τῶι] δὲ ἐν Ἀγκύρῃ ἑκ[α]|τόνβ[ην ἔθυσε]ν, θέας καὶ πομπὴν ἔ|δω[κεν], ὁμοίως δὲ ταυρομαχίαν | καὶ [ταυρ]οκαθ[άπτ]ας καὶ μονομάχω[ν] | ζεύ[γη] ν´. ἤλι[ψε]ν δι᾽ ὅλου τοῦ ἐνιαυ||τοῦ [τὰ τ]ρία ἔθ[νη], θηρομαχίαν ἔ|δω[κεν] |

Similar gifts [ἐπὶ] Σιλουανο[ῦ] (*ll.* 56–71) *and* ἐπὶ Βασιλᾶ (*ll.* 72–96).

110. Puteoli. *CIL.* x. 1613.

[L. C]alpurnius L. f. templum Augusto cum ornamentis d. s. f.

111. Masculula (Africa). *ILS.* 6774/5.

divo Augusto sacrum conventus civium Romanor. et Numidarum qui Mascululae habitant

112. Emerita (Lusitania). *Mem. museos archeol. prov.* 1943, 45 (new reading of *ILS.* 6892).

divo Augusto | Albinus Albui f. flamen | divae Aug. provinciae Lusitan[iae]

113. Corinth. *Corinth,* viii. 2, no. 110.

Callicrateae Philesi fil. sacerdoti in perpet. Providentiae Aug. et Salutis publicae tribules tribus Agripp[i]ae bene meritae

114. Alabanda (Caria). *BCH.* 1934, 300.

[ὁ] δῆμος ἐτείμησεν πάλιν ταῖς | [μ]εγάλαις τειμαῖς καὶ ἀνέθηκεν | [Ἀ]ριστογένην Μενίσκου τοῦ Ἀριστογέ|[ν]ους ἱερέα διὰ γένους Ὑγιείας τε καὶ || [Σ]ωτηρίας αὐτοκράτορος Καίσαρος | καὶ Ἡλίου, ἄνδρα μεγαλόφρονα | καὶ εὐσεβῆ̣α̣ καὶ δικαιοσύνῃ διαφέ|ροντα καὶ εὐεργέτην τῆς πόλεω[ς] | ἀρχιερατεύσαντα ἐν τῇ πατρίδι || τῆς τε Ῥώμης καὶ τοῦ Σεβαστοῦ | [Κ]αίσαρος καὶ τὰς μεγίστας καὶ με|[γ]αλομέρις ἐπιτελέσαντα φιλοδο|ξίας

115. (*a*) Between 9 B.C. and A.D. 2, reinscribed (*b*) between A.D. 19 and 23, Ammochostus (Cyprus). *BSA.* xlii (1947), p. 222, no. 9.

(*a*) *[αὐτοκράτορι Καίσαρι θεοῦ υἱῶι θεῶι Σεβαστῶι ὁ δεῖνα τοῦ δεῖνος ἀρχιερεὺς] διὰ βίου αὐτοῦ καὶ τῶν διδύμων υἱῶν [αὐτοῦ] Γαΐου καὶ Λουκίου Καισά[ρων] γυμνασιαρχῶν τῶι ἑαυτ[οῦ εὐ]εργέτη[ι* L]κ̣δ̣ʹ (?)

(*b*) *[Τιβερίωι Καίσαρι θεοῦ υἱῶι θεῶι Σεβαστῶι ὁ δεῖνα τοῦ δεῖνος ἀρχιερεὺς] διὰ βίου αὐτοῦ καὶ τῶν διδύμων υἱῶν Δρ̣ο̣ίσ. Κα[ίσ.] Τιβερίου καὶ Γερμανικοῦ Καισά[ρων] γυμνασιαρχῶν τῶι ἑαυτ[οῦ εὐ]εργέτη[ι* L]κ̣δ̣ʹ (?)

116. A.D. 1, Tentyrae (Egypt). *OGIS.* 659.

ὑπὲρ αὐτοκράτορος Καίσαρος θεοῦ υἱοῦ Διὸς Ἐλευθερίου Σεβαστοῦ, ἐπὶ Ποπλίου Ὀκταυίου ἡγεμόνος καὶ Μάρκου Κλωδίου Ποστόμου ἐπιστρατήγου, Τρύφωνος στρατηγοῦντος, οἱ ἀπὸ τῆς μητροπόλεως καὶ τοῦ νομοῦ τὸ πρόπυλον Ἴσιδι θεᾶι μεγίστηι καὶ τοῖς συνναίοις θεοῖς. ἔτους λα' Καίσαρος, Θωὺθ θ' Σεβαστῆι

117. A.D. 37, Papyrus. *P. Oxyrh.* ii, p. 184, no. 240; cf. 253, also Wilcken, *Chrestomathie*, no. 111.

[. . . . κω]μογραμματεὺς | [. . . . .]τοου Ἐρήμου. | [ὀμνύω Τιβέριον Καί]σαρα νέον Σεβαστὸν αὐτοκράτορα | [θεοῦ Διὸς Ἐλευθε]ρ̣[ίου] Σεβαστοῦ υἱὸν εἶ μὴν || [μὴ συνε]ιδέναι με μηδενὶ διασεσεισμέ|[νωι ἐπὶ] τῶν προκειμένων κωμῶν ὑπὸ | [. . . .]ο̣ς στρατιώτου καὶ τῶν παρ' αὐτοῦ. | [εὐορκοῦ]ντι μέμ μοι εὖ εἴη, ἐφιορκοῦντι δὲ | [τὰ εναν]τία. (ἔτους) κγ' Τιβερίου Καίσαρος Σεβαστοῦ || Μεχ(εὶρ) ιζ'

118. Association for imperial cult, 6 B.C., Papyrus. Wilcken, *Chrestomathie*, no. 112.

ἔτους κε' Καίσαρος Ἀθὺρ κ̣β̄ ἐ̣π̣ὶ̣ τ̣ῆ̣ς̣ γε̣[νη]|θείσης συναγωγῆς ἐν τῷ̣ Παρα̣τόμωι συνόδου | Σεβαστῆς τοῦ θεοῦ αὐτοκράτορος Καίσαρος, ἧς συνα[γωγεὺς] | καὶ προστάτης Πρῖμος Καίσαρος, ἱερεὺς Ἰουκοῦνδ[ος] || Καίσαρος, γυμνασίαρχος Ἀλέξανδ[ρο]ς [συμπαρ]όν|των τῶν πλ̣ε̣ίστων. ἐπεὶ συντ̣ε̣τ̣ά̣χ̣αμεν [τῶι] | προκιμένωι ἱερεῖ Ἰουκούνδωι [ἀφ'] ὧν ἔχει τῆς | συνόδου κεφαλαίων ἐπιδέξασθαι [.]υ̣ισω Καίσαρος | ἀποδοῦ[ν]αι ὑπὲρ Συντρόφου το̣ῦ̣ Κ̣α̣ί̣σ̣α̣ρ̣ο̣ς̣ συνοδε̣ί̣του || [ἕως] μ[ι]ᾶς (?) τριακάδος τ̣[ο]ῦ ἐνεστῶτος ἔ̣τ̣ο̣υ̣ς̣ ἃ̣ς̣ [ὀ|φεί]λ̣ε̣ι̣ αὐτῶι ἀργυρίου Πτολεμαϊ[κ]οῦ (δραχμὰς) ρκ', | ἔδοξε κοινῇ γνώμῃ τὸν μὲν Ἰουκοῦνδον ἐ[ξο]|διάσαι ἕως τῆς τριακάδος το̣ῦ̣ Ἀθύρε̣ω̣ς̣ ὑπὲρ τοῦ | Συντρόφ[ου] τὰς τ[οῦ] ἀργ(υρίου) (δραχ.) ρ[κ'] ἀτόκους, τοὺς δὲ ἀπὸ τῆς || συνόδου π[α]ραδέξασθαι τῶι Ἰουκούνδῳ̣ ταύτας | εἰ[ς] ἃ ὀ̣φ[ειλ]ε̣[ι τ]ῆι συνόδωι κεφάλαια, εἶναι δὲ | [ἀνυ]πεύθυ̣ν̣[ον τ]ὸν Ἰουκ[οῦνδο]ν περὶ τούτων | [μη]δενὶ ἐξόντος ἐπ' ἀ[ναγ]ω̣γῇ τούτων λ̣όγο̣ν | [ποιεῖσ]θ̣α[ι] ἢ̣ τὸν τοιο̣ῦ̣[τον. . . .] . α̣σθαι, βεβ[αι||οῦν δὲ] τὸ ὑπογραφὲν δισσὸν [χειρόγραφον. . . . . | . . . .] ὧν τὸ μὲν ἓν κα̣[. . . . . | . . . . τ]ὸ δὲ ἕτερον ἐπ̣[. . . .

119. Sestertius, 10–6 B.C. (?), Lugdunum. Mattingly, p. 92, nos. 548 ff.; cf. 565 ff.

Obv. Head of Augustus. CAESAR PONT. MAX.
Rev. Altar at Lugdunum. ROM. ET AVG.

120. Divona Cadurcorum. *ILS.* 7041.

M. Lucter. Lucterii Sen[e]ciani f. Leoni omnibus honoribus in patria functo sacerd. arae Aug. inter confluent. Arar. et Rhodani civitas Cad. ob merit. eius publ. posuit

121. Tarracina, temple. *CIL.* x. 6305.

Romae et Augusto Caesari divi [f.] A. Aemilius A. f. ex pecunia sua f. c.

122. Tetradrachm, 19–18 B.C., Pergamum. Mattingly, p. 114, no. 705 f.

Obv. Head of Augustus. IMP. IX TR. PO. V

Rev. Temple. ROM. ET AVGVST. COM. ASIAE

123. Anticaria (Baetica). *CIL.* ii. 2038.

Iuliae Aug. Drusi [fil.] div[i Aug.] matri Ti. Caesaris Aug. principis et conservatoris et Drusi Germanici [g]en[etric]is orbis M. Cornelius Proculus pontufex Caesarum

124. Bronze coin, Colonia Romula (Baetica). Heiss, p. 393, no. 2; Vives, p. 124, no. 3.

Obv. Head of Augustus radiate with star and thunderbolt. PERM. DIVI AVG. COL. ROM.

Rev. Head of Livia with crescent on globe. IVLIA AVGVSTA GENETRIX ORBIS

125. Rome, tomb of freedmen and slaves of Livia. *ILS.* 4995.

dis manibus [. . . . .] Aug. lib. Bathyllus aeditus templi divi Aug. [e]t divae Augustae quod est in Palatium, inmunis et honoratus

126. Gaulus, near Malta. *ILS.* 121; cf. J. Guey, *JdS.* 1938, p. 74.

Cereri Iuliae Augustae divi Augusti, matri Ti. Caesaris Augusti, Lutatia C. f. sacerdos Augustae ⌈imp. perpet.⌉[1] uxor M. Livi M. f. Qui. Optati flaminis G[a]ul. Iuliae Augusti[2] ⌈imp. perpet.⌉[1] cum V liberis[3] s. p. consacravit

[1] ⌈ ⌉ *added later after erasure: Guey proposes to read:* im{p}perpet.
[2] Augustae *Guey*. [3] cum v(iro et) liberis *or* cum (quinque) liberis

127. A.D. 3, Africa. *ILS.* 120.

Iunoni Liviae Augusti sacrum, L. Passieno Rufo imperatore Africam obtinente Cn. Cornelius Cn. f. Cor. Rufus et Maria C. f. Galla Cn. conservati vota l. m. solvont

128. Athens. *IG.*[2] ii. 3, 3238.

Ἰουλίαν θεὰν Σεβαστὴν Πρόνοιαν ἡ βουλὴ ἡ ἐξ Ἀρήου πάγου καὶ

ἡ βουλὴ τῶν ἑξακοσίων καὶ ὁ δῆμος ἀναθέντος ἐκ τῶν ἰδίων Διονυσίου τοῦ Αὔλου Μαραθωνίου ἀγορανομούντων αὐτοῦ τε Διονυσίου Μαραθωνίου καὶ Κοΐντου Ναιβίου Ῥούφου Μελιτέως

129. Lampsacus. *IGRR.* iv. 180 (*CIG.* 3642).

Ἰουλίαν Σεβαστὴν Ἑστίαν νέαν Δήμητρα ἡ γερουσία, τὸ δὲ εἰς τὸ ἄγαλμα καὶ τὴν βάσιν καὶ τὴν ἀνάστασιν αὐτοῦ δαπάνημα ποιησαμένου ἐκ τῶν ἰδίων ὑπὲρ τῆς εἰς τοὺς στεφάνους εὐσεβείας τοῦ ἱερέως τῶν Σεβαστῶν καὶ στεφανηφόρου τοῦ σύμπαντος αὐτῶν οἴκου καὶ ταμίου τοῦ δήμου τὸ δεύτερον Διονυσίου τοῦ Ἀπολλωνοτείμου

130. Corinth. *Corinth,* viii. 2, no. 15.

[Dianae] Pacilucife[rae Aug]ustae sacrum [pro salut]e Ti. Caesaris [Augusti] P. Licinius P. l. [. . . . . . .] Philosebastos [d. s.] p. f. c.

130a. Bronze coin, Asia Minor. *BMC. Lydia,* p. 251, no. 104.

Obv. Younger Drusus and Germanicus on curule chairs. ΔΡΟΥΣΟΣ ΚΑΙ ΓΕΡΜΑΝΙΚΟΣ ΝΕΟΙ ΘΕΟΙ ΦΙΛΑΔΕΛΦΟΙ

Rev. Wreath. Inside: ΚΟΙΝΟΥ ΑΣΙΑΣ Round: ΕΠΙ ΑΡΧΙΕΡΕΩΣ ΑΛΕΞΑΝΔΡΟΥ ΚΛΕΩΝΟΣ ΣΑΡΔΙΑΝΟΥ

131. Olisipo (Lusitania). *ILS.* 6896.

Q. Iulio Q. f. Gal. Ploto aed. IIvir. flamini Germ. Caesaris flamini Iuliae Aug. in perpetum

132. Aquitania. *Bull. société hist. du Périgord,* 1941, 402.

[Io]vi ọpṭịṃ. ṃạx. [Ti]b. Caesari Aug. sacrum [. . V]aler. Silvanus d. s. p. d.

133. A.D. 27, Rome. *ILS.* 6080.

genio Ti. Caesaris divi Augusti fili Augusti C. Fulvius Chryses mag. pagi Amentini minor. donum dedit V k. Iun. L. Calpurnio Pisone M. Crasso Frugi cos.

134. Nov. 16, A.D. 29, Lapethus (Cyprus). *OGIS.* 583.

Τιβερίωι Καίσαρι Σεβαστῶι θεῶι θεοῦ Σεβαστοῦ υἱῶι | αὐτοκράτορι ἀρχιερεῖ μεγίστωι δημαρχικῆς ἐξουσίας | τὸ λα', ἐπὶ Λευκίου Ἀξίου Νάσωνος ἀνθυπάτου καὶ Μάρκου | Ἐτρειλίου Λουπέρκου πρεσβευτοῦ καὶ Γαΐου Φλαβίου Φίγλου ταμία{ι} || Ἄδραστος Ἀδράστου Φιλοκαῖσαρ 5 *ὁ ἐνγενικὸς ἱερεὺς τοῦ | ἐν τῷ γυμνασίωι κατεσκευασμένου ὑπὸ αὐτοῦ ἐκ τοῦ ἰδίου | Τιβερίου Καίσαρος Σεβαστοῦ ναοῦ καὶ ἀγάλματος, ὁ φιλόπατρις | καὶ πανάρετος καὶ δωρεὰν καὶ αὐθαίρετος γυμνασίαρχος καὶ | ἱερεὺς τῶν ἐν γυμνασίωι θεῶν, κατεσκεύασεν τὸν ναὸν καὶ || τὸ ἄγαλμα ἰδίοις ἀναλώμασιν τῶι ἁτοῦ θεῶι, ἐφηβαρχοῦντος | Διονυσίου τοῦ Διονυσίου τοῦ καὶ Ἀπολλοδότου Φιλοκαίσαρος. | Ἄδραστος Ἀδράστου Φιλοκαῖσαρ καθιέρωσεν, συνκαθιεροῦντος | καὶ τοῦ υἱοῦ αὐτοῦ Ἀδράστου Φιλοκαίσαρος, τοῦ καὶ αὐτοῦ δωρεὰν | καὶ αὐθαιρέτου γυμνασιάρχου τῶν παίδων, τῆι γενεσίῳ || Τιβερίου ∟ις Ἀπογονικοῦ κδ´*

134a. Bronze coin, Corinth. Grant, *Asp.* p. 14 f., nos. 42 ff.

Obv. Head of Augustus, radiate. L. ARRIO PEREGRINO IIVIR. *Rev.* Temple, inscribed: GE̅N̅T. IVLI. Round edge: L. FVRIO LABE̅O̅NE IIVIR. COR.

135. Altar, Byrsa, Carthage. *CRAcInscr.* 1913, 680; cf. *RA.* xxiii (1926), 40 ff.

genti Augustae P. Perelius Hedulus sac. perp. templum solo privato primus pecunia sua fecit

136. Athens. *IG.*^{2} ii. 3, 3257.

ἡ βουλὴ καὶ ὁ δῆμος Δροῦσον Καίσαρα θεοῦ υἱὸν νέον θεὸν Ἄρη

137. Nasium (Belgica). *CIL.* xiii. 4635.

Tib. Caesar[i Aug.] f. Augusto et pro perpetua salute divinae domus

138. Wall of inner enclosure of Herod's Temple, now in Istanbul. *Revue biblique*, xx (1921), p. 263. Other copies: *OGIS.* 598 and *Quarterly of the Dept. Ant. Palestine*, vi (1938), p. 1.

μηθένα ἀλλογενῆ εἰσπορεύεσθαι ἐντὸς τοῦ περὶ τὸ ἱερὸν τρυφάκτου καὶ περιβόλου· ὃς δ' ἂν λήφθῃ ἑαυτῶι αἴτιος ἔσται διὰ τὸ ἐξακολουθεῖν θάνατον

139. Probably 7 B.C., Rome. *ILS.* 3612.

Larib. Aug. ministri qui k. Aug. primi inierunt Antigonus M. Iuni Erotis, Anteros D. Poblici Barnai, Eros A. Poblici Damae, Iucundus M. Ploti Anterotis

140. Cippus, 2 B.C., Rome. *ILS.* 9250.

Laribus Augustiis ministri anni VI: Felix L. Crautani, Florus

Sex. Avieni, Eudoxsus C. Caesi, Polyclitus Sex. Anchari, L. Caninio Gallo C. Fufio Gemino cos. XIIII k. Octobr.

[La]ribus Aug. vicei Statae matris ministri anni VI: {L. et N. Savoni}[1] Felix C. Crautani Ptolomaei, Eudoxus C. Caesi L. f. Nigri, Polyclitus Sex. Anchari Fausti, L. Caninio Gallo C. Fufio Gemino XIV k. Oct.

[1] *Later addition in smaller letters, unexplained.*

141. A.D. 12, Rome. *ILS.* 3308.

Germanico Caesare C. Fonteio [Cap]itone cos. k. Ian. Statae Fortunae Aug. sacr. Sex. Fonteius Ↄ. l. Trophimus, Cn. Pompeius Cn. l. Nicephor. mag. vici sandaliari reg. IIII anni XVIII d. d.

142. A.D. 1, Rome. *ILS.* 3090.

Mercurio[1] aeterno deo I[ovi I]unoni regin. Min[ervae So]li Lunae Apol[lini Dia]nae Fortuna[e . .]nae Opi Isi Pi[etati[2] . . .] Fatiis d[ivinis quod bo]num [faustum feli]xque [sit] imp. Caesari Augus[to, imperio[2]] eius, senati populi[que Romani] et gentibus, nono [anno] introeunte felic[iter] C. Caesare L. Pau[llo cos.], L. Lucretius L. l. Zethus iussu Iovis aram Augustam posuit. Salus Semonia.[1] Populi Victoria[1]

[1] *Later additions.* [2] *Supplements uncertain.*

VI

IMPERIAL DEPENDANTS, FREEDMEN, AND SLAVES

See also nos. 125, 333

143. Smyrna. *IGRR.* iv. 1444 (*CIG.* 3285).

Μᾶρκον Ἀρτώριον Ἀσκληπιάδην, θεοῦ Καίσαρος Σεβαστοῦ ἰατρόν, ἡ βουλὴ καὶ ὁ δῆμος τῶν Σμυρναίων ἐτίμησαν ἥρωα, πολυμαθίας χάριν

144. Smyrna. *IGRR.* iv. 1392.

[Ti. Claudius Ti. Cl]audi Thrasylli [l. Ti. C]aesari Augus[to et Augustae Caesaris Augusti matri]

[Τιβέριος Κλαύδι]ος Τιβερίου Κλα[υδίου Θρασύλλου ἀπελεύθερος Τιβερίῳ̣ Καίσαρι Σεβαστῷ̣ κ]αὶ Σεβαστῆι Καί[σαρος Σεβαστοῦ μητρί̣]

145. Funeral urn, Rome. *Bull. Comm.* 1939, 24.

Ti. Claudi Athenodori f. Qui. Melitonis Germanici medici

146. Urbinum. *ILS.* 1847.

[T]i. Iulius Latinus [. .] Iuli Leonidae f. [p]raeceptoris Caesaru[m] trib. mil. leg. IIII Scythic. [vixit a]nn. XXXVII [. . . .

147. Rome. *ILS.* 1948.

C. Iulius divi Aug. l. Niceros Vedian. acce(n)s. Germanico Caisar. cos.[1] et Calvisio Sabino cos.[2] Iulia L. f. Helice vix. ann. XX

C. Iulius Aug. l. Amaranthus sibi et Iuliae C. l. Clarie et Iuliae C. l Mercatillae delicio meo. Iulia Euheteria Helices mater

[1] *A.D. 12 or 18.* [2] *A.D. 26.*

148. Probably A.D. 37, Philippi. *BCH.* 1934, 449.

A[. . . . .] | Ti. C[aesa]r divi Augusti f. | divi [Iuli] n. trib. potes[t.] XXXIIX | Dru[sus] Caesar Ti. Aug. f. || divi [Aug. n.] divi Iuli pro[n.] tr. pot. II. | Caḍ[m]us Atimetus Marti[alis?] | C. Iuli [A]ugusti liberti mo. ḍ. [s. f. c.?][1]

[1] mo(numentum) d(e) s(uo) f(aciendum) c(uraverunt)

149. Rome. *ILS.* 1877.

C. Octavius Octaviae Augusti sororis l. Auctus scr. libr. Viccia C. l. Gnome uxor

150. Rome. *Bull. Comm.* 1928, 298.

M. Iulius Augustae l. Cnismus sibi et uxori Liviae M. l. Helpidi et (*vac.*) Secundo et Iuliae Augustae l. Acte et Ti. Caesaris Aug. l. Aegle libertis libertabus posterisque eorum

151. Rome. *ILS.* 1926.

Q. Fabius Africani l. Cytisus	et
viator quaestorius ab aerario	Liviae divae
scr. libr. tribunicius scr. libr.	Aug. l.
quaestorius trium decuriarum.	Culicinae.
C. Calpetanus C. l. Cryphius viator	Plasidiena L. f.
pullarius prior vir Culicinae.	Agrestina
L. Numpidius L. l. Philomelus scr. libr.	Calpetani Liviani
q. III decuriarum Cytisi	primi pil.
frater pius et fidelis.	
C. Proculeius C. l. Heracleo	
Culicinae pater.	
Proculeia Stibas mater Culicinae	

152. Rome. *ILS.* 7888 a and b.

(*a*) M. Vipsanius M. l. Zoticus cur. III[1] ol. XIV sibi et Vipsaniae M. l. Stibadi coll.

(*b*) Vipsania M. M. l. Acume Zotici M. Agrippae ex monumentis[2] M. Agrippae

[1] cur(ator) (tertium) *of the burial club.*

[2] *Probably Zoticus' office in Agrippa's household.*

153. Sarcophagus, Rome. *CIL.* vi. 8409 c.

Antemo Ti. Caesaris Aug. l. a rationi[b.] accenso delat. ab Aug.

154. Rome, Monumentum Marcellae. *CIL.* vi. 4776.

[I]ulia Bolae l. Glycera Dardani Ti. Caesaris Aug. et Augustae ser. Archelaiani mulier v. a. XXXVII vitalis delicium eorum

155. Rome. *NdS.* 1922, 418.

[Ti. Iu]lius Ti. Iuli Aug. lib. Medates | fecit sibi et Iuliae Pryneni (*a goose*) | (*a hen*) coniugi suae gallinarius

156. Rome. *NdS.* 1922, 417.

(*a*) Ti. Iulio Diogeni Remothalciano

(*b*) Ti. Iuli Fausti. Vipsaniae Vrbanae. ollae quae fuerunt Diogenis Remothalciani

157. A.D. 43, Rome. *ILS.* 1795.

genio Coeti Herodian. praegustator. divii Augusti, idem postea vilicus in hortis Sallustianis, decessit non. Augustis M. Cocceio Nerva C. Vibio Rufino cos. Iulia Prima patrono suo

158. Rome. *ILS.* 1514.

Musico Ti. Caesaris Augusti Scurrano disp. ad fiscum Gallicum provinciae Lugdunensis ex vicaris eius qui cum eo Romae cum decessit fuerunt benemerito:

Venustus negot.	Agathopus medic.	Facilis pediseq.
Decimianus sump.	Epaphra ab argent.	Anthus ab arg.
Dicaeus a manu	Primio ab veste	Hedylus cubicu.
Mutatus a manu	Communis a cubic.	Firmus cocus
Creticus a manu	Pothus pediseq.	Secunda
	Tiasus cocus	

159. Rome. *ILS.* 1802.

Diocles Ti. Caesaris ministr. Germanicianus natione Gallograe[c]. vixit ann. XXXV

160. Territory of the Rutaeni (Aquitania). *CIL.* xiii. 1550.

Zmaragdo vilico quaest. magistro ex decurion. decr. familiae Ti. Cae[sa]ris quae est in me[tal]lis

161. Bronze plaque attached to a lamp, A.D. 11, Samnium. *ILS.* 3806.

T. Statilio Tauro M'. Aemilio Lepido cos. Tricunda Ti. Claudi Neronis ser. vilic. magist. Bellonae lucerna(m) cum suis ornament. libens animo donum dat idib. Iun. in Ligures Baebianos

VII

FOREIGN KINGS

Kings are also recorded in nos. 21, 48, 109, 241, 352. Slaves of kings: 154, 156–7.

162. Carthago Nova. *ILS.* 840.

regi Iubae re[gis] Iubae filio regi[s] Iempsalis n. regis Gau[dae] pronepoti regis Masiniss[ae] pronepotis nepoti IIvir. quinq. patrono coloni

162a. Silver coin, Mauretania. Head, *HN.*², p. 888, fig. 399.

Obv. Head of Juba II. REX IVBA
Rev. Bust of Cleopatra Selene. ΒΑΣΙΛΙΣΣΑ ΚΛΕΟΠΑΤΡΑ

163. A.D. 29–30, Caesarea (Mauretania). *Mél. Gautier* (1937), 332.

[pro salute r]egis Ptlemaei (*sic*) [r]egis Iubae f. reginante anno decimo Antistia Galla votum Saturno solvi libens merito victuma accepta [a]b Iulia Respecti f. Vitale Rusguniense

164. Athens. *OGIS.* 197; *IG.*² ii. 3445.

ὁ δῆμος βασιλ[έ]α Πτολεμαῖον, βασιλέως Ἰούβα υἱ[ό]ν, βασιλέως Πτολεμαίου ἔκγονον, ἀρετῆς ἕνεκεν καὶ εὐνοίας τῆς εἰς ἑαυτόν

165. Segusio (Cottian Alps). *BFC.* xi (1904), 89.

M. Agrippae L. f. [cos III tri]b. potest. [. . . . . .] Do[nnus] et Cotti(us?) Cotti(i) f.

166. 9–8 B.C., Segusio (Cottian Alps), arch. *ILS.* 94.

imp. Caesari Augusto divi f. pontifici maxumo tribunic. potestate XV imp. XIII M. Iulius regis Donni f. Cottius praefectus ceivitatium quae subscriptae sunt. Segoviorum Segusinorum Belacorum Caturigum Medullorum Tebaviorum Adanatium Savincatium Ecdiniorum Veaminiorum Venisamorum Iemeriorum Vesubianiorum Quadiatium et ceivitates quae sub eo praefecto fuerunt

167. A.D. 1–2, Byzantium. *Ath. Mitt.* 1911, 287; 1912, 180.

Ἴσιδι Σαράπιδι βασιλεύοντος Ῥοιμετάλκου, μεγαρχοῦντος δὲ

Ἀρτεμιδώρου τοῦ Φιλοστράτου ἔτους λβʹ Ἀρτεμίδωρος Συνίστορος υἱὸς ναυαρχήσας τὰ μεγάλα Πλ[οι]αφέσια[1] τὸν τελάμωνα[2] ἀνέθηκεν

[1] *Festival of Isis* (*5 March, beginning of sailing season*). [2] =στήλην

168. Philippi. *BCH.* 1932, 203.

C. Iulio Roeme[talci] regi regis Raescu[po]ris f. M. Acculeius M. f. Vol. amico bene merito f. c.

169. Near Neapolis (Thrace). Θρακικά 1935, 302.

Διὶ Ὑψίστωι εὐχαρισ[τή]ριον ὑπὲρ κυρίου βασιλέος Θρακῶν Ῥοιμητάλκα Κότυος καὶ τῶν τέκνων αὐτοῦ Εὔτυχος ὁ ἐπὶ τῶν λατόμων καὶ οἱ ὑπ' αὐτὸν πάντες

170. Panticapeum. *IGRR.* i. 874 (*IPEux.* ii, no. 25).

βα[σιλεύοντος βασιλέως βασιλέων] μεγάλου Ἀσάνδρου [Φιλ]ορωμαίου Σωτῆρος καὶ βασιλίσσης Δυνάμεως, Πανταλέων ναύαρχος Ποσιδῶνι Σωσινέωι καὶ Ἀφροδίτηι Ναυαρχίδι

171. Phanagoria. *IGRR.* i. 901 (*IPEux.* ii, no. 354).

αὐτοκράτορα Καίσαρα θεοῦ υἱὸν Σεβαστὸν τὸν [π]άσης γῆς καὶ [πάσης] θαλάσσης ἄρ[χ]οντα, τὸν ἑαυτῆς σωτ[ῆρα καὶ εὐ]εργέτη[ν], βασίλισσα Δύν[αμις Φιλορώ]μαι(ος)

172. Panticapaeum. *IGRR.* i. 879 (*IPEux.* ii, no. 36).

βασιλέα μέγαν Ἀσποῦργον Φιλορώμαιον τὸν ἐκ βασιλέως Ἀσανδρόχου Φιλοκαίσαρα καὶ Φιλορώμαιον βασιλεύοντα παντὸς Βοοσπόρου, Θεοδοσίης καὶ Σινδῶν καὶ Μαιτῶν καὶ Ταρπείτων καὶ Τορετῶν Ψησῶν τε καὶ Τανα[ε]ιτῶν, ὑποτάξαντα Σκύθας καὶ Ταύρους, Μενέστρατος βʹ ὁ ἐπὶ τῆς νήσσου τὸν ἑαυτοῦ σωτῆρα καὶ εὐεργέτην

173. Smyrna (?). *OGIS.* 377.

ὁ δῆμος Ζήνωνα βασιλίσσης Πυθοδωρίδος Φιλομήτορος καὶ βασιλέως Πολέμωνος υἱόν, θυγατριδῆ δὲ τῆς εὐεργέτιδος Ἀντωνίας, ἐτείμησεν

174. Probably epitaph, shortly after March 43 B.C., east of Ancyra. *RA.* 1935, ii, 140.

[βασιλεὺς Δηι]όταρος Φιλο[πάτ]ωρ κ[αὶ Γ]αλατῶν Τολισ[τοβ]ωγ[ίω]ν καὶ Τρόκμων [τ]ετρ[άρ]χης ὁ ἐγ βασιλέως [Δ]ηιοτάρου Φιλορωμαίου καὶ Γαλατῶν Τολιστοβωγίων καὶ Τρόκμων τετράρχο[υ] καὶ ἐγ βασιλίσσης Βερενίκης

175. Athens. *OGIS.* 357; *IG.*[2] ii. 3430.

[ὁ] δῆμος [βασιλέα Καπ]ποδοκί[ας καὶ τῆς τραχεία]ς Κιλικίας Ἀ[ρχέλαον Φι]λόπατριν ἀρε[τῆς] ἕνεκα

176. Athens. *IG.*[2] ii. 3437–8; cf. *OGIS.* 363.

ἡ βουλὴ καὶ [ὁ δ]ῆμος [β]ασίλισσαν Γλαφύραν βασιλέω[ς] Ἀρχελάου θυγατέρα βασιλέως Ἰόβ[α] γυναῖκ[α ἀρε]τῆς ἕνε[κ]α

177. Anazarbus (Cilicia). *IGRR.* iii. 895.

Δροῦ[σον] Καίσαρα Τιβερίου [Σεβα]στοῦ υἱὸν [θεοῦ Σεβ]αστοῦ υἱωνὸν Ἕλενος βασ[ι]λέως Φιλοπάτορος ἀπελεύθερος

178. Athens. *OGIS.* 414; *IG.*[2] ii. 3440.

ὁ δῆμο[ς] βασιλέα Ἡρώδην Φιλορώμαιον εὐεργεσίας ἕνεκεν καὶ εὐνοίας τῆς εἰς ἑαυτόν

179. Delos. *OGIS.* 417; *Inscr. de Délos*, no. 1586.

ὁ δῆμος ὁ Ἀθ[η]ν[αίων καὶ οἱ] κατοικοῦ[ντ]ε[ς] τὴ[ν νῆσον] Ἡρώδην βασιλέω[ς Ἡ]ρ[ώδου] τετράρχην ἀρετῆς [ἕνεκεν καὶ εὐνοί]ας τῆς εἰς ἑαυτοὺ[ς Ἀπόλλωνι . . .] ἐπὶ ἐπιμ[ελητοῦ τῆς νήσου Ἀπολλωνίου τοῦ Ἀπολ]λωνίου Ῥα[μνουσίου]

180. Abila (Syria). *OGIS.* 606.

ὑπὲρ τῆς τῶν κυρίων Σε[βαστῶν] σωτηρίας καὶ τοῦ σύμ[παντος] αὐτῶν οἴκου Νύμφαιος Ἀέ[του] Λυσανίου τετράρχου ἀπελε[ύθερος] τὴν ὁδὸν κτίσας ἄστε[ι]π[τ]ο[ν οὖσαν καὶ] τὸν ναὸν οἰκο[δομ]ή[σας τὰς περὶ αὐτὸν] φυτείας πάσας ἐφύ[τευσεν ἐκ τ]ῶν ἰδίων ἀναλ[ωμάτων θεῷ] Κρόνῳ κυρίῳ κα[ὶ . . . .] Εὐσεβία γυνή

181. Silver Coin, A.D. 14 (?), Armenia. *BMC. Galatia*, &c., p. 101.

Obv. Head of Augustus. ΘΕΟΥ ΚΑΙΣΑΡΟΣ ΕΥΕΡΓΕΤΟΥ

Rev. Head of Artavasdes III. ΒΑΣΙΛΕΩΣ ΜΕΓΑΛΟΥ ΑΡΤΑΥΑΞΔΟΥ

182. Didrachm, A.D. 37–38 (?), Caesarea (Cappadocia). Mattingly, p. 162, no. 104.

Obv. Head of Germanicus. [GERMANIC]VS CAESAR TI. AVG. F. COS. II

Rev. Germanicus placing tiara on head of Artaxias. ARTAXIAS [G]ERMANICVS

183. Rome. *ILS*. 842.

Seraspadanes Phraatis Arsacis regum regis f. Parthus. Rhodaspes Phraatis Arsacis regum regis f. Parthus

184. Arsinoe (Egypt). Preisigke, *Sammelbuch griech. Urkunden*, i, 1570.

ὑπὲρ βασιλίσσης Κλεοπάτρας θεᾶς Φιλοπάτορος καὶ βασιλέως Πτολεμαίου τοῦ καὶ Καίσαρος θεοῦ Φιλοπάτ⟨ορ⟩ος καὶ Φιλομήτορος καὶ τῶν προγόνων Σούχωι θεῷ μεγάλῳ πατροπάτορι

185. Tetradrachm, 36–30 B.C., Antioch. *BMC. Galatia*, &c., p. 158, nos. 53 ff.

Obv. Head of Antony. ΑΝΤΩΝΙΟΣ ΑΥΤΟΚΡΑΤΩΡ ΤΡΙΤΟΝ ΤΡΙΩΝ ΑΝΔΡΩΝ
Rev. Bust of Cleopatra. ΒΑΣΙΛΙΣΣΑ ΚΛΕΟΠΑΤΡΑ ΘΕΑ ΝΕΩΤΕΡΑ

186. 13 B.C., Pselcis (Upper Egypt). *IGRR*. i. 1359.

Ἁρποκρὰς ἥκω ἀναβαίνων μετὰ Ἐ[μάτου] πρεσβευτοῦ καὶ Ταμίου γραμματέως [πρὸς] τὴν κυρίαν βασίλισσαν καὶ τὸ προσ[κύνημα] ἐπόησα ὧδε παρ[ὰ] τῷ κυρίῳ Ἑρμ[ῇ θεῷ μεγίστῳ] καὶ Ἐμάτου καὶ Ἀνθούσης καὶ [Ἀλε]ξανδρήας, ἔτους ιζ' Καί[σα.] Μεχ[είρ]

VIII

SENATORS

Senators are also recorded as proconsuls or legates in nos. 43, 52, 58, 81a, 98, 127, 134, 241, 264–5, 268–9, 284, 290–2, 294, 316–17, 320a, 321, 330, as *curatores* in nos. 296, 298, as patrons or honorary magistrates of towns in 234, 238, 347, 355–6, and in the preambles of the SCC. in nos. 30, 307. Cf. also no. 94a.

187. After 22 B.C., near Gaeta. *ILS.* 886.

L. Munatius L. f. L. n. L. pron. Plancus cos. cens. imp. iter. VIIvir epulon., triump: ex Raetis, aedem Saturni fecit de manibis, agros divisit in Italia Beneventi, in Gallia colonias deduxit Lugudunum et Rauricam

188. Rome. *ILS.* 887.

L. Memmius C. f. Gal. q. tr. p[l.] frumenti curator ex s.c., praefectus leg. XXVI et VII Lucae ad agros dividundos, pontifex Albanus. Memmia filia testamento suo fieri iussit

189. Mytilene. *ILS.* 891.

cives Romani qui Mytileneis negotiantur M. Titio L. f. procos. praef. classis cos. desig.[1] patrono honoris causa

[1] *cos. suff. 31* B.C.

189a. Bronze coin, Magnesia ad Sipylum. *BMC. Lydia,* p. 139, no. 13.

Obv. Head of M. Tullius Cicero (son). ΜΑΡΚΟΣ ΤΥΛΛΙΟΣ ΚΙΚΕΡΩΝ
Rev. Hand with vine-wreath and corn-ears. ΜΑΓΝΗΤΩΝ ΤΩΝ ΑΠΟ ΣΙΠΥΛΟΥ ΘΕΟΔΩΡΟΣ

190. Athens. *ILS.* 8810; *IG.*² ii. 4118.

ὁ δῆμος Μᾶρκον Λικίνιον Μάρκου ὑὸν Κράσσον ἀνθύπατον καὶ αὐτοκράτορα ἀρετῆς ἕνεκεν καὶ εὐνοίας

190a. Bronze coin, Hippo Diarrhytus (Africa). Grant, *FITA.* p. 224.

Obv. Head of Tiberius. CLAVDIO NERONI HIPPONE LIBERA
Rev. Head of Africanus Fabius Maximus. FABIO AFRICANO

190b. Bronze coin, Temnus (Asia). *BMC. Troas, Aeolis and Lesbos*, p. 146, no. 24.

Obv. Head of C. Asinius Gallus. ΑΣΙΝΙΟΣ ΓΑΛΛΟΣ ΑΓΝΟΣ

Rev. Head of Dionysus. ΑΠΟΛΛΑΣ ΦΑΙΝΙΟΥ ΤΑΜΝΙΤΑΝ.

191. Near Rome. *ILS.* 901.

[. . .] Fonteio Q. f. q. mancup. stipend. ex Africa

192. Near Rome. *ILS.* 903.

Cn. Baebio Cn. [f.] Tampilo Valae Numoniano q. pr. pro cos. IIIvir. a. a. a. f. f.[1] viro

[1] a(ere) a(rgento) a(uro) f(lando) f(eriundo)

193. Aquileia. *ILS.* 906.

C. Appulleius M. f. Tappo pr. aed. tr. pl. q. iudex quaestionis rerum capital.

194. Rome. *ILS.* 909.

C. Papirius C. f. Clu. Carbo tr. mil. XXVIvir q. pro pr. Antullia Q. f. uxsor

195. Rome. *ILS.* 911.

P. Numicio Picae Caesiano praef. equitum VIvir. q. pro pr. provinc. Asiae tr. pl. provincia Asia

P. Numicio Picae Caesiano praef. eq. VIvir. q. pro pr. provinc. Asiae tr. pl. P. Cornelius Rufinus, C. Autronius Carus, L. Pomponius Aeschin., Sex. Aufidius Euhodus, Q. Cassidienus Nedym., T. Manlius Inventus, C. Valerius Albanus, Sex. Aufidius Primigen., patrono

196. Rome. *ILS.* 914.

Q. Propertius Q. f. Fab.

C. Propertius Q. f. T. n. Fab. Postumus IIIvir cap. et insequenti anno pro IIIvir. q. pr. desig. ex s. c. viar. cur. pr. ex s. c. pro aed. cur. ius dixit procos.

Q. Properti [. . . . .

197. Histonium. *ILS.* 915.

P. Paquius Scaevae et Flaviae filius Consi et Didiae nepos Barbi et Dirutiae pronepos Scaeva, quaestor decemvir stlitibus iudicandis ex s. c. post quaesturam, quattuorvir capitalis ex s. c.

post quaesturam et decemviratum stlitium iudicandarum, tribunus plebis aedilis curulis iudex quaestionis praetor aerarii, pro consule provinciam Cyprum optinuit, viar. cur. extra u. R. ex s. c. in quinq.,[1] procos. iterum extra sortem auctoritate Aug. Caesaris et s. c. misso[2] ad componendum statum in reliquum provinciae Cypri, fetialis, consobrinus idemque vir Flaviae Consi filiae Scapulae neptis Barbi proneptis simul cum ea conditus

Flavia Consi et Sinniae filia Scapulae et Sinniae neptis Barbi et Dirutiae proneptis consobrina eademque uxor P. Paquii Scaevae filii Scaevae Consi nepotis Barbi pronepotis simul cum eo condita

[1] viar(um) cur(ator) extra u(rbem) R(omam) ex s(enatus) c(onsulto) in quinq(uennium) [2] *read* missus

198. Forum Clodii (Etruria). *ILS.* 916. Cf. E. Groag, *Die röm. Reichsbeamten von Achaia*, p. 20 f.

Cn. Pullio [. . . .] Pollioni feti[ali q. ? Xviro] stlitib. iud. ex s.c. tr. pl. pr. aḍ ạ[erar.] procos. [pr]ovinciae Narb. [comiti ? imp. Caes.] Augus[ti i]n Gallia Comat[a itemque] in Aquita[nia], Athena[s missus ? ab imp. Caes.] August[o] legatus in [. . . . .], IIvir. quinquenna[li Claudienses ex praef.] Claudi[a patrono]

199. Tibur. *ILS.* 918; cf. *CAH.* x, p. 877 f.

. . . . | r]egem, qua redacta in pot[estatem imp. Caesaris] | Augusti populique Romani senatu[s dis immortalibus] | supplicationes binas ob res prosp[ere gestas, et] | ipsi ornamenta triumph[alia decrevit]; | pro consul. Asiam provinciam op[tinuit; legatus pr. pr.] | divi Augusti iterum Syriam et Ph[oenicen optinuit]

200. Near Tibur. *ILS.* 921.

M. Plautius M. f. A. n. Silvanus cos.[1] VIIvir epulon. huic senatus triumphalia ornamenta decrevit ob res in Ilyrico bene gestas. Lartia Cn. f. uxor. A. Plautius M. f. Urgulanius vixit ann. IX

[1] 2 B.C.

201. Attalea (Pamphylia). *SEG.* vi. 646.

Μᾶρκον Πλαύτιον Σιλουανὸν πρεσβευτὴν ἀντιστράτηγον αὐτοκράτορος Καίσαρος Σεβαστοῦ ὁ δῆμος καὶ οἱ συνπολιτευόμενοι Ῥωμαῖοι τὸν ἑαυτῶν πάτρωνα καὶ εὐεργέτην

202. Athens. *ILS.* 928; *IG.*[2] ii. 4126.

L. Aquillio C. f. Pom. Floro Turciano Gallo Xvir. s[t]l. iud. tribuno mil. leg. VIIII Macedonic. quaestor. imp. Caesar. Aug. proquaest. provinc. Cypri tr. pl. pr. procos. Achaiae. ἡ βουλὴ ἡ ἐξ Ἀρείου πάγου καὶ ἡ βουλὴ τῶν χ κα[ὶ] ὁ δῆμος Λ. Ἀκύλλιον Φλῶρον Τουρκιανὸν Γάλλον ἀνθύπατον εὐνοίας ἕνεκεν τῆς πρὸς τὴν πόλιν. ἐπὶ ἱερίας Ἱπποσσθενίδος τῆς Νικοκλέ[ους Π]ιραιέως θυγατρός

203. Tenos. *OGIS.* 463; *IG.* xii. 5, 940.

ὁ δῆμος Πόπλιον Κοινκτίλιον Οὐᾶρον τὸν ταμίαν τοῦ αὐτοκράτορος Καίσαρος [θεοῦ Σεβα]στοῦ τὸν πάτ[ρωνα καὶ εὐεργέτην, θεοῖς]

204. Carthago Nova. *CIL.* ii. 3414; cf. *Bull. Comm.* lxxi (1943–5), 68 ff.

P. Silio leg. pro pr. patrono colonei

205. Superaequum of the Paeligni. *ILS.* 932.

Q. Vario Q. f. Gemino leg. divi Aug. II procos. pr. tr. pl. q. quaesit. iudic. praef. frum. dand. Xvir. stl. iudic. curatori aedium sacr. monumentor.que public. tuendorum. is primus omnium Paelign. senator factus est et eos honores gessit. Superaequani publice patrono

206. Luna. *ILS.* 935.

[Sex.] Appuleio Sex. f. Gal. Sex. n. Sex. pron. Fabia Numantina nato, ultimo gentis suae

207. Treia (Picenum). *ILS.* 937.

M'. Vibio M'. f. Vel. Balbino tr. mil. pr. fabr. pr. eq. q. aed. pl. praet. aerari leg. divi Aug. et Ti. Caesaris Aug. procos. provinc. Narbonensis

208. Epidaurus (Dalmatia). *ILS.* 938.

P. Cornelio Dolabellae cos.[1] VIIviro epuloni sodali Titiensi leg. pro pr. divi Augusti et Ti. Caesaris Augusti civitates superioris provinciae Hillyrici

[1] A.D. *10*.

209. Ipsus (Asia). *ILS.* 9483.

. . . .] Favonio cos. pro cos. Asiae XVviro sacr. faciendis sodali Augustal. IIIvir. centur. equit. recognosc. censoria potestat. leg. divi Augusti et Ti. Caesaris Augusti[. . .

209a. Bronze coin, Hippo Diarrhytus (Africa). Grant, *Asp.* p. 8, no. 20.

Obv. Head of Tiberius. TI. CAESAR DIVI AVGVSTI F. AVGVSTVS

Rev. Head of L. Apronius. L. APRONIVS·HIPPONE LIBERA

209b. Bronze coin, Galatia. Grant, *Num. Chron.* 1950, p. 45, nos. 4 ff.

Obv. Head of Tiberius. ΤΙΒΕΡΙΟΣ ΚΑΙΣΑΡ

Rev. Temple. ΕΠΙ ΒΑΣΙΛΑ[1] ΠΡΕΣ. ΣΕΒ.

[1] *Cf. no. 109, l. 72.*

209c. Bronze coin, A.D. 22–23, Thapsus. Grant, *Asp.* p. 10, no. 27.

Obv. Head of Tiberius. TI. CAE. DIVI AVG. F. AVG. IMP. VIII COS. IIII

Rev. Livia seated as Vestal. PERMIS. Q. IVN. BLAESI PROCOS. IT. C.[1] P. GAVIO CASCA C.P.I.[2]

[1] c(urante) [2] C(oloniae) P(iae ?) I(uliae)

210. Brixia. *ILS.* 940.

P. Cornelio Len[tulo] Scipioni cos.[1] pr. aerari legato Ti. Caesaris Aug. leg. VIIII Hispan. pontif. fetiali d. d.

[1] A.D. *24.*

211. Brixia. *ILS.* 942.

C. Pontio C. [f.] Paeligno trib. m[il.] leg. X Gem. q. cur. locorum public. iterum aed. cur. legato pro pr. iter. ex s. c. et ex auctorit. Ti. Caesaris d.

212. Rome. *ILS.* 943.

Q. Caerellius Q. f. Qui. IIIvir cap. quae. pro pr. tr. pl. legato (*sic*) pro pr. ter pr. praef. frum. ex s. c. {s.} leg. Ti. Caesaris Aug. procos. ex testamento

Q. Caerellio M. f. Qui. patri tr. milit. quae. tr. pl. praetori leg. M. Antoni procos.

213. Allifae (Samnium). *ILS.* 944; cf. Tibiletti, *Principe e magistrati repubbl.*, 188.

. . . . . . viacure[1] . . . . . [q. tr. p]l. pr. leg. [pro pr. imp. C]aesaris Augusti [i]ter. per commendation. Ti. Caesaris Augusti ab senatu cos. dest. patrono

[1] via(rum) cur(atori) ?

214. Tibur. *ILS.* 950.

memoriae Torquati Novelli P. f. Attici Xviri stlit. iud. [tr.] mil. leg. I trib. vexillar. [leg. q]uattuor I V XX XXI q. aed. [praet.] ad hast. cur. loc. public. [leg. a]d cens. accip. et dilect. et [proco]s. provinciae Narbon. [in cui]us honoris fine [annum] agens XXXXIIII [For]o Iulii decessit

215. Rome, Forum. *ILS.* 3783.

pro salute Ti. Caesar[is Au]g[u]st. pontifi[cis maxi]mi principis [optimi] et ius[tissimi ex] v[oto suscep]to C. Fulviu[s .....]us procos. [pr. prae]f. frum. da[nd.] ex s. [c. le]g. pro pr. [.....] q. pro pr. tr. mil. leg. IX Hisp. Concordiae. auri p. V, arg. p. XXIII[1]

[1] *See note, no. 225.*

216. Rome. *Bull. Comm.* 1928, 318.

L. Cassio Longino cos. XVvir. sacris faciundis legato pro pr. Ti. Caesaris Augusti Sextani Arelatenses patrono

217. Ruscino (Narbonensis). E. Espérandieu, *Inscr. latines de Gaule* (*Narbonnaise*), no. 633.

P. Mem[mio P. f.] Reg[ulo] quaesto[ri Ti.] Caesari[s praet.] cos.[1] [septem]viro epulo[n]um [s]odali [August]ali frat. [Arv. legat]o Caes. [Aug. pat]rono

[1] *cos.* A.D. *31.*

218. Delphi. *ILS.* 8815; *Fouilles de Delphes*, iii. 1, 532.

[Πόπ]λιον Μέμμιον Ποπλίου υἱὸν Ῥῆγλον ὕπατον[1] πρεσβευτὴν Σεβαστῶν ἀντιστράτηγον ἱερέα ἐν τρισὶ συστήμασι ἱερωσυνῶν ἀνθύπατον Ἀσίας καὶ τὸν υἱὸν αὐτοῦ

[1] *cos.* A.D. *31.*

218a. A.D. 35–36, Lepcis Magna. *ITrip.*, no. 330.

Ti. Caesari divi Aug. f. Augusto divi Iuli n. pont. max. cos. V imp. VIII trib. potest. XXXVII C. Rubellius Blandus q. divi Aug. tr. pl. pr. cos. procos. pont. patronus ex reditibus agrorum quos Lepcitanis resti[tui]t vias omnis civitatis Lepcitanae sternendas silice [curavit.] M. Etrilius Lupercus leg. pro pr. patronus s[ub hasta f. l.[1]]

[1] f(aciendum) l(ocavit).

IX

EQUESTRIAN ORDER

For other equestrian careers see nos. 242–3, 245, 247 (centurions promoted into the order), 21, 62, 116, 285 (prefects and other officials of Egypt), 11, 146, 270, 354 (military officers). For more general allusions to the order see 94a, 209, 358–9.

219. Rome. *ILS.* 7848.

leibertorum et leibertar. C. Maecenatis L. f. Pom. postereisque eorum et qui ad id tuendum contulerunt contulerint

219a. Bronze coin, Tralles (Caesarea). Grant, *FITA.* p. 382, no. 2.

Obv. Head of P. Vedius Pollio. ΠΩΛΛΙΩΝ ΚΑΙΣΑΡΕΩΝ
Rev. Head of Zeus. ΜΕΝΑΝΔΡΟΣ ΠΑΡΡΑΣΙΟΥ

220. Volsinii. *ILS.* 8996.

[L. Seius Strabo][1] praefectus Aegypt[i et] Terentia A. f. mater eiu[s et] Cosconia Lentulii Malug[inensis f.] Gallitta uxor eius ae[dificiis] emptis et ad solum de[iectis] balneum cum omn[i ornatu Volsiniens]ibus ded[erunt ob publ]ica co[mmoda]

[1] *Name of Seianus' father inserted from other evidence.*

221. Aeclanum (Samnium). *ILS.* 1335.

M. Magio M. f. Maximo praef. Aegypti Tarraconenses

222. Verona. *ILS.* 1336.

P. Graecinio P. f. Pob. Laconi ornamentis consularibus

223. Rome. *ILS.* 1337.

Laco praef. vig. XIII

224. Superaequum Paelignorum. *ILS.* 9007.

Q. Octavius L. f. C. n. L. pron. Ser. Sagitta IIvir quinq. III praef. fab. prae. equi. trib. mil. a populo procurator Caesaris Augusti in Vindalicis et Raetis et in valle Poenina per annos IIII et in Hispania provincia per annos X et in Suria biennium

225. Silver bust of Tiberius, posthumous, Teate Marrucinorum. *Arch. Anz.* 1940, 521.

Ti. Caesari divi Aug. f. | Augusto pontif. maximo | trib. potest. XXXVIII cos. V | ex testamento M. Pulfenni || Sex. f. Arn. Ↄ leg. VI Ferr. | C. Herennius T. f. Arn. Capito | trib. milit. III praef. alae | praef. veteranorum | proc. Iuliae Augustae || proc. Ti. Caesaris Aug. | proc. C. Caesaris Aug. | Germanici. | arg. (*vac.*) p. X[1]

[1] arg(enti) p(ondo) (decem)

226. Cos, Asclepieum. *Bull. Comm.* 1933, App., 17.

[ὁ δ]ᾶμος ἀνέθηκεν Γν[αῖ]ον Καπίτωνα Τιβερ[ίου] Καίσαρος Σεβαστ[οῦ θε]οῦ ἐπίτροπον [ἀρετᾶς ἕ]νεκα καὶ εὐνοίας [τᾶς ἐς αὐ]τόν

227. Ilium. *IGRR.* iv. 219.

ἡ βουλὴ καὶ ὁ δῆμος ἐτείμησαν Τίτον Οὐ[α]λέριον Πρόκλον τὸν φροντιστὴν Δρούσου Καίσαρος, καθελόντα τὰ ἐν Ἑλλησπόντῳ ληστήρια καὶ ἐν ἅπασιν ἀνεπιβάρητον φυλάξαντα τὴν πόλιν

228. Sestinum (Umbria). *ILS.* 2691.

L. Voluseno L. f. Clu. Clementi trib. mil. praef. equit. praef. tir. Gall. Na[rbonen]sis II[. . . . .]noi[. . . . .] accepit missus a divo Aug. hic cum mitteretur a Ti. Caes. Aug. in Aegypt. ad iur. dict. decessit provinc. Aquitania

229. Aquinum (Latium). *ILS.* 6286.

Q. Decio Q. f. M. n. Saturnino pontif. minori Romae tubicini sacror. publ. p. R. Quirit. praef. fabr. cos. ter curatori viarum Labic. et Latinae trib. mil. praef. fabr. i. d. et sortiend. iudicibus in Asia IIIIvir. i. d. Veronae q. bis IIvir. i. d. IIvir. iter. quinq. praef. quinq. Ti. Caesaris Augusti, iter. Drusi Caesaris Ti. f., tertio Neronis Caesaris Germanici f. pontif. flamini Romae et divi August. perpetuo ex auctor. Ti. Caesaris Augusti et permissu [e]ius cooptato coloniae patrono, publice d. d.

230. Hasta (Etruria). *ILS.* 6747.

P. Vergilio P. f. P. n. Pol. Laureae aed. IIvir. i. d. praef. fabr. iudici de IIII decuriis equiti selectorum publicis privatisq. praef. Drusi Caesaris German. [f.] IIvir. quinq., P. Vergilio P. f. P. n. Pol. Paullino equo publico iudici de IIII decu[r]. praef. fabrum praef. chortis II v[et]era[nae . . . .]iorum exercitus [. . . . . .

230a. Rome. *ILS.* 1320.

dis manibus sacrum C. Caesio Q. f. Ter. Nigr. ex prima admissione ex qua[t]tuor decuris curio minor. Caesia C. l. Theoris patrono et sibi

231. Origin unknown. *ILS.* 2683.

Q. Aemilius Q. f. | Pal. Secundus [in] | castris divi Aug. s[ub] | P. Sulpi[c]io Quirinio le[gato] || C[a]esaris Syriae honori|bus decoratus pr[a]efect. | cohort. Aug. I pr[a]efect. | cohort. II classicae. idem | iussu Quirini censum egi || Apamenae civitatis mil|lium homin. civium CXVII, | idem missu Quirini adversus | Ituraeos in Libano monte | castellum eorum cepi, et ante || militiem praefect. fabrum | delatus a duobus cos. ad ae|rarium et in colonia | quaestor, aedil. II, duumvir II, | pontifexs. || ibi positi sunt Q. Aemilius Q. f. Pal. | Secundus f. et Aemilia Chia lib. | h. m. amplius h. n. s.[1]

[1] h(oc) m(onumentum) amplius h(eredem) n(on) s(equetur)

232. A.D. 10, Mons Claudianus, Egypt. *Proc. Soc. Bibl. Archaeology* 1909, 323; cf. *OGIS.* 660.

ἔτους μ' Καίσαρος Παῦνι α' | ἀγαθῇ τύχῃι. ἐπεὶ Ποπλίου | Ἰουεντίου Ῥούφου χιλιάρ|χου τῆς τερτιανῆς λε||γέων. καὶ ἐπάρχου Βερνίκη|ς καὶ ἀρχιμεταλλάρχου | τῆς Ζμαράγδου καὶ Βα|ζίου καὶ Μαργαρίτου καὶ | πάντων τῶν μεταλλῶν || τῆς Αἰγύπτου ἀνέθηκε | ἐν τῶι Ὀφιάτηι ἱερὸν | Πᾶνι θεῶι μεγίστωι | καὶ αὐτῶι Ποπλίωι Ἰουεντ[ίωι] | Ἀγαθόποδι ἀπελευθ[έ]||ρου καὶ ἐπιτρόπωι καὶ προ|νοήτου καὶ εὐεργέτηι | πάντων τῶν μεταλλῶν | τῆς Αἰγύπτου. | τὸ προσκύνημα Θολεμαί||ου κουράτορος σπίρης Φλώ|ρου κεντυρίας Βάσσου ὁ καὶ | ἐπιστήσας

232a. Milestone, A.D. 13–14, Sardinia. *ILS.* 105.

imp. Caesar August. divi f. pater patriae pontifex maximus trib. potestat. XXXVI obtinente T. Pompio [P]roculo. pro leg. X

233. Emona. *Bull. assoc. mus. de Slovénie* 1937, 134.

T. Iunius D. f. Ani. Montanus tr. mil. VI praef. equit. VI praef. fabr. II pro leg. II

234. Dyrrhachium. *ILS.* 2678.

L. Ti[t]inio L. f. Aem. Sulpiciano pontif. praef. pro IIvir. et IIvir. quinq. tr. mil. et tr. mil. pro legato et praef. quinq. T. Statili Tauri patri

235. Lanuvium. *ILS.* 2676; iii 2, p. clxxix.

A. Castricius Myriotalenti f. tr. mil. praef. eq. et classis mag. colleg. Lupercor. et Capitolinor. et Mercurial. et paganor. Aventin. XXVIvir [.........]moni per plures [.......... ...]i sortitionibus [...............]dis redemptis

236. Luceria, Amphitheatre. *JdS.* 1938, 73.

M. Vecilius M. f. L. n. Campus praef. fabr. tr. mil. IIv[ir iure] dic. pontifex amphitheatrum loco privato suo et maceriam circum it sua pec. in honor. imp. Caesaris August[i] coloniaeque Luceriae f. c.

237. Formiae. *ILS.* 6285.

L. Arrio Salano praef. quinq. Ti. Caesaris praef. quinq. Neronis et Drus[i] Caesarum designato tub. sac. p. R.[1] aed. III auguri interreg[i] trib. milit. legion. III August. leg. X Geminae praef. equit. praef. castror. praef. fabr. Oppia uxor

1 tub(icini) sac(rorum) p(opuli) R(omani)

238. Antioch (Pisidia). *ILS.* 9503.

C. Caristani[o C. f. Ser.] Frontoni Caesiano Iulio praef. fabr. trib. mil. leg. XII Fulm. praef. coh. Bos[p]. pontif. praef. P. Sulpici Quirini IIvir. praef. M. Servili praef. [....

239. Near Aquileia. *ILS.* 2703.

Ti. Iulio C. f. Fab. Viatori subprae[f.] coh. III Lusitanorum IIIIvir. iur. dic. praef. coh. Ubior. equitatae. Erboniae Sex. f. Gratae uxori C. Iulius Aug. l. Linus filio et nurui

240. Rome. *ILS.* 1314.

C. Pompeius C. f. Ter. Proculus trib. mil. leg. XVIII praefectus fabrum sevir centur. equit. hic sepultus est

241. Alpine valley above Brixia. *ILS.* 847.

Staio Esdragass. f. Voben. principi Trumplinorum praef. [c]ohort. Trumplinorum [s]ub C. Vibio Pansa legato pro [pr. ite]m Vindol. i[m]munis Caesaris [.......] et suis. Messava Veci f. uxor

X

ARMY AND NAVY

Legions are also recorded in nos. 45, 146, 188, 210–11, 214–15, 225, 232, 237–8, 240, 290, 339, 342–3, 361, soldiers in 45, 225, 232, 239, 361. For veterans see 302, 347a, for the fleet 189, 235, 301.

242. Venafrum. *ILS.* 2021.

L. Ovinius L. f. Ter. Rufus prim. ordo cohortium praet. divi Augusti prim. pil. leg. XIIII Gem. trib. mil. cohort. XI urb. trib. mil. coh. [. .] III praet. praef. fabr. IIvir L. Ovinio M. f. Ter. patri, M. Ovinio L. f. Ter. Vopisco fratri, Allidiae L. f. Rufae matri, Pulliae Primae uxori

243. Iulium Carnicum (Venetia). *ILS.* 1349.

C. Baebio P. f. Cla. Attico IIvir. i. [d.] primopil. leg. V Macedonic. praef. civitatium Moesiae et Treballia[e pra]ef. [ci]vitat. in Alpib. maritumis t[r.] mil. coh. VIII pr. primopil. iter. procurator. Ti. Claudi Caesaris Aug. Germanici in Norico civitas Saevatum et Laiancorum

244. Paeligni. *ILS.* 2689.

[S]ex. Pedio Sex. f. An. Lusiano Hirruto prim. pil. leg. XXI pra[ef]. Raetis Vindolicis valli[s P]oeninae et levis armatur. IIIIvir. i. d. praef. Germanic[i] Caesaris quinquennalici [i]uris ex s. c. quinquen. iterum. hic amphitheatrum d. s. p. fecit. M. Dullius M. f. Gallus

245. Venafrum. *ILS.* 2690.

Lusia M. f. Paullina Sex. Vettuleni Cerialis sibi et M. Vergilio M. f. Ter. Gallo Lusio patri prim. pil. leg. XI praef. cohort. Ubiorum peditum et equitum donato hastis puris duabus et coronis aureis ab divo Aug. et Ti. Caesare Aug. praef. fabr. III trib. mil. cohort. primae idio[lo]go ad Aegyptum IIvir. iterum pontif. A. Lusio A. f. Ter. Gallo fratri trib. mil. leg. XXII Cyrenaicae praef. equit.

246. Venafrum. *ILS.* 2688.

Sex. Aulieno Sex. f. Ani. primo pil. II tr. mil. praef. levis armat. praef. castr. imp. Caesar. Aug. et Ti. Caesaris Augusti praef. classis praef. fabr. IIvir. Venafri et Foro Iuli flamini Augustali Nedymus et Gamus lib.

247. Sora (Latium). *ILS.* 2226.

L. Firmio L. f. prim. pil. tr. mil. IIIIvir. i. d. colonia deducta prim. pontifici legio IIII Sorana honoris et virtutis caussa

248. Varia (near Tibur). *ILS.* 2637.

M. Helvius M. f. Cam. Rufus Civica prim. pil. balneum municipibus et incolis dedit

249. Near Praeneste. *ILS.* 2684.

Sex. Iulius S. f. Pol. Rufus evocatus divi Augusti praefectus ⟨I⟩ cohortis Corsorum et civitatum Barbariae in Sardinia

250. Rome. *ILS.* 2014.

[C. P]etronius C. f. Fal. Varia speculator Caesari[s]. Hordionia T. l. Egist[e] uxor

251. Rome. *ILS.* 2028.

d. m. Q. Caetronius Q. f. Pub. Passer mil. coh. III pr. annis XVIII, missus duobus Geminis,[1] sibi et Masuriae M. f. Marcellae

vixi quod volui semper bene pauper honeste,
fraudavi nullum, quod iuvat ossa mea

In f.[2] p. XIS, in agr. p. XIIIS

[1] A.D. *29*. [2] f(ronte)

252. Ostia. *ILS.* 9494.

[. . . . . .]u[. .] militi cohor. VI pr. Ostienses locum sepult. dederunt publicoque funere efferun. decrerunt quod in incendio restinguendo interit. in f. p. XII, in ag. p. XXV

253. Rome. *CIL.* vi. 2993.

L. Aufusti L. f. Subura Rufini cen. cohor. VII vigil. Rom. candidat. Ti. Caesar. et Aufustiae Superantiae et Aufusti et Aufustiae Gemel. oll. IIII L. Aufustius L. f. Sub. Fusculus Maior L. Aufustius L. f. Palatina Serenus m. ex caussa leg. faciun. cur.[1]

[1] m(onumentum) ex caussa leg(ati) faciun(dum) cur(averunt)

254. Ateste. *ILS.* 2243.

M. Billienus M. f. Rom. Actiacus legione XI proelio navali facto in coloniam deductus ab ordine decurio allec[tus . . . .]mo Eruc[. . . . .

255. Moesia Inferior. *ILS.* 2270.

L. Plinius Sex. f. Fab. domo Trumplia mil. leg. XX annorum XLV stipendiorum XVII hic situs est. testamento fieri iussit. Secundus L. Plin. et P. Mestri libertus fecit

256. Nemausus. *ILS.* 2267.

Ti. Caesaris divi Aug. f. Augusti miles missicius T. Iulius Festus militavit annos XXV in legione XVI decreto decurion. accepit frumenti $\overline{\text{m}}$. L, balneum et sui[1] gratuitum in perp. et aream inter duos (*sic*) turres per P. Pusonium Peregrinum IIIIvir. et $\overline{\text{XI}}$ vir. adsignatam

[1] *Perhaps* et balnei usum (*Hirschfeld*).

257. Near Salonae (Dalmatia). *ILS.* 2252–3.

(*a*) T. Ancharenus T. f. Ser. dom. Laranda mil. leg. VII an. XLV stip. XXIII h. s. e.

(*b*) Cn. Domitius Cn. f. Vel. Pessinunte an. XLIV stip. XXV veteran. ex leg. VII h. s. e. testamento fieri iussit

258. Near Burnum (Dalmatia). *ILS.* 2259.

A. Sentius A. f. Pom. Arreti. vet. leg. XI h. s. e., t. f. i., hic est occisus finibus Varvarinorum in agello secus Titum flumen ad Petram Longam. f. c. her.[1] Q. Calventius L. f. Vitalis

[1] f(aciundum) c(uravit) her(es)

259. Near Philippi. *BCH.* 1923, 87.

Sex. Volcasio L. f. Vol. leg. XXVIII domo Pisis

260. Simitthu (Africa). *ILS.* 2305.

L. Flaminius D. f. Arn. mil. leg. III Aug. ꓶ Iuli Longi dilecto lectus ab M. Silano[1] mil. annis XIX in praecidio ut esset in salto Philomusiano ab hostem in pugna occissus vixit pie annis XL h. s. e.

[1] *proconsul Africae* A.D. *33–38.*

261. Coptos (Egypt). *ILS.* 2483.

[coh. IIII]

¬Longi:
C. Marcius C. f. Pol. Alexand.
¬Catti:
L. Longinus L. f. Ser. Tavio
¬Vedi:
L. Licinius L. f. Pol. Sebastop.
¬Servati:
M. Lollius M. f. Pol. Ancyr.
¬Caecili:
C. Cornelius C. f. Pol. Anc.
¬Aquilae:
C. Sossius C. f. Pol. Pompeiop.

[coh. IIII]

¬Etri:
L. Longinus L. f. Pol. Ancyr.
¬Vetti Rufi:
C. Longinus C. f. Pol. Alex.
¬Casti:
M. Cassius M. f. Pol. Isinda
¬C. Mammi:
M. Petronius M. f. Pol. Alex.
¬P. Mammi:
Cn. Otacilius Cn. f. Pol. Anc.
¬Oeniana:
M. Longinus M. f. Pol. Eten.

coh. V

¬Publili:
C. Didius C. f. Pol. Ancyr.
¬Gavisidi:
C. Helvius C. f. Pol. Gang.
¬Iustiana:
T. Antonius T. f. Ser. Tavio
¬Licini Veri:
C. Sentius C. f. Ser. Tavio
¬Numeri:
C. Iulius C. f. Pol. Alexan.
¬Lucretiana:
L. Iulius L. f. Gal. Lugdun.

coh. V

¬Canini:
C. Valerius C. f. Pol. Anc.
¬M. Corneli:
M. Iulius M. f. Pol. Alex.
¬Materni:
M. Lollius M. f. Pol. Ancyr.
¬Cliterniana:
Sex. Lusius Sex. f. Pol. Tavio
¬Clementis:
C. Vibius C. f. Ani. Verg.
¬Gavisidiana:
C. Aufidius C. f. Pol. Anc.

coh. VI

¬Treboni:
M. Valerius M. f. Pol. Sid.
¬Curti:
C. Valerius C. f. Pap. Nicae.
¬Mini:
C. Granius C. f. Pol. Anc.
¬Coti:
C. Valerius C. f. Gal. Lugd.
¬Curiati:
C. Trebius C. f. Pup. Paraet.
¬Galbae:
C. Aufidius C. f. Pol. cast.

coh. VI

¬Firmi:
C. Spedius C. f. Pol. Cyren.
¬Longi:
C. Antonius C. f. Pol. Alex.
¬Flacci:
P. Papirius P. f. Pol. Anc.
¬Vari:
C. Longinus C. f. Pol. cast.
¬Pacci:
P. Flavius P. f. Anien. Paph.
¬Hordioni:
C. Romanius C. f. Fab. Ber.

coh. VII

(*large part lost*)

[. . . . . f. s. s.[1]]
alarum III dec. V,
dupl. I, sesquiplic. IIII,
equites CCCCXXIIII

coh. V[II]

(*large part lost*)

coh. I Theb., cui praeest
Sex. Pompeius Merula:
¬C. Terentius Maximus,
¬C. Iulius Montanus,
¬L. Domitius Aper
sum.: ¬III;
f. s. s.[1] coh. VII ¬ X,
eq. LXI, mil. DCCLXXXIIX

per eosdem, qui supra scripti sunt, lacci aedificati et dedicati sunt: Apollonos hydreuma VII k. Ianuar., Compasi k. Augustis, Berenicide XVIII k. Ianuar., Myoshormi idus Ianuar.; castram (*sic*) aedificaverunt et refecerunt

[1] f(it) s(umma) s(ummarum)

262. Contract, 5 B.C., Papyrus. *BGU*. iv. 1108.

Ἀρτεμιδώρωι ἀρχιδικαστῆι καὶ πρὸς τῇ ἐπιμελείαι τῶν χρηματιστῶν καὶ τῶν ἄλλων κριτηρίων | παρὰ Μάρκου Σενπρωνίου Μά[ρκου υἱοῦ] φυλῆς Αἰμιλίας στρατιώτου τῶν ἐκ τῆς | δευτέρ[ας καὶ εἰ]κοστῆς λ[ε]γεῶν[ο]ς σπ[είρης . . . .]κα[. .]ρε[. . . καὶ] παρὰ | Ἐ[ρωταρίου τῆς . . .]κομει[. . . μετὰ κυρίου καὶ ἐν]γύου τοῦ συγγενο(ῦς) [Λ]ο[υ]κίου [. .]ομυσίου || Λουκίου υἱοῦ [. . . . . .] συνχωρεῖ ἡ Ἐρωτάριον ἐπὶ μῆνας δέκα [π]έντε ἀπὸ | Φαῶφι τοῦ ἐνε(στῶτος) ἕκτου καὶ εἰκοστοῦ ἔτους Καίσαρος τροφεύσειν καὶ θηλάσειν ἔξω παρ' ἑατῇ κατὰ πόλ(ιν) | τῷ ἰδίῳ αὐ(τῆς) γάλ(ακτι) καθ(αρῷ) καὶ ἀφθ(όρῳ) ὃ ἐνκεχείρικεν αὐτῇ ὁ Μᾶρκος ἔτι ἀπὸ Ἐπεὶφ τοῦ διεληλυθότος ἔτους δουλικὸν παιδίον | ᾧ ὄνομα Πρεῖμος (*there follow the terms of payments, &c.*)

263. Boundary stones, Cantabria. *ILS*. 2454–5.

(*a*) ter. August. dividit prat. leg. IIII et agrum Iuliobrig.

(*b*) [t]er. Aug[u]st. dividit [p]rat. leg. IIII [et] agrum Se[gisa]mon.

264. A.D. 29–30, boundary stone, Africa. *ILS*. 9375.

leg. III A[ug.] leimitavit C. Vibio Marso procos. III d. d.[1] LXX, u. k.[2] CCLXXX

[1] d(extra) d(ecumanum) [2] u(ltra) k(ardinem)

265. A.D. 18–19, Iader (Dalmatia). *ILS*. 2280.

Ti. Caesar divi Aug. f. Augustus imp. pontif. max. trib. potest. XX cos. III leg. VII leg. XI P. Cornelio Dolabella leg. pro pr.

266. Salonae. *ILS.* 2478.

. . .] cuius viai millia passus sunt CLXVII munit per vexillarios leg. VII et XI. item viam Gabinianam ab Salonis Andetrium aperuit et munit per leg. VII

267. A.D. 33–34, Iron Gate, Danube (Moesia Superior). *ILS.* 2281.

T. Caesare Aug. f. Augusto imperator. pont. max. tr. pot. XXXV leg. IIII Scyt. leg. V Maced.

268. Strymon Valley. *Ἀρχ. Ἐφημ.* 1932, 3.

imp. Caesare divi f. Aug. L. Tario Ruf. pro̩ pr. leg. X Fret. pontem fecit

269. Palmyra, temple of Bêl. *Syria* 1932, 275.

[Dr]uso Caesari ⌊Ti. Aug. f. divi nepoti⌋ Ti. Caesari divi Aug. f. Augusto divi Iuli nepoti, Ger[manico Caesari] ⌊Ti. Aug. f. divi nepoti⌋ ⌜imperatoribus posuit [Min]ucius T. f. Hor. Rufus legatus leg. X Fretensis⌝

⌜ ⌝ = *later addition*, ⌊ ⌋ = *still later addition.*

269a. Mediolanum Santonum (Gaul). *ILS.* 2531.

C. Iulio Agedil[li f. Fabi]a Macro Sant. duplicario alae Atectorigiana[e] stipendis emeritis XXXII aere incisso, evocat[o] gesatorum DC Raetorum castello Ircavio, clup[eo] coronis aenulis aureis donato a commiliton[ibus.] Iulia Matrona f. C. Iul. Primulus l. h. e. t.[1]

[1] h(eredes) e(x) t(estamento)

270. Velitrae. *SEG.* iv. 102.

M. Mindio M. f. Marcell[o] praefecto classis quei militant Caesari nauarchi et trierarchi patrono

οἱ στρατευόμενοι Καίσαρι ναύαρχοι καὶ τριήραρχοι Μᾶρκον Μίνδιον Μάρκελλον τὸν ἔπαρχον τοῦ στόλου

271. Near Tuder (Umbria). *ILS.* 2231.

C. Edusius Sex. f. Clu. natus Mevaniae centurio legion. XXXXI Augusti Caesaris et centurio classicus ex testamento

272. Misenum. *ILS.* 2817.

C. Iulio Caesaris l. Automato trierar. Iulia C. l. Plusia soror fecit et sibi et suis

273. Naples. *ILS.* 2818.

Ti. Iulius Aug. et August. l. Diogenes tr. sibi et Nigidiae Eutychiae coniugi et suis. Nigidia Eutychia S[ta]beriae C. l. Margaritae amicae suae. h. m. h. n. s.[1]

[1] h(oc) m(onumentum) h(eredem) n(on) s(equetur)

274. Brundisium. *ILS.* 2819.

Iulia Cleopatra quae et Lezbia C. Iuli Menoetis f. Antiochensis Syriae ad Daphnem, uxor Malchionis Caesaris trierarchi de triere Triptolemo

275. Puteoli. *NdS.* 1913, 24.

[C. Iuli]us Malchio[nis Caes]aris [Augus]ti lib. lib. Dama C[. . .]sis sibi [et Iuliae ?] Tertiae coni[ugi s]anctae [. . . . e]t [suis l]iberti[s lib]ertabusque [posterisque eorum . . . . in fronte pedes . .] [in agr]o pedes L

276. Forum Iulii (Narbonensis). *ILS.* 2822.

Antho Caesaris trierarcho Liviano C. Iulius Iaso f. c.

277. Rome. *ILS.* 2823.

Ti. Iulio Aug. l. Hilaro nauarcho Tiberiano Claudia Basilea viro suo

XI

PUBLIC WORKS

See also nos. 266, 268, 320a, 363a.

278. SCC. de aquaeductibus, 11 B.C. Frontinus, *de aquis urbis Romae*, ch. 100, 104, 106, 108, 125, 127; *FIR.* no. 41.

A

quod Q. Aelius Tubero Paulus Fabius Maximus cos. v. f.[1] de iis qui curatores aquarum publicarum ex consensu senatus a Caesare Augusto nominati essent ordinandis, d. e. r. q. f. p.,[2]

d. e. r. i. c.:[3] placere huic ordini eos qui aquis publicis praeessent, cum eius rei causa extra urbem essent, lictores binos et servos publicos ternos, architectos singulos et scribas et librarios, accensos praeconesque totidem habere, quot habent ii per quos frumentum plebei datur; cum autem in urbe eiusdem rei causa aliquid agerent, ceteris apparitoribus iisdem, praeterquam lictoribus, ⟨uti⟩; utique quibus apparitoribus ex hoc S.c. curatoribus aquarum uti liceret, eos diebus X proximis quibus S.c. factum esset ad aerarium deferrent; quique ita delati essent, iis praetores aerarii mercedem cibaria, quanta praefecti frumento dando dare deferreque solent, annua darent et adtribuerent, iisque eas pecunias sine fraude sua facere liceret: utique tabulas chartas ceteraque, quae eius curationis causa opus essent iis curatoribus praeberi, ea[4] Q. Aelius Paulus Fabius cos. ambo alterve, si iis videbitur, adhibitis praetoribus qui aerario praesint, praebenda locent. itemque, cum viarum ⟨quo⟩que curatores frumentique parte quarta anni publico fung⟨eb⟩antur ministerio, ut curatores aquarum iudiciis vacent privatis publicisque

B

quod Q. Aelius Tubero Paulus Fabius Maximus cos. v. f.[1] de numero publicorum salientium qui in urbe essent intraque aedificia urbi coniuncta, quos M. Agrippa fecisset, q. f. p.[2],

d. e. r. i. c.:[3] neque augeri placere neque minui ⟨numerum⟩ publicorum salientium, quos ⟨CVI⟩[5] nunc esse retulerunt ii quibus negotium a senatu est imperatum ut inspicerent aquas publicas inirentque numerum salientium publicorum. itemque placere curatores aquarum, quos Caesar Augustus ex senatus auctoritate nominavit, dare operam ut salientes publici quam adsiduissime interdiu et noctu aquam in usum populi funderent

C

quod Q. Aelius Tubero Paulus Fabius Maximus cos. v. f.[1] quosdam privatos ex rivis publicis aquam ducere, q. d. e. r. f. p.,[2]

d. e. r. i. c.:[3] ne cui privato aquam ducere ex rivis publicis liceret, utique omnes ii quibus aquae ducendae ius esset datum ex castellis ducerent, animadverterentque curatores aquarum, quibus locis intra extra urbem apte castella privati facere possent, ex quibus aquam ducerent, quam ex castello communem accepissent a curatoribus aquarum; neve cui eorum quibus aqua daretur publica ius esset intra quinquaginta pedes eius castelli ex quo aquam ducerent laxiorem fistulam subicere quam quinariam

D

quod Q. Aelius Tubero Paulus Fabius Maximus cos. v. f.[1] constitui oportere, quo iure intra extraque urbem ducerent aquas ii quibus adtributae essent, q. d. e. r. f. p.,[2]

d. [e. r.] i. [c.]:[3] uti usque eo maneret adtributio aquarum, exceptis quae in usum balnearum essent datae aut haustus nomine, quoad iidem domini possiderent id solum in quod accepissent aquam

E

quod Q. Aelius Tubero Paulus Fabius Maximus cos. v. f.[1] de rivis specibus fornicibus aquae Iuliae Marciae Appiae Tepulae Anienis reficiendis, q. d. e. r. f. p.,[2]

d. e. r. i. c.:[3] uti cum ii rivi ⟨specus⟩ fornices, quod Augustus Caesar se refecturum impensa sua pollicitus senatui est, reficerentur, ex agris privatorum terra limus lapides testa harena ligna ceteraque quibus ad eam rem opus esset, unde quaeque eorum proxime sine iniuria privatorum tolli sumi portari possint viri boni arbitratu aestimata darentur tollerentur sumerentur exportarentur: et ad eas res omnes exportandas earumque rerum reficiendarum causa, quotiens opus esset, per agros privatorum sine iniuria eorum itinera actus paterent darentur

F

quod Q. Aelius Tubero Paulus Fabius Maximus cos. v. f.,[1] aquarum quae in urbem venirent itinera occupari monumentis et aedificiis et arboribus conseri, q. f. p.,[2]

d. e. r. i. c.:[3] cum ad reficiendos rivos specusque per⟨tineat, ut spatium circa eos pateat neve quicquam ad eos ponatur, quo impediantur a⟩[6]quae et opera publica corrumpantur, placere circa fontes et fornices et muros ⟨extra urbem?⟩ utraque ex parte quinos denos pedes patere, et circa rivos qui sub terra essent et specus intra urbem et urbi continentia[7] aedificia utraque ex parte quinos pedes vacuos relinqui ita, ut neque monumentum in is locis neque aedificium post hoc tempus ponere neque conserere arbores liceret: si quae nunc essent arbores intra id spatium, exciderentur, praeterquam si quae villae continentes et inclusae aedificiis essent. si quis adversus ea conmiserit, in singulas res poena HS dena milia essent, ex quibus pars dimidia praemium accusatori daretur, cuius opera maxime convictus esset qui adversus hoc s. c. conmisisset, pars autem dimidia in aerarium redigeretur: deque ea re iudicarent cognoscerentque curatores aquarum

[1] v(erba) f(ecerunt) [2] q(uid) d(e) e(a) r(e) f(ieri) p(laceret) [3] d(e) e(a) r(e) i(ta) c(ensuerunt) [4] praebenda *cod.* [5] *Added from Plin.* nat. hist. *36. 15. 121.* [6] *Supplied by Mommsen.* [7] specus extra urbem continentia *cod.*

279. Lex Quinctia de aquaeductibus, 9 B.C. Frontinus, *de aquis urbis Romae*, ch. 129; *FIR.* no. 14. Cf. Syme, *JRS.* 1949, 17.

T. Quinctius Crispinus consul [de s(ua) s(ententia)?] populum iure rogavit populusque iure scivit in foro pro rostris aedis divi Iulii pr. ⟨k.⟩ Iulias. tribus Sergia principium fuit, pro tribu {S.} Sex(tus) ⟨Vibidius?⟩ L. f. Virro ⟨primus scivit⟩

quicumque post hanc legem rogatam rivos specus fornices fistulas tubulos castella lacus aquarum publicarum, quae ad urbem ducuntur, sciens dolo malo foraverit ruperit foranda rumpendave curaverit peiorave fecerit, quo minus eae aquae earumve quae queat[1] in urbem Romam ire cadere fluere pervenire duci quove minus in urbe Roma et qua[2] aedificia urbi continentia sunt erunt, in is hortis praediis locis quorum hortorum praediorum locorum dominis possessoribus u.f.[3] aqua data vel adtributa est vel erit, saliat distribuatur dividatur in castella lacus inmittatur, is populo Romano ⟨HS.⟩ centum milia dare damnas esto; et qui d(olo) m(alo) quid[4] eorum ita fecerit, id omne sarcire reficere restituere aedificare ponere excidere[5] demolire damnas esto sine dolo malo; eaque[6] omnia ita ut

⟨recte factum esse volet⟩ quicumque curator aquarum est erit, ⟨aut⟩ si curator aquarum nemo erit, tum is praetor, qui inter cives et peregrinos ius dicet, multa pignoribus cogito coerceto; eique curatori aut, si curator non erit, tum ei praetori eo nomine cogendi coercendi multae dicendae sive pignoris[7] capiendi ius potestasque esto. si quid eorum servus fecerit, dominus eius HS. centum milia populo d. d. e.[8] si qui locus circa[9] rivos specus fornices fistulas tubulos castella lacus aquarum publicarum, quae ad urbem Romam ducuntur et ducentur, terminatus ⟨e⟩st et erit,[10] neve[11] quis in eo loco post hanc legem rogatam quid obponito molito obsaepito figito statuito ponito conlocato arato serito neve in eum quid immittito, praeterquam rerum[12] faciendarum reponendarum causa quod hac lege licebit oportebit. qui adversus ea quid fecerit et adversus eum siremps lex ius[13] causaque omnium rerum omnibusque esto, atque uti esset esseve oporteret, si is adversus hanc legem rivum specum rupisset forassetve. quo minus in eo loco pascere herbam fenum secare sentes [tollere liceat, e(ius) h(ac) l(ege) n(ihilum) r(ogato).][14] curatores aquarum qui nunc sunt quique erunt ⟨faciunto, ut in eo loco qui⟩ circa fontes[15] et fornices et muros et rivos et specus terminatus est, arbores vites vepres sentes ripae maceriae salicta harundineta tollantur excidantur effodiantur excodicentur, uti quod recte factum esse volet; eoque nomine iis pignoris capio multae dictio coercitioque esto, idque iis sine fraude sua facere liceto, ius potestasque esto.[16] quo minus vites arbores, quae villis aedificiis maceriisque inclusae sunt, maceriae quas curatores aquarum causa cognita ne demolirentur dominis permiserunt, quibus inscripta insculptave essent ipsorum qui permisissent curatorum nomina, maneant, hac lege nihilum rogato.[17] quo minus ex iis fontibus rivis specibus fornicibus aquam sumere haurire iis quibuscumque curatores aquarum permiserunt permiserint, praeterquam rota calice machina liceat, dum ne qui puteus neque foramen novum fiat, eius hac lege nihilum rogato.

[1] qua *cod.* [2] in iis locis quae *cod.* [3] u(su)f(ructuariis) ? [4] quidaquid *cod.* [5] et celere *cod.* [6] aquae *cod.* [7] coge. decoercenda. multa dicenda sunt. pignoris *cod.* [8] d(are) d(amnas) e(sto) [9] si quis circa *cod.* [10] steterit *cod.* [11] neque *cod.* [12] earum *cod.* [13] eum si rem publicam ex iussu *cod.* [14] *gap of 15 letters in cod.* [15] qui nunc sunt circa fontes quique erunt *cod.* [16] isto, *followed by gap of 12 letters in cod.* [17] rogatio *cod.*

280. Cippi, near Rome. *ILS.* 5746.

(*a*) Iul. Tep. Mar. | imp. Caesar | divi f. | Augustus | ex s.c. | CIII | p. CCX⊥

(*b*) Mar. | imp. Caesar | divi f. | Augustus | ex s. c. | ∞ C⊥II p. CCX⊥

(*c*) Iul. | imp. Caesar | divi f. Augustus | ex s. c. | CCCII | p. CCX⊥

281. 5–4 B.C., Rome, on the Aqua Marcia. *ILS.* 98.

imp. Caesar divi Iuli f. Augustus pontifex maximus cos. XII tribunic. potestat. XIX imp. XIIII rivos aquarum omnium refecit

282. Edict of Augustus de aquaeductu Venafrano, between 18 and 11 B.C., near Venafrum. *ILS.* 5743; *FIR.* no. 67.

[ed]ict[um im]p. Ca[esaris Augusti] . . | . . (*six lines missing*) . . . . | Venafranorum nomin[e . . . . . . ius sit lice]atque | qui rivi specus saepta fon[tes . . . . .]que aquae [ducend]ae reficiundae || causa supra infrave libram [facti aedi]ficati structi sunt, sive quod | aliut opus eius aquae ducendae ref[ici]undae causa supra infrave libram | factum est, uti quidquid earum r[er]um factum est, ita esse habere itaque | reficere reponere restituere resarcire semel saepius, fistulas canales | tubos ponere, aperturam committere, sive quid aliut eius aquae ducen||dae causa opus [er]it, facere placet, dum qui locus ager in fundo, qui | Q. Sirini (?) L. f. Ter. [est esseve] dicitur, et in fundo qui L. Pompei M. f. Ter. Sullae | est esseve dicitur, m[acer]ia saeptus est, per quem locum subve quo loco | specus eius aquae p[er-ve]nit, ne ea maceria parsve quae eius maceriae | aliter diruat[ur tollat]ur, quam specus reficiundi aut inspiciendi cau||sa: [neve quid ibi pri]vati sit, quominus ea aqua ire fluere ducive poss[it | . . . .]. dextra sinistraque circa eum rivom circaque | ea o[pera quae eius aqu]ae ducendae causa facta sunt, octonos pedes agrum | [v]acuo[m esse placet], p[e]r quem locum Venafranis eive qui Venafranorum | [nomine . . . . .], iter facere eius aquae ducendae operumve eius aquae || [ductus faciendor]u[m] reficiendorum ⟨causa⟩, quod eius s. d. m.[1] fiat, ius sit liceatque, | quaeque ea[rum rer]um cuius faciendae reficiendae causa opus erunt, quo | proxume poterit, advehere adferre adportare, quaeque inde exempta erunt, | quam maxime aequaliter dextra

sinistraque p.[2] VIII iacere, dum ob eas res damn[i] | infecti iurato promittatur. earumque rerum omnium ita habendarum || colon. (?) Ven[afra]nis ius potestatemque esse placet, dum ne ob id opus domi|nus eorum cuius agri locive, per quem agrum locumve ea aqua ire fluere | ducive solet, invius fiat; neve ob id opus minus ex agro suo in partem agri | quam transire transferre transvertere recte possit; neve cui eorum, per quo|rum agros ea aqua ducitur, eum aquae ductum corrumpere abducere aver||tere facereve, quo minus ea aqua in oppidum Venafranorum recte duci |· fluere possit, liceat |

quaeque aqua in oppidum Venafranorum it fluit ducitur, eam aquam | distribuere discribere vendundi causa, aut ei rei vectigal inponere consti|tuere, IIviro IIviris praefec.[3] praefectis eius coloniae ex maioris partis decuri||onum decreto, quod decretum ita factum erit, cum in decurionibus non | minus quam duae partes decurionum adfuerint, legemque ei dicere ex | decreto decurionum, quod ita ut supra scriptum est decretum erit, ius po|testatemque esse placet; dum ne ea aqua, quae ita distributa discripta deve qua | ita decretum erit, aliter quam fistulis plumbeis d.t.[4] ab rivo p.[2] L ducatur; neve || eae fistulae aut rivos nisi sub terra, quae terra itineris viae publicae limi|tisve erit, ponantur conlocentur; neve ea aqua per locum privatum in|vito eo cuius is locus erit ducatur. quamque legem ei aquae tuendae op[e]||ribusve, quae eius aquae ductus ususve causa facta sunt erunt, tuendis | [IIviri praefect]i [e]x decurion. decreto, quod ita ut s. s. e. factum erit, dixeri[nt, || eam . . . . fir]mam ratamque esse placet| [. . . (*eleven lines missing*) . . . | . . . . .] Venafranae s[. . . . . | . . . . . .]atio quam colono aut incola[e . . . . .] | da[. . .]i[. . . .] is cui ex decreto decurionum ita ut supra comprensum est, ne||gotium datum erit, agenti, tum, qui inter civis et peregrinos ius dicet, iudicium | reciperatorium in singulas res HS X reddere, testibusque dumtaxat X denun|tiand[o q]uaeri placet; dum reciperatorum reiectio inter eum qui aget et | eum quocum agetur ita fi[et ut ex lege, q]uae de iudicis privatis lata est, | licebit oportebit.

[1] s(ine) d(olo) m(alo) [2] p(edes) [3] praefec(to) [4] d(um)t(axat)

283. Two Cippi, with identical inscriptions, Volturno Valley, near aqueduct of Venafrum. *ILS*. 5744; cf. *NdS*. 1926, 437.

iussu imp. Caesaris Augusti circa eum rivom qui aquae

ducendae causa factus est octonos ped. ager dextra sinistraq. vacuus relictus est

284. Between A.D. 21 and 30, Nicopolis (Syria). *CIL.* iii. 6703.

[Ti. Caesar] imp. divi Aug. f. Augustus divi Iuli n. [pontif.] maxim. cos. IIII tr. potest. [aquam] Augustam Nicopoli[m] adducendam curavit [cur. Cn.] Saturnino leg. Cae[s]aris Augusti

285. A.D. 10–11, Alexandria. *ILS.* 9370; Breccia, *Cat. mus. d'Aless. Iscr. gr. e lat.*, 49.

imp. Caesar divi f. August. pontif. maxim. flumen Sebaston ab Schedia induxit a milliario XXV quod per se toto oppido flueret, praefecto Aegypti C. Iulio Aquila anno XXXX Caesaris

αὐτοκράτωρ Καῖσαρ θεοῦ υἱὸς Σεβαστὸς ἀρχιερεὺς ποταμὸν Σεβασ-[τὸν] ἀπὸ Σχεδίας ἤγαγεν ἐπὶ σταδίους διακοσίους ῥέοντα δι' ὅλης τῆς πόλεως, ἐπὶ ἐπάρχου τῆς Αἰγύπτου Γαΐου Ἰουλίου Ἀκύλα ∟ *μ' Καίσαρος*

286. 27 B.C., Ariminum, arch. *ILS.* 84.

senatus populusq[ue Romanus imp. Caesari divi f. Augusto imp. sept.] cos. sept. designat. octavom v[ia Flamin]ia [et reliquei]s celeberrimeis Italiae vieis consilio [et sumptib]us [eius mu]niteis

287. Denarius, 16 B.C., Rome. Mattingly, p. 15, nos. 79 ff.; cf. 432 ff.

Obv. Head of Augustus. AVGVSTVS TR. POT. VII

Rev. Cippus with inscription: S. P. Q. R. IMP. CAE. QVOD V. M. S. EX EA P. Q. IS AD A. DE.[1] Outside cippus: L. VINICIVS L. F. IIIVIR

[1] quod v(iae) m(unitae) s(unt) ex ea p(ecunia) q(uam) is ad a(erarium) de(tulit)

288. Milestone, 2–1 B.C., near Bononia. *ILS.* 9371.

imp. Caesar Augustus pontifex maximus cos. XIII tribunicia potestate XXII viam Aemiliam ab Arimino ad flumen Trebiam muniendam curavit. ⊥XXIX

289. Milestone, 2 B.C., Baetica. *ILS.* 102.

imp. Caesar divi f. Augustus cos. XIII trib. potest. XXI pontif. max. a Baete et Iano August. ad Oceanum ⊥XIII

290. Milestone, A.D. 14, Africa. *ILS.* 151.

imp. Caes. Augusti f. Augustus tri. pot. XVI. Asprenas cos. pr. cos. VIIvir epul[o]num viam ex cast. hibernis Tacapes muniendam curavit. leg. III Aug. CI[. .]

291. Milestone, Lepcis Magna. *ITrip.* no. 930.

imp. Ti. Caesaris Aug. iussu L. Aelius Lamia pro cos. ab oppido in mediterraneum direxsit m. p. $\overline{\text{XLIV}}$

292. A.D. 16–17, Salonae. *ILS.* 5829.

$\overline{\text{V}}$. [Ti. C]aesar divi Augusti f. [Aug]ustus imp. pont. max. [trib.] potest. XIIX cos. II [viam] a colonia Salonitan. [. . . m]unit[. . . . .]vici[. . . . . et idem . . . . . . mu]nit ad [sum]mum montem Ditionum Ulcirum per millia passuum a Salonis LXXVIID P. Dolabella leg. pro pr.

293. A.D. 19–20, Salonae. *ILS.* 5829a.

[Ti. C]aesar divi Augusti f. [Au]gustus imp. pontif. max. trib. potest. XXI [c]os. III viam a Salonis ad [. . . . . . c]astel. Daesitiatium per m[ill. pass]uum CLVI munit et idem viam ad Ba[. . . . flu]m[e]n quod divid[. . . . . a . . . .]ibus, a Salonis muni[t mil. pas]suum CLVIII

294. 6 B.C., Comama (Pisidia). *ILS.* 5828.

imp. Caesar divi f. Augustus pont. ma[x]. cos. XI desig. XII imp. XV trib. potes. XIIX viam Sebasten curante Cornuto Aquila leg. [su]o pro praetore [f]ecit

295. Rome. *ILS.* 5923d.

⌜C. Asinius C. f. Gallus⌝[1] C. Marcius L. f. Censorinus cos.[2] ex s. c. termin. r. r.[3] prox. cipp. p. XIIXS. curatores riparum qui primi terminaver. ex s. c. restituerunt

[1] ⌜ ⌝ *name erased and later restored.* [2] *8* B.C. [3] r(ecta) r(egione)

296. Ostia. *NdS.* 1921, 260.

C. Antistius C. f. C. n. Vetus | C. Valerius L. f. Flacc. Tanur. | P. Vergilius M. f. Pontian. | P. Catienus P. f. Sabinus || Ti. Vergilius Ti. f. Rufus | curatores riparum et alvei | Tiberis ex s. c. terminaver. | r. r. l. p.[1] [. . . . .]

[1] r(ecta) r(egione) l(ongum) p(edes)

297. 27–23 B.C., Rome. *Bull. Comm.* 1939, 13; cf. *ILS.* 5935.

(*a*) Id quod intra cippos ad campum versus soli est Caesar Augustus redemptum a privato publicavit

(*b*) Id quod intra cippos ad campum versus soli est publicum est

298. Rome. *ILS.* 5939.

T. Quinctius Crispinus Valerianus, C. Calpetanus Statius Rufus, C. Pontius P[a]elignus, C. Petronius Umbrinus, M. Crassus Frugi, curatores locor. publicor. iudicand. ex s. c. causa cognita ex privato in public. restituer.

XII

ADMINISTRATION OF THE EMPIRE

SEE also the SCC. in 30, 37, 278, edicts in 31, 282, laws in 279, 364–5, imperial letters in 99(II), 102, and letters of proconsuls in 20, 98. Cf. also nos. 58a, 130a, 209b–c.

299. Letter of Antony and S. C. de Aphrodisiensibus, 42 B.C., Aphrodisias (Caria). *OGIS*. 453–5; *FIR*. no. 38.

A. [*Μᾶρκος Ἀντώνιος Μάρκου υἱὸς αὐτοκράτωρ ὕπατος ἀποδεδει*]|*γμένος τὸ β′ καὶ* [*τὸ γ′* | *τῶν*] *τριῶν ἀνδρῶν τῆς* | *τῶν δημοσίων πρα*|*γμάτων διατάξεως* || *Πλαρασέων καὶ Ἀφρο*|*δεισιέων ἄρχουσιν* | *βουλῇ δήμῳ χαίρειν·* | *εἰ ἔρρωσθε, εὖ ἂν ἔ*|*χοι· ὑγιαίνω δὲ καὶ* || *αὐτὸς μετὰ τοῦ στρα*|*τεύματος. Σόλων Δημητρίου* [*ὑ*]*μέτερος* | *πρεσβευτής, ἐπι*|*μελέστατα πεφρον*||*τικὼς τῶν τῆς πό*|*λεως ὑμῶν πραγ*|*μάτων, οὐ μόνον* | *ἠρκέσθη ἐπὶ τοῖς* | *γεγονόσιν οἰκονο*||[*μή*]*μασιν, ἀλλὰ καὶ* | *ἡμᾶς παρεκάλεσ*|*εν εἰς τὸ τοῦ γεγο*|*νότος ὑμεῖν ἐπι*|*κρίματος καὶ δόγμα*||*τος καὶ ὁρκίου καὶ νό*|*μου ἀντιπεφωνημέ*|*να ἐκ τῶν δημοσίων* | *δέλτων ἐξαποστεῖ*|*λαι ὑμεῖν τὰ ἀντίγρα*||*φα. ἐφ' οἷς ἐπαινέ*|*σας τὸν Σόλωνα μᾶλ*|*λον ἀπεδεξάμην ἔσ*|*χον τε ἐν τοῖς ὑπ' ἐμοῦ* | *γεινωσκομένοις,* || *ᾧ καὶ τὰ καθήκοντα* | *ἀπεμέρισα φιλάν*|*θρωπα, ἄξιον ἡγη*|*σάμενος τὸν ἄν*|*δρα τῆς ἐξ ἡμῶν τει*||*μῆς, ὑμεῖν τε συ*|*νήδομαι ἐπὶ τῷ ἔχειν* | *τοιοῦτον πολείτην.* | *ἔστιν δὲ ἀντίγραφα* | *τῶν γεγονότων ὑ*||*μεῖν φιλανθρώπων* | *τὰ ὑπογεγραμμένα·* | *ἃ ὑμᾶς βούλομαι* | *ἐν τοῖς δημοσίοις* | *τοῖς παρ' ὑμεῖν* || *γράμμασιν ἐντάξαι*

B. *γράμματα Καίσαρος* | [. . . . .]

C. [*περὶ ὧν* . . . . *λόγους ἐποιήσαντο* . . . . . . *περὶ τούτου τοῦ πράγματος οὕτως ἔδοξεν· ἀρέσκειν τῇ συγκλήτῳ Πλαρασεῖς καὶ Ἀφροδεισιεῖς, ὡς ἔκρινε Γάιος Καῖσαρ αὐτοκράτωρ, κατὰ τὰ* | *δί*]*καια ἐσθλά τε* [*πάντ*]*α ἐλευθέρους εἶναι, τῷ* [*τε*] *δικαίῳ καὶ ταῖς* [*κρίσεσιν ταῖς ἰδίαις τὴν πό*|*λιν*] *τὴν Πλαρασέων καὶ Ἀφροδεισιέων χρῆσθαι μήτε ἐγγύην ε*[*ἰς Ῥώμην αὐτοὺς κατὰ δόγμα τι* | *κ*]*αὶ κέλευσιν ὁμολογεῖν· ἅ τέ τινα ἔπαθλα τειμὰς φιλάνθρω*[*πα* . . . . *τρεῖς ἄνδρες* | *ο*]*ἱ τῆς τῶν δημοσίων πραγμάτων διατάξεως τῷ ἰδίῳ ἐπικρίματι Πλ*[*αρασεῦσι καὶ Ἀφροδεισιεῦ*||*σι*] *προσεμέρισαν προσμεριοῦσιν, συνεχώρησαν συνχωρήσουσιν, τα*[*ῦτα πάντα κύρια εἶναι* | *γ*]*ενέσθαι. ὁμοίως τε ἀρέσκειν τῇ συγκλήτῳ τὸν δῆμον τὸν Πλα*[*ρασέων καὶ Ἀφροδεισιέ*]||*ων τὴν* ἐλευθερίαν καὶ τὴν ἀτέλειαν αὐτοὺς πάντων τῶν πραγ[μάτων ἔχειν καρπίζεσθαι, | καθ]άπερ καί τις πολιτεία τῷ καλλίστῳ δικαίῳ καλλίστῳ τε νόμῳ ἐστίν, [ἥτις παρὰ τοῦ | δήμο]υ τοῦ Ῥωμαίων τὴν ἐλευθερίαν καὶ τὴν ἀτέλειαν ἔχει φίλη τε καὶ σύ[μμαχος γεγέ||νηται. τὸ δὲ] τέμενος θεᾶς Ἀφροδίτης ἐν πόλει Πλαρασέων καὶ Ἀφροδεισιέω[ν ἄσυλον | ἔ]στω ταὐτῷ {τῷ} δικαίῳ ταὐτῇ τε δεισιδαιμονίᾳ, ᾧ δικαίῳ καὶ ᾗ δεισ[ιδαιμονίᾳ τὸ ἱερὸν θε|ᾶς Ἐφε]σίας ἐστὶν ἐν Ἐφέσῳ· κύκλῳ τε ἐκείνου τοῦ ἱεροῦ εἴτε τέμενος εἴτ[ε ἄλσος ἐστίν, οὗ|τος ὁ] τόπος ἄσυλος ἔστω. ὅπως τε ἡ πόλις καὶ οἱ πολεῖται οἱ Πλαρασέων [καὶ Ἀφροδεισιέων | μεθ' ὧ]ν κωμῶν χωρίων ὀχυρωμάτων ὀρῶν προσόδων πρὸς τὴν φιλίαν το[ῦ δήμου προσῆλθον, ταῦτα || ἔχωσ]ιν κρατῶσιν χρῶνται καρπίζωνταί τε πάντων πραγμάτων ἀτε[λεῖς ὄντες. μηδέ τινα | φόρον δ]ιά τινα αἰτίαν ἐκείνων διδόναι μηδὲ [σ]υνεισφέρειν ὀφείλωσιν, [ἀλλ' αὐτοὶ πᾶ|σι τούτ]οις κατ' οὖσαν μετὰ ταῦτα ἐν ἑαυτοῖς κύρωσιν χρῶν[ται καρπίζωνται κρατῶσιν. ἔδοξεν]

300. Letter of Antony to the Koinon of Asia, 42/1 or 33/2 B.C., Papyrus. Preisigke, *Sammelbuch*, i. 4224.

Μᾶρκος Ἀντώνιος αὐτοκράτωρ | τριῶν ἀνδρῶν δημοσίων πραγμάτων | ἀποκαταστάσεως[1] τῶι κοινῶι τῶν ἀ|πὸ τῆς Ἀσίας Ἑλλήνων χαίρειν. καὶ || πρότερον ἐντυχόντος μοι ἐν Ἐφέσωι | Μάρκου Ἀντωνίου Ἀρτεμιδώρου τοῦ | ἐμοῦ φίλου καὶ ἀλείπτου, μετὰ τοῦ ἐ|πωνύμου τῆς συνόδου τῶν ἀπὸ τῆς | οἰκουμένης ἱερονικῶν καὶ στεφα||νειτῶν ἱερέως Χαροπείνου Ἐφεσίου, | περὶ τοῦ <τὰ> προυπάρχοντα τῆι συνό|δωι μένειν ἀναφαίρετα, καὶ περὶ τῶν | λοιπῶν ὧν ᾐτεῖτο ἀπ' ἐμοῦ τιμίων | καὶ φιλανθρώπων[2] τῆς ἀστρατευσίας || καὶ ἀλειτουργεσίας πάσης καὶ ἀνεπι|σταθμείας καὶ τῆς περὶ τὴν πανή|γυριν ἐκεχειρίας καὶ ἀσυλίας καὶ | πορφύρας, ἵνα συνχωρήσω γράψαι | παραχρῆμα πρὸς ὑμᾶς, συνχωρῶ{ν} || βουλόμενος καὶ διὰ τὸν ἐμὸν φί|λον Ἀρτεμίδωρον καὶ τῶι ἐπωνύ|μωι αὐτῶν ἱερεῖ εἴς τε τὸν κόσμον τῆς | συνόδου καὶ τὴν αὔξησιν αὐτῆς χα|ρίσασθαι. καὶ τὰ νῦν πάλιν ἐντυ||χόντος μοι τοῦ Ἀρτεμιδώρου ὅπως | ἐξῇ αὐτοῖς ἀναθεῖναι δέλτον χαλ|κῆν καὶ ἐνχαράξαι εἰς αὐτὴν περὶ | τῶν προγεγραμμένων φιλανθρώπων, | ἐγὼ προαιρούμενος ἐν μηδενὶ καθ||υστερεῖν τὸν Ἀρτεμίδωρον περί τ<ιν>ων | ἐντυχόντ<α> ἐπεχώρησα τὴ[ν κά]|θεξιν τῆς δέλτο(υ) ὡς παρακαλεῖ [με]. || ὑμῖν (δὲ) γέγραφα περὶ τούτων

[1] ἀπὸ καταστάσεως? ἀπὸ *mistaken for* ἐπὶ?

[2] φιλανθρώπου *pap.*

For the date cf. Brandis, Hermes, *1897*, *516*; *Robert,* Hellenica, *vii*, *122*.

301. Letters and edict of Octavian to the Rhosians, between 41 and 30 B.C., Rhosos (Syria). *ISyr.* iii. 1 (1950), no. 718; cf. *FIR.* no. 55 (except part III).

I

ἔτους [...] μηνὸς Ἀπελλαίου [..... | αὐτοκρά]τωρ Καῖσαρ θεοῦ Ἰουλίου υἱός, αὐτοκράτωρ τὸ τέταρτον ὕπ[ατος | τὸ δεύτ]ερον καὶ τὸ τρίτον ἀποδεδειγμένος, Ῥωσέων τῆς ἱερᾶς καὶ ἀσύλου καὶ | [αὐτονό-μ]ου ἄρχουσι βουλῆι δήμωι χαίρειν· ‹εἰ ἔρρωσθε καλῶς ἂν ἔχοι›· καὶ αὐτὸς δὲ μετὰ τοῦ στρατεύματος || [ὑγίαινον. τ]ὰ ὑπογεγραμμένα ἐξελήφθη{ι} ἐκ στήλης ἐκ τοῦ ἐν Ῥώμῃ Καπετωλίου, | [ἅπερ ἀξιῶ] καταχωρίσαι εἰς τὰ παρ' ὑμῖν δημόσια γράμματα· πέμψατε δὲ καὶ ἀντίγραφον | [αὐτῶν εἰς] Ταρσέων τὴν βουλὴν καὶ τὸν δῆμον, Ἀντιοχέων τὴν βουλὴν καὶ τὸν δῆμον | [Σελευκέω?]ν τὴν βουλὴν καὶ τὸν δῆμον, ὅπως καταχωρίσωσιν. ἔρρωσθε |

II

[Καῖσαρ α]ὐτοκράτωρ τριῶν ἀνδρῶν ἐπὶ τῆς καταστάσεως τῶν δημοσίων πραγμά||[των, κατὰ ν]όμ̣ο̣ν Μουνάτιον καὶ Αἰμίλιον πολειτείαν καὶ ἀνεισφορίαν πάντων τῶν | [ὑπαρχόντ]ων ἔδωκεν[1] εἰς τούτους τοὺς λόγους· | [ἐπεὶ Σέλευ]κος Θεοδότου Ῥωσεὺς συνεστρατεύσατο ἡμεῖν ἐν τοῖς κατὰ τὴν | [ἀνατολὴν τόπ]οις,[2] ὄντων αὐτοκρατόρων ἡμῶν, πολλὰ καὶ μεγάλα περὶ ἡμῶν ἐκακοπά|[θησεν ἐκιν]δύνευσέν τε, οὐδενὸς φεισάμενος τῶν πρὸς ὑπομονὴν δεινῶν, || [καὶ πᾶσαν] προαίρεσιν πίστιν τε παρέσχετο τοῖς δημοσίοις πράγμασιν, τούς τε | [ἰδίους καιρ]οὺς τῆι ἡμετέραι σωτη[ρίαι] συνέζευξεν πᾶσάν τε βλάβην περὶ τῶν | [δημοσίων πρα]γμάτων τοῦ δήμ[ου τ]ο[ῦ Ῥωμ]αίων ὑπέμεινε, παροῦσιν καὶ ἀποῦσιν | [ἡμεῖν χρη]στὸς ἐγένετο· |

1. [αὐτῶι καὶ γ]ονεῦσι τέκνοις ἐκγόνοις τε αὐτοῦ γυναικί τε τούτου ἥτις με||[τ' αὐτοῦ] ἔστ[αι . . . *c. 16 letters* . . .] πολειτείαν καὶ ἀνεισφορίαν τῶν ὑπαρχόν|[των δίδ]ομεν οὕτω[ς ὡς οἵτινες τῶ]ι ἀρίστωι νόμωι ἀρίστωι τε δικαίωι πολεῖται | [ἀνείσφο]ροί [εἰσιν, καὶ στρατείας λει]του[ργία]ς τε δημοσίας ἁπάσης πάρε|[σις ἔστω]. |

2. [αὐτὸς ὁ ἐπ]άνω γεγρ[αμμένος καὶ γονεῖς τέκ]ν[α] ἔκγ[ο]νο[ί τε] αὐτοῦ φυλῆς Κορνηλίας ἔστω{ι} || [καὶ? ψῆφ]ός τε ἐ[ν]τ[α]ῦθα [φερέσθω? καὶ φέρειν καὶ τειμᾶσθαι? ἐξ]έστω{ι}· καὶ ἐὰν ἀπόντες τει|[μᾶσθαι θ]έλωσιν[...] α[..........]ιας Ἰταλίας εἶναι θέλωσιν | [.......]ος τειμο[......] |

3. [καθόσον] ὁ προγεγρ[α]μ[μένος καὶ γυνὴ καὶ γονεῖς τ]έκνα ἔ[κ-γονοί] τ[ε] αὐτοῦ πρὸ τοῦ πολείτης [Ῥωμαῖο]ς ἀνείσφορος ε[ἶν]αι [ἀτελὴς ἦ̣ν? .....], καὶ πολεί[της Ῥω]μαῖος ἀνείσφορος γεγονὼς ||

[κατὰ τὸ?] δίκαιον ἐὰν χ[ρῆ]σθ[αι? θέλῃι, ἐξεῖναι, τὰς] ἱε[ρω]σ[ύνας ....]ις τείμια φιλάνθρωπα | [.......] τά τε ὑ[πάρχοντα? ἔχειν καρπίζεσθαι καθάπερ τις τῶι ἀρίστωι νό]μωι [ἀ]ρίστωι τε δικαίωι ἔχει | [καρπίζεται].

ch. 4–7 (ll. 33–52) badly mutilated. The words οὔτε χειριστὴν εἰσφ[ορῶν δη]μοσιώ[νην τε] *occur.*

8. [ἐάν τις α]ὐτῶν κατηγορεῖν θέλ[ῃι ἔγκ]λημά τ[ε εἰς?]άγειν κριτήριόν τε κατ' αὐτῶν λαμβά||[νειν κρί]σιν τε συνίστασθ[αι... *c. 20 letters*...]ειν, ἐπὶ τούτων τῶν πραγμάτων πάντων || [ἐάν τε ἐ]ν οἴκωι τοῖς ἰδίοις [νόμοις ἐάν τε ἐν πόλεσιν] ἐλευθέραις ἐάν τε πρὸς ἄρχοντας ἢ ἀν||[τάρχοντα]ς ἡμετέρους [. . . *c. 20 letters* . . . κρί]νεσθαι θέλωσιν, αὐτῶν τὴν αἵρεσιν εἶναι | [ἀρέσκει?] μήτε τις ἄλλω[ς ἢ ἐν τ]ούτ[οις γεγραμμένον ἐστὶ ποιήσ?]ηι περί τε αὐτῶν κρίνη<ι> προσανε[ν]έγ||[κας γνώ]μην τε εἴπῃι· [ἐὰν δὲ κριτήριόν τι περὶ αὐτῶν ὑπ]εναντίως τούτοι[ς γεί]νηται, τοῦτο κύριον | [μὴ εἶνα]ι. ||

9. [ἐὰν δέ τι]ς τούτου [τ]οῦ προγεγραμμένου, γ[ονέ]ω[ν γυναικὸς τ]έκνων ἐκγόνων τε αὐτοῦ[3] ὄνομα δέξασθαι | [θελήσηι?] πρό[κ]ριμά τε κεφαλῆς ποιήσα[σθαι . . . *c. 17 letters* . . .]ειν π[ρ]εσβευτάς τε πρὸς τὴν [σύ]νκλητον | [τὴν ἡμετέ]ραν [πρός] τε ἄρχοντας ἀντά[ρχοντάς τε τοὺς ἡμετέρ]ους παραγείνεσθ[αι πρ]εσβευτάς τε πέμ||[πειν περὶ τῶν ἰδίων πραγμάτω[ν τοῖς προγεγραμμένοις ἐξ]ουσίαν εἶναι [ἀρέ]σκει. ἥτις ἂν πολει||[τεία ὅστις] τε ἄρχων ὅσα τ[ε κατὰ ταῦτα δεῖ, μὴ ποιήσηι καὶ ὑπεναντίον] τούτοις ποιήσηι ἢ ἐκ προαγωγῆς γνῶι || [ἢ ....]οίηι ἢ ἐνεχυράση<ι> δόλωι τε πο[ν]η[ρ]ῶ[ι κωλύση]ι ὧ<ι> ἔλασσον οὗτοι οἱ προγεγραμμένοι τοῖς | [φιλανθρώ]ποις [τ]οῖς δεδογμένοις χ[ρῆ]σθ[αι δυνή]σονται, τῶι δήμωι τῶν Ῥωμαίων νο<ύμ>μων ση||[στερτίω]ν δέκα μυριάδας δοῦναι κατ[άδικοι ἔσ]τωσαν τούτου τε τοῦ χρήματος τῶι | [θέλοντι?] αἴ[τημ]α ἔκπραξίς τε ἔστω [ἐάν τε] ἐν τῆι ἐπαρχείαι παρὰ ἄρχουσιν ἀντάρχ[ου|σίν τε ἡμε]τέροις ἐάν τε ἐν Ῥώμηι [πρ]ο<σ>α[ἰτ]εῖν ἐ[κ]πράσσειν τε θέλῃι περὶ δὲ τούτων τῶν || [χρημάτω]ν ἐγγύας ἱκανῶ[ς δι]δομένωι [δικάζε]σθαι ἀρέσκει. ταῦτα τὰ προγεγραμμέ||[να ὅπως οὕτ]ως γείνηται, ἄρ[χοντες ἀντάρχοντέ]ς τε ἡμέτεροι οἵτινες <ἂ>ν ἐκε<ῖ> ἐπὶ τῆς δί||[κης κατα]σ<τ>ῶσιν ἐπικρειν[έτ]ω[σ]αν φροντιζέτωσάν τε

III

[ἔτους...] μηνὸς Δύστρου ιε'· αὐτοκράτωρ Καῖσαρ θεοῦ υἱός, αὐτοκράτωρ τὸ ἕκτον ὕπατος | [τὸ τρί]τον ἀποδεδειγμένος τὸ τέταρτον, Ῥωσέων τῆς ἱερᾶς καὶ ἀσύλου καὶ αὐτονόμου || [ἄρχουσι] βουλῆι δήμωι χαίρειν· εἰ ἔρρωσθε, καλῶς ἂν ἔχοι· καὶ αὐτὸς δὲ μετὰ τοῦ στρατεύ||[ματος ὑγί]αινον· οἱ πεμφθέντες πρεσβευταὶ ὑφ' ὑμῶν Σέλευκος ναύαρχος ἐμὸς Ἡρᾶς Καλλι|[...]έρως Σύμμαχος ἄνδρες ἀγαθοὶ παρὰ δήμου ἀγαθοῦ φίλου συμμάχου τε ἡμετέρου | [ἀποδημήσ]αντες εἰς Ἔφεσον πρός με διελέχθησαν περὶ ὧν εἶχον τὰς ἐντολάς· ἐγὼ οὖν τοὺς | [ἄνδρας ἀπ]εδεξάμην εὑρὼν φιλοπατρίδας καὶ ἀγαθοὺς καὶ τὰς τιμὰς καὶ τὸν στέφανον δέδεγμαι || [πειράσομ]αί τε ἐπὶ τοὺς τόπους ἐλθὼν ἀγαθοῦ τινος ὑμεῖν γείνεσθαι παραίτιος καὶ συντηρῆσαι | [τὰ φιλάνθ]ρωπα τῆι πόλει καὶ ταῦτα ἥδειον διὰ Σέλευκον τὸν ναύαρχόν μου ποιήσω{ι} συνεστρατευμέ|[νον μοι π]άντα τὸν τοῦ πολέμου χρόνον καὶ διὰ παντὸς ἠριστευκότα καὶ πᾶσαν ἀπόδειξιν εὐνοίας | [τε καὶ πίσ]τεως παρεσχημένον, ὃς οὐδένα καιρὸν παραλέλοιπεν ἐντυγχάνων ὑπὲρ ὑμῶν καὶ πᾶ|[σαν εἰσφ]ερόμενος σπουδὴν καὶ προθυμίαν ὑπὲρ τῶν ὑμεῖν συμφερόντων. ἔρρωσθε ||

IV

[ἔτους ....μ]ηνὸς Ἀπελλαίου θ'. αὐτοκράτωρ Καῖσαρ, θεοῦ υἱός, αὐτοκράτωρ τὸ ἕκτον, ὕπατος τὸ τέταρ|[τον, Ῥωσέ]ων τῆς ἱερᾶς καὶ ἀσύλου καὶ αὐτονόμου ἄρχουσι βουλῆι δήμωι χαίρειν. εἰ ἔρρωσθε, καλῶς | [ἂν ἔχοι· καὶ] αὐτὸς δὲ μετὰ τοῦ στρατεύματος ὑγίαινον. Σέλευκος ὁ καὶ ὑμέτερος πολεί|[της καὶ ἐμ]ὸς ναύαρχος ἐμ πᾶσι τοῖς πολέμοις συνεστρατευμένος μοι καὶ π[ολλ]ὰς ἀπο|[δείξεις κ]αὶ τῆς εὐνοίας καὶ τῆς πίστεως καὶ τῆς ἀνδρείας δεδωκώς, ὡς καθῆκο[ν ἦ]ν τοὺς || [συνστρατευ]σαμένους ἡμεῖν καὶ κατὰ πόλεμον ἀριστεύσαντας, κεκόσμηται φιλανθρώποις | [καὶ ἀνεισφ]ορίαι καὶ πολιτείαι. τοῦτον οὖν ὑμεῖν συνίστημι· οἱ γὰρ τοιοῦτοι ἄνδρες καὶ τὴν πρὸς τὰς | [πατρίδας] εὔνοιαν προθυμοτέραν ποιοῦσιν· ὡς οὖν ἐμοῦ πάντα δυνατὰ ποιήσοντος ὑμεῖν ἥδει|[ον διὰ Σέλ]ευκον, θαρροῦντες περὶ ὧν ἂν βούλεσθε πρός με ἀποστέλλετε. ἔρρωσθε

[1] ἔδωκαν *inscr.* [2] *Suppl. Guarducci,* APont. *1938, 53.* [3] αὐτῶν *inscr.*

302. Edict of Octavian, Papyrus, 37–30 B.C. (?). Wilcken, *Chrestomathie,* no. 462; new reading: *FIR.* p. 315, no. 56.

p. cum Manius Valens veteranus ex.[.]ter recitasserit | partem edi[c]ti hoc quod infra scriptum est. imp. Caesar | [d]ivi filius trium[v]ir rei publicae consultor[1] dicit: visum | [est] edicendum mi[hi vete]ranis dare om[nibus], ut tributis || [. . . *lines 5–7 mutilated, more missing* . . . | . .] ipsis parentibu[s lib]erisque eorum e[t uxo]ribus qui sec[um]|que erunt im[mu]nitatem omnium rerum d[a]re, utique || optimo iure optimaq[u]e legis[2] cives Romani sunt[3] immunes | sunto liberi s[unto mi]litiae muneribusque publicis fu[ngen|d]i vocat[i]o,[4] item in [quavi]s tribu s. s.[5] suffragium | [fe]rendi c[e]nsendi[que] potestas esto et si a[b]sentes | voluerint [ce]nseri detur quod[cum]que iis qui s. s.[6] sun[t i]psis parentes[7] || [co]n[iu]ges[7] liberisq[ue] eorum. item quem[.]ṃọtum[8] veterani | immune[s] esint[9] eor[um] esse volui quẹc̣[u]ṃque sacer{tia}|[do]tia qu[o]sque hon[or]es quaeque praemia [b]eneficia commoda | habuerunt, item ut habeant utantur fruanturque permit[t]i | [d]o. invitis iis neq[ue] magistr[at]us cete[ros] neque laegatum || [n]eque procuratorem [ne]que em[p]torem t[ri]butorem esse | [p]lace[t] neque in domo eorum divertendi ⟨h⟩iemandique causamque[10] | [a]b ea quem detuci[11] place[t]

[1] *Corrupt; read either* const. iter. *or* consul ter (*or* iter.). [2] *Read* lege [3] sunt *or* sunto *written above* sint [4] *Read* vacatio ⟨esto⟩ [5] s(upra) s(cripta) [6] s(upra) s(cripti) [7] *Read* parentibus coniugibus [8] quemadmodum? [9] essent [10] *Read* causa neque [11] deduci

303. Letter of Octavian to Mylasa (Caria), 31 B.C., Mylasa. *Syll.*³ 768.

(*a*) αὐτοκράτωρ Καῖσαρ θεοῦ Ἰουλίου | υἱὸς ὕπατός τε τὸ τρίτον καθεσ|ταμένος Μυλασέων ἄρχουσι βου|λῆι δήμωι χαίρειν· εἰ ἔρρωσθε κ[α]||λῶς ἂν ἔχοι· καὶ αὐτὸς δὲ μετὰ τ[οῦ] | στρατεύματος ὑγίαινον. κα[ὶ πρό]|τερον μὲν ἤδη περὶ τῆς κατ[ασχού]|σης ὑμᾶς τύχης προσεπέ[μψατέ] | μοι, καὶ νῦν παραγενομένω[ν τῶν] || πρεσβευτῶν, Οὐλιάδ[ου .....]

(*b*) [.....]ς τῶν πολεμίων πταῖσαι καὶ πρατη[θεί]|σης τῆς πόλεως, πολλοὺς μὲν αἰχμαλώτο[υς] | ἀποβαλῖν πολίτας, οὐκ ὀλίγους μὲν φονευθέ[ν]|τας, τινὰς δὲ καὶ συνκαταφλεγέ⟨ν⟩τας τῇ πόλε[ι], || τῆς τῶν πολεμίων ὠμότητος οὐδὲ τῶν | ναῶν οὐδὲ τῶν ἱερῶν τῶν ἁγιωτάτων ἀ|ποσχομένης· ὑπέδιξαν δέ μοι καὶ περὶ| τῆς χώρας τῆς λελεηλατημένης καὶ τῶν | ἐπαύλεων τῶν ἐμπεπρησμένων, ὥστε ἐμ || πᾶσιν ὑμᾶς ἠτυχηκέναι· ἐφ' οἷς πᾶσιν συνε[ῖ|δον παθόντας] ταῦτα πάσης τειμῆς καὶ χάρι|[τος ἀξίους ἄνδρας γενομέν]ους ὑμᾶς πε[ρὶ Ῥωμαίους.......

304. Letter of Octavian to C. Norbanus Flaccus, proconsul of Asia. Josephus, *Ant. Iud.* xvi. 166.

Καῖσαρ Νωρβανῷ Φλάκκῳ χαίρειν· Ἰουδαῖοι ὅσοι ποτ' οὖν εἰσίν, οἳ δι' ἀρχαίαν συνήθειαν εἰώθασι χρήματά τε ἱερὰ φέροντες ἀναπέμπειν ἀκωλύτως τοῦτο ποιείτωσαν εἰς Ἱεροσόλυμα

305. Letter of C. Norbanus Flaccus, proconsul of Asia, to Sardis. Josephus, *Ant. Iud.* xvi. 171.

Γάϊος Νωρβανὸς Φλάκκος ἀνθύπατος Σαρδιανῶν ἄρχουσι καὶ βουλῇ χαίρειν. Καῖσάρ μοι ἔγραψε κελεύων μὴ κωλύεσθαι τοὺς Ἰουδαίους ὅσοι ἂν ὦσιν κατὰ τὸ πάτριον αὐτοῖς ἔθος συναγαγόντες χρήματα ἀναπέμπειν εἰς Ἱεροσόλυμα. ἔγραψα οὖν ὑμῖν ἵν' εἰδῆτε ὅτι Καῖσαρ κἀγὼ οὕτω θέλομεν γίνεσθαι

306. Letter of C. Norbanus Flaccus, proconsul of Asia, to Ephesus. Philo, *Leg. ad Gaium*, 40 § 315.

Γάϊος Νωρβανὸς Φλάκκος ἀνθύπατος Ἐφεσίων ἄρχουσιν χαίρειν· Καῖσάρ μοι ἔγραψεν Ἰουδαίους οὗ ἂν ὦσιν ἰδίῳ ἀρχαίῳ ἐθισμῷ νομίζειν συναγομένους χρήματα φέρειν ἃ πέμπουσιν εἰς Ἱεροσόλυμα. τούτους οὐκ ἠθέλησε κωλύεσθαι τοῦτο ποιεῖν. ἔγραψα οὖν ὑμῖν, ἵν' εἰδῆτε ὡς ταῦτα οὕτως γίνεσθαι κελεύει

307. SCC. de foedere cum Mytilenaeis, 25 B.C., Mytilene. *IG.* xii. 2, 35. Cf. *RFil.* 1942, 125.

The inscription first contains two letters of Julius Caesar (47 and 45 B.C.), *in which he accepts Mytilene's offers of peace and alliance and sends them the text of a SC. on this alliance (col. a, col. b, 1–35).*

[δόγμ]ατα συγκλήτου περὶ ὁρκίου. | [αὐτοκράτορος Καίσαρος] Σεβαστοῦ τὸ ἔνατον, Μάρκου Σιλανοῦ ὑ[πάτων | προτεθὲν? ...... ἐπι]ταγῇ Μάρκου Σιλανοῦ ἐκ συγκλήτου δό[γματος | ..... Ἰ]ουνίων ἐν κουρίᾳ Ἰουλίᾳ γραφομένῳ παρ[ῆσαν || Παῦλος Αἰμίλιος Λευ]κίου υἱὸς Παλατίνᾳ Λέπεδος, Γάϊος Ἀσίν[ιος Γναΐ|ου υἱὸς ..... Πωλ-λίω]ν, Λεύκιος Σεμπρώνιος Λευκίου υἱὸς Φαλ[έρνᾳ Ἀ|τρατινός, Μᾶρκος Τερέντ]ιος Μάρκου υἱὸς Παπειρίᾳ Οὐάρρων, Γάϊο[ς Ἰού|νιος .... Σι]λανός, Κοΐντος Ἀκούτιος Κοΐντου υἱὸς [.......

Col. c.

περὶ ὧν [Μᾶ]ρκος Σιλανὸς λόγ[ο]υς [ἐποιήσατο ἐπὶ αὐτοκράτορα Καίσαρα Σεβασ]|τὸν [τ]ὸν συνάρχοντα γράμμ[ατα πεμφθῆναι καὶ ἀπόκρισιν ἐλθεῖν, ὥστε | ἐ]ὰν τῆι συγκλήτωι ἀρέσκῃ μετ[ὰ τῶν Μυτιληναίων τὰ ὅρκια γενέσθαι, | τ]ούτου τοῦ πράγματος αὐτῶ[ι τῶι Σιλανῶι ἡ φροντὶς ἐπιτρέπηται, πε||ρ]ὶ τούτου τοῦ πράγματος ο[ὕτως ἔδοξεν· ὅπως Μᾶρκος Σιλανὸς | ὕ]πατος, ἐὰν αὐτῶι φαίνηται, ὅρκ[ια τῶν Μυτιληναίων γενέσθαι φροντίσηι ἄλ|λο] τε ὁποῖον ὥστε ἂν ἐκ τῶν [δημοσίων πραγμάτων πίστεώς τε τῆς αὐ]|τοῦ φαίνηται. ἔδοξεν. | [π]ρὸ ἡμέρων τριῶν καλανδῶν Ἰο[υλίων ἐν .... γραφομένῳ παρῆ]||σαν Γάϊος Νωρβα[νὸς] Γαΐ[ου υἱὸς Φλάκκος, ... Ἀπ]|πίου υἱὸς Παλα[τίνᾳ ....., ... | Κ]ηνσωρῖνος [.......], | Μᾶρκος Οὐα[λέριος ......]|κου υἱὸ[ς ...., ...ο]υ υἱὸς Κλοστο||μίνᾳ Λ[......, Μᾶρκος Τερέντιος Μάρκου υἱὸς Παπε]ιρίᾳ Οὐάρρων, Γάϊος Κ[........].| περὶ ὧν Μ[ᾶρκος Σιλανὸς λόγους ἐποιήσατο, τῶι τῆς συγκλήτου] δόγματι ἑαυτῶι | δεδο[μένωι, ὅπως ἐὰν ἑαυτῶι φαίνηται τὰ ὅρκια τῶν Μυτ]ιληναίων γενέσ|θαι φροντ[ίσηι ἄλλο τε ὁποῖον ὥστε ἂν ἐκ τῶν δημοσ]ίων πραγμάτων || πίστεώς τ[ε τῆς ἰδίας φαίνηται, πάντα ἑαυτὸν πείσασθ]αι· λοιπὸν εἶναι | ἵνα τούτ[ου τοῦ πράγματος τὰ ἀκόλουθα πράττηται], περὶ τούτου τοῦ | πράγματ[ος οὕτως ἔδοξεν· ὅπως Μᾶρκος Σιλανὸς] ὕπατος ἐὰν αὐτῶι φαίνη[ται τὰ ὅρκια πεμφθῆναι πρὸς τοὺς Μυτιληναί]ους ὡς ἔστακε | γενέσθαι [καὶ ταῦτα καὶ τὰ τῆς συγκλήτου δόγματα τ]ὰ περὶ τούτου || τοῦ πράγ[ματος γενόμενα ἐν δέλτῳ χαλκῇ . . . . . ἐγ]χαραχθῆναι καὶ | εἰς δημό[σιον ἀνατεθῆναι φροντίσῃ. ἔδοξεν]. | αὐτοκράτ[ορος Καίσαρος Σεβαστοῦ τὸ ἔνατον, Μάρκ]ου Σιλανοῦ ὑπά|των [. . . *about 30 lines missing*]

Col. d.

ὁ [δῆμ]ο[ς ὁ] Μυτιληναίων ἀρχὴ[ν τὴν ἑαυτοῦ . . . . . .] | φυλασσέτω οὕτως ὡς ἄν τι κ[. . . . .]. | τοὺς πολεμίους τοῦ δήμου τ[οῦ Ῥωμαίων ὁ δῆμος ὁ Μυτιληναίων διὰ τῆς ἰδίας ἐ]|πικρατείας μὴ ἀφειέτω{ι} δημοσ[ίᾳ βουλῇ διελθεῖν, ὥστε τῷ δήμῳ τῷ] || Ῥωμαίων ἢ τοῖς ἀρχομένοις ὑπ' [αὐτοῦ ἢ τοῖς συμμάχοις τοῦ δήμου τοῦ Ῥωμαί]|ων πόλεμον ποιῆσαι, μήτε αὐτοῖς [ὅπλοις χρήμασι ναυσὶ βοηθείτω]. | ὁ δῆμος ὁ Ῥωμαίων τοὺς πολεμί[ους τοῦ δήμου τοῦ Μυτιληναίων διὰ τοῦ ἰδίου] | ἀγροῦ καὶ τῆς ἰδίας ἐπικρατεία[ς μὴ ἀφειέτω δημοσίᾳ βουλῇ διελθεῖν], | ὥστε τῶι δήμῳ τῶι Μυτιληνα[ίων ἢ τοῖς ἀρχομένοις ὑπ' αὐτοῦ ἢ τοῖς συμμά]||χοις τοῦ δήμου τοῦ Μυτιλην[αίων πόλεμον ποιῆσαι, μήτε αὐτοῖς] | ὅπλοις χρήμα[σι ν]αυσὶ βοηθ[είτω]. | ἐάν τις πρότερος πόλεμον πο[ιήσῃ τῷ δήμῳ τῷ Μυτιληναίων ἢ τῷ δή]|μῳ τῷ Ῥωμαίων [καὶ] τοῖ[ς συμμάχοις τοῦ δήμου τοῦ Ῥωμαίων, βοηθείτω ὁ δῆμος ὁ Ῥωμαίων τῷ δήμῳ τῷ Μυτιληναίων καὶ ὁ δῆμος ὁ Μυτιληναί||ων τῷ δήμῳ τῷ Ῥωμαίων καὶ τοῖς συμμάχοις το]ῦ δήμου τοῦ Ῥωμαίων | [. . . . .] βέβαιός τε ἔστω. εἰρήνη | [ἔστω εἰς τὸν ἅπαντα χρόνον] |

ll. 18–27 and col. e contain further clauses, but they are too mutilated to be restored.

308. Letter of Agrippa to the Gerusia of Argos. *Mnemosyne* 1919, 263.

γερόντων. | Ἀγρίππας Ἀργείων γέρουσι τοῖς ἀπὸ | Δαναοῦ καὶ Ὑπερμήστρας χαίρειν· | ἐγὼ τοῦ τε διαμεῖναι τὸ σύστημα || ὑμῶν καὶ φυλάξαι τὸ παλαιὸν ἀξίωμα | τὴν αἰτίαν ἐματῷ σύνοιδα παρεσχη-|μένωι καὶ πολλὰ τῶν καταλελυμένων | ὑμεῖν ἀποδεδωκότι δικαίων πρός τε | τοὐπιὸν προνοεῖν ὑμ[ῶν προθύμως] || ἔχω καὶ τὴ[ν. . . . .] | νομιζ[. . . . .

309. Letter of Agrippa to Ephesus. Josephus, *Ant. Iud.* xvi. 167–8.

Ἀγρίππας Ἐφεσίων ἄρχουσι βουλῇ δήμῳ χαίρειν· τῶν εἰς τὸ ἱερὸν τὸ ἐν Ἱεροσολύμοις ἀναφερομένων ἱερῶν χρημάτων τὴν ἐπιμέλειαν καὶ φυλακὴν βούλομαι τοὺς ἐν Ἀσίᾳ Ἰουδαίους ποιεῖσθαι κατὰ τὰ πάτρια. τούς τε κλέπτοντας ἱερὰ χρήματα τῶν Ἰουδαίων καταφεύγοντάς τε εἰς τὰς ἀσυλίας βούλομαι ἀποσπᾶσθαι καὶ παραδίδοσθαι τοῖς Ἰουδαίοις, ᾧ δικαίῳ ἀποσπῶνται οἱ ἱερόσυλοι. ἔγραψα δὲ καὶ Σιλανῷ τῷ στρατηγῷ ἵνα σάββασιν μηδεὶς ἀναγκάζῃ Ἰουδαῖον ἐγγύας ὁμολογεῖν

310. Letter of Agrippa to Cyrene. Josephus, *Ant. Iud.* xvi. 169–70.

Μᾶρκος Ἀγρίππας Κυρηναίων ἄρχουσι βουλῇ δήμῳ χαίρειν· οἱ ἐν Κυρήνῃ Ἰουδαῖοι, ὑπὲρ ὧν ἤδη ὁ Σεβαστὸς ἔπεμψε πρὸς τὸν ἐν Λιβύῃ στρατηγὸν τότε ὄντα Φλάουιον καὶ πρὸς τοὺς ἄλλους τοὺς τῆς ἐπαρχίας ἐπιμελουμένους, ἵνα ἀνεπικωλύτως ἀναπέμπηται τὰ ἱερὰ χρήματα εἰς Ἱεροσόλυμα, ὡς ἔστιν αὐτοις πάτριον. ἐνέτυχόν μοι νῦν ὡς ὑπό τινων συκοφαντῶν ἐπηρεάζοιντο καὶ ὡς ἐν προφάσει τελῶν μὴ ὀφειλομένων κωλύοιντο· οἷς ἀποκαθιστάνειν κατὰ μηδένα τρόπον ἐνοχλουμένοις, καὶ εἴ τινων ἱερὰ χρήματα ἀφῄρηνται τῶν πόλεων τοὺς εἰς ταῦτα ἀποκεκριμένους καὶ ταῦτα διορθώσασθαι τοῖς ἐκεῖ Ἰουδαίοις κελεύω

311. Edicts of Augustus and S. C. de repetundis, 7–6 B.C. and 4 B.C., Cyrene. *SEG.* ix. 8. Cf. Oliver, *MemAmAcR.* 1949, 105.

I

αὐτοκράτωρ Καῖσαρ Σεβαστὸς ἀρχιερεὺς δημαρχικῆς | ἐξουσίας ἑπτακαιδέκατον αὐτοκράτωρ τεσσερασκαιδέκατον | λέγει· | ἐπειδὴ τοὺς πάντας εὑρίσκω Ῥωμαίους ἐν τῆι περὶ Κυρήνην || ἐπαρχήαι πέντε καὶ δέκα καὶ διακοσίους ἐκ πάσης ἡλικίας | δισχειλίων καὶ πεντακοσίων διναρίων ἢ μείζω τίμησιν ἔχοντας, | ἐξ ὧν εἰσιν οἱ κριταί, καὶ ἐν αὐτοῖς τούτοις εἶναί τινας συνωμοσίας | αἱ πρεσβῆαι τῶν ἐκ τῆς ἐπαρχήας πόλεων ἀπωδύραντο τὰς ἐπιβαρού|σας τοὺς Ἕλληνας ἐν ταῖς θανατηφόροις δίκαις, τῶν αὐτῶν ἐμ μέρει κα||τηγορούντων καὶ μαρτυρούντων ἀλλήλοις, κἀγὼ δὲ αὐτὸς ἔγνωκα ἀ|ναιτίους τινὰς τῶι τρόπῳ τούτῳ καταβεβαρημένους καὶ ἐς τὴν ἐσχά|την ἠγμένους τιμωρίαν, ἄχρι ἂν ἡ σύνκλητος βουλεύσηται περὶ τούτου | ἢ ἐγὼ αὐτὸς ἄμεινον εὕρω τι, δοκοῦσί μοι καλῶς καὶ προσηκόντως ποιήσειν | οἱ τὴν Κρητικὴν καὶ Κυρηναικὴν ἐπαρχήαν καθέξοντες προτιθέντες ἐν τῆι κατὰ || Κυρήνην ἐπαρχήαι τὸν ἴσον ἀριθμὸν Ἑλλήνων κριτῶν ἐκ τῶν μεγίστων τιμημά|των ὅσον καὶ Ῥωμαίων, μηδένα νεώτερον πέντε καὶ εἴκοσι ἐτῶν, μήτε Ῥωμαῖον μή|τε Ἕλληνα, μηδὲ ἔλασ<σ>ον ἔχοντα τίμημα καὶ οὐσίαν, ἂν γε εὐπορία τοιούτων ἀν|θρώπων ἦι, δειναρίων ἑπτακισχειλίων καὶ πεντακοσίων, ἢ ἂν τούτωι τῶι τρόπωι | μὴ δύνηται συμπληροῦσθαι ὁ ἀριθμὸς τῶν ὀφειλόντων προτίθεσθαι κριτῶν, τοὺς ‖ τὸ ἥμισυ καὶ μὴ ἔλασ<σ>ον τούτου τοῦ τιμ<ήμ>ατος ἔχοντας προτιθέτωσαν κριτὰς ἐν | τοῖς θανατηφόροις τῶν Ἑλλήνων κριτηρίοις. ἐὰν δὲ Ἕλλην κρινόμε|νος, πρὸ μιᾶς ἡμέρας ἢ τὸν κατήγορον ἄρξασθαι λέγειν, δοθείσης ἐξου|σίας αὐτῷ πότερον ἅπαντας βούλεται κριτὰς αὐτῶι Ῥωμαίους εἶναι ἢ τοὺς | ἡμίσους Ἕλληνας, ἕληται τοὺς ἡμίσεις Ἕλληνας, τότε σηκωθεισῶν τῶν ‖ σφαιρῶν καὶ ἐπιγραφέντων αὐταῖς τῶν ὀνομάτων, ἐγ μὲν τοῦ ἑτέρου κλη|ρωτηρίου τὰ τῶν Ῥωμαίων ὀνόματα, ἐγ δὲ τοῦ ἑτέρου τὰ τῶν Ἑλλήνων κληρο[ύ]|σθω, ἕως ἂν {αν} ἐφ' ἑκατέρου γένους ἀνὰ εἴκοσι πέντε ἐκπληρωθῶσιν, ὧν ἀνὰ ἕ|να ἐξ ἑκατέρου γένους ὁ διώκων, ἂν βούληται, ἀπολεγέτω, τρῖς δὲ ἐξ ἁπάντων | [ὁ] φεύγων, ἐφ' ὧι οὔτε [Ῥ]ωμαίους πάντας οὔτε Ἕλληνας πάντας ἀπολέξει· εἶτα οἱ ‖ ἄλλοι πάντες ἐπὶ τὴν ψηφοφορίαν ἀπολυέσθωσαν καὶ φερέτωσαν ἰδίαι μὲν εἰς ἑτέ|ραν κίστην οἱ Ῥωμαῖοι τὴν ψῆφον, ἰδίαι δὲ οἱ Ἕλληνες εἰς ἑτέραν· εἶτα γενομένης ἰδί|αι τῆς διαριθμήσεως τῶν ἑκατέρωθεν ψήφων, ὅ τι ἂν οἱ πλείους ἐξ ἁπάντων δικάσω|σιν, τοῦτο ἐμφανῶς ὁ στρατηγὸς ἀποφαινέσθω. καὶ ἐπεὶ τοὺς ἀδίκους θανάτους ὡ|ς τὸ πολὺ οἱ προσήκοντες τοῖς ἀπολωλόσιν οὐκ ἀτειμωρήτους περιορῶσιν, εἰκός τέ ἐστιν ‖ τοῖς ἐνόχοις μὴ ἐνλίψειν Ἕλληνας κατηγόρους τοὺς δίκην ὑπὲρ τῶν ἀπολωλότων | οἰκήων ἢ πολειτῶν πραξομένους, ὀρθῶς καὶ προσηκόντως μοι δοκοῦσιν ποιή|σειν ὅσοι Κρήτης καὶ Κυρήνης στρατηγήσουσιν, εἰ ἐν τῇ κατὰ Κυρήνην ἐπαρχήαι ὑπὲρ | Ἕλληνος ἀνδρὸς ἢ γυναικὸς ἀναιρέσεως μὴ προσίοιντο κατήγορον Ῥωμαῖον Ἕλλη|νος, πλὴν εἰ μή τις Ῥωμαιότητι τετειμημένος ὑπέρ τινος τῶν οἰκήων ἢ πο‖λειτῶν θανάτου δικάζοιτο

II

αὐτοκράτωρ Καῖσαρ Σεβαστὸς ἀρχιε|ρεὺς δημαρχικῆς ἐξουσίας τὸ ἑπτακαιδέκατον λέγει· φθόνος ψόγος | τε εἶναι Ποπλίωι Σεξστίωι Σκεύαι οὐκ ὀφείλει, ὅτι Αὖλον Στλάκκιον Λευ|κίου υἱὸν Μάξιμον καὶ Λεύκιον Στλάκκιον Λευκίου υἱὸν Μακεδόνα καὶ Πόπλι|ον Λακουτάνιον Ποπλίου ἀπελεύθερον Φιλέρωτα, ἐπειδὴ ἑατοὺς οὗτοι, ‖ ὃ πρὸς τὴν ἐμὴν σωτηρίαν τά τε δημόσια πράγματα ἀνῆκεν, ἐπίστασθαι καὶ | βούλεσθαι εἰπεῖν ἔφησαν, δεσμίους πρός με ἐκ τῆς Κυρηναικῆς ἐπαρχήας{α} | ἀναπεμφθῆναι ἐφρόντισεν· τοῦτο γὰρ ἐποίησεν Σέξστιος καθηκόντως καὶ ἐ|πιμελῶς. λοιπὸν ἐπειδὴ τῶν πρὸς ἐμὲ καὶ τὰ δημόσια πράγματα ἀνηκόν|των οὐδὲν γεινώσκουσι, τοῦτο δὲ ἐν τῆι ἐπαρχήαι εἶπαν ἑατοὺς πε‖πλάσθαι καὶ ἐψεῦσθαι φανερόν <τε> ἐποίησάν μοι, ἐλευθερωθέντας | αὐτοὺς ἐκ τῆς παραφυλακῆς ἀφείημι. Αὖλον δὲ

Στλάκκιον | Μάξιμον, ὃν Κυρηναίων οἱ πρέσβεις αἰτιῶνται ἀνδριάντας ἐκ τῶν | δημοσίων τόπων ἠρκέναι, ἐν οἷς καὶ τὸν ὧι ἡ πόλεις τὸ ἐμὸν ὄνομα ὑπέγραψεν, ἕως | {s} ἂν περὶ τούτου τοῦ πράγματος διαγνῶ, ἀπελθεῖν ἄνευ τῆς ἐμῆς ἐπιταγῆς κω||λύω

III

αὐτοκράτωρ Καῖσαρ Σεβαστὸς ἀρχιερεὺς δημαρχικῆς ἐξουσίας | τὸ ἑπτακαιδέκατον{ι} λέγει· εἴ τινες ἐκ τῆς Κυρηναικῆς ἐπαρχή|ας πολειτήαι τετείμηνται, τούτους λειτουργεῖν οὐδὲν ἔλασ<σ>ον ἐμ μέρει τῷ τῶν | Ἑλλήνων σώματι κελεύω, ἐκτὸς τ[ο]ύτ{ι}ων οἷς κατὰ νόμον ἢ δόγμα συνκλή<του ἢ> | τῶι τοῦ πατρός μου ἐπικρίματι ἢ τῶι ἐμῶι ἀνεισφορία ὁμοῦ σὺν τῆι πολειτήαι || δέδοται· καὶ τούτους αὐτούς, οἷς ἡ ἀνεισφορία δέδοται, τούτων τῶν πρα|γμάτων εἶναι ἀτελεῖς ὧν τότε εἶχον ἀρέσκει μοι, ὑπὲρ δὲ τῶν ἐπικτήτων | πάντων τελεῖν τὰ γεινόμενα

IV

αὐτοκράτωρ Καῖσαρ Σεβαστὸς ἀρχιε|ρεὺς δημαρχικῆς ἐξουσίας τὸ ἑπτακαιδέκατον λέγει· αἵτινες | ἀμφισβητήσ<ε>ις ἀνὰ μέσον Ἑλλήνων ἔσονται κατὰ τὴν Κυρηναικὴν ἐπαρχήαν, || ὑπεξειρημένων τῶν ὑποδίκων κεφαλῆς, ὑπὲρ ὧν ὃς ἂν τὴν ἐπαρχήαν διακατέχῃ | αὐτὸς διαγεινώσκειν κ[αὶ] ἱστάναι ἢ συμβούλιον κριτῶν παρέχειν ὀφείλει, | ὑπὲρ δὲ τῶν λοιπῶν πραγμάτων πάντων Ἕλληνας κριτὰς δίδοσθαι ἀρέσκει, εἰ μή τις | ἀπαιτούμενος ἢ ὁ εὐθυνόμενος πολείτας Ῥωμαίων κριτὰς ἔχειν βούληται· ὧν δ' ἀνὰ | {να} μέσον ἐκ τοῦδε τοῦ ἐμοῦ ἐπικρίματος Ἕλληνες[1] κριταὶ δοθήσονται, κριτὴν δίδοσθαι || οὐκ ἀρέσκει ἐξ ἐκείνης τῆς πόλεως οὐδὲ ἕνα ἐξ ἧς ἂν ὁ διώκων ἢ ὁ εὐθύνων ἔσται ἢ ἐκεῖ|νος ὁ {π} ἀπαιτούμενος ἢ ὁ εὐθυνόμενος |

V

αὐτοκράτωρ Καῖσαρ Σεβαστὸς ἀρχιερεὺς μέγιστος | δημαρχικῆς ἐξουσίας ιθʹ λέγει· | δόγμα συνκλήτου τὸ ἐπὶ Γαΐου Καλουισίου καὶ Λευκίου || Πασσιήνου ὑπάτων κυρωθὲν ἐμοῦ παρόντος καὶ συν|επιγραφομένου, ἀνῆκον δὲ εἰς τὴν τῶν τοῦ δήμου τοῦ | Ῥωμαίων συμμάχων ἀσφάληαν, ἵνα πᾶσιν ᾖ γνωστὸν | ὧν κηδόμεθα, πέμπειν εἰς τὰς ἐπαρχήας διέγνων καὶ τῶι | ἐμῶι προγράμματι ὑποτάσσειν, ἐξ οὗ δῆλον ἔσται πᾶσιν || τοῖς τὰς ἐπαρχήας κατοικοῦσιν ὅσην φροντίδα ποιούμε|θα ἐγώ τε καὶ ἡ σύνκλητος τοῦ μηδένα τῶν ἡμῖν ὑποτασ<σ>ο|μένων παρὰ τὸ προσῆκόν τι πάσχιν ἢ εἰσπρατ<τ>εσθαι |

δόγμα συνκλήτου· |

ὑπὲρ ὧν Γάϊος Καλουίσιος Σαβεῖνος Λεύκιος Πασσιῆ||νος Ῥοῦφος ὕπατοι λόγους ἐποιήσαντο περὶ ὧν | αὐτοκράτωρ Καῖσαρ Σεβαστός ἡγεμὼν ἡμέτερος | ἐξ ξυμβουλίου γνώμης ὃ ἐκ τῆς συνκλήτου κληρωτὸν ἔσχεν, | ἀνενεχθῆναι δι' ἡμῶν· {ι} πρὸς τὴν βουλὴν ἠθέλησεν, ἀνηκόντων | ἐς τὴν τῶν συμμάχων τοῦ δήμου τοῦ Ῥωμαίων ἀσφάλειαν, ἔδο||ξε τῆι βουλῆι· τῶν προγόνων τῶν ἡμετέρων δίκας χρημάτων | {ξε τη} ἀπαιτήσεως νομοθετησάντων, ὅπως ῥᾷον οἱ σύμμαχοι ὑ|πὲρ ὧν ἂν ἀδικηθῶσιν ἐπεξελθεῖν καὶ κομίσασθαι χρήματα ἀφαι|ρεθέντες δύνωνται, ὄντος δὲ τοῦ γένους τῶν τοιούτων δικασ|τηρίων ἔστιν ὅτε βαρυτάτου καὶ ἀηδεστάτου αὐτοῖς δι' οὓς ἐγρά||φη ὁ νόμος, τῶν ἐπαρχηῶν μακρὰν ἀπεχουσῶν ἕλκεσθαι μάρτυ|ρας πένητας ἀνθρώπους καί τινας ἀσθ<ε>νῖς διὰ νόσον ἢ διὰ γῆρας, ἀρέσ|κει τῆι βουλῆι, ἐάν τινες τῶν συμμάχων μετὰ τὸ γενέσθαι τοῦτο τὸ | δόγμα τῆς συνκλήτου χρήματα δημοσίαι ἢ ἰδίαι πραχθέντες ἀπαι|τεῖν βουληθῶσιν, χωρὶς τοῦ κεφαλῆς εὐθύνειν τὸν εἰληφότα, καὶ ὑπὲρ || τούτων καταστάντες ἐνφανίσωσι τῶν ἀρχόντων τινί, ὧι ἐφεῖται συν[ά]|γειν τὴν σύν[κλ]ητον, τούτους τὸν ἄρχοντα ὡς τάχιστα πρὸς τὴν βουλὴν | προσαγαγεῖν καὶ συνήγορον, ὃ<ς> ὑπὲρ αὐτῶν ἐρεῖ ἐπὶ τῆς {η} συνκλήτου, ὃν ἂ[ν] | αὐτοὶ αἰτήσωσιν, διδόναι· ἄκων δὲ μὴ συνηγορείτω ὧι ἐκ τῶν νόμων παρ|αίτησις ταύτης τῆς λειτουργίας δέδοται. ὧν ἂν ἐν τῇ συνκλήτωι αἰ||τίας ἐπιφέρουσιν ἀκουσθῶσιν ὅπως ἄρχων,[2] ὃς ἂν αὐτοῖς πρόσοδον εἰς τὴν | σύνκλητον δῶι, αὐθημερὸν παρούσης τῆς βουλῆς, ὥστε μὴ ἐλάττους διακο|σίων εἶναι, κληρούσθω{ι} ἐκ πάντων τῶν ὑπατικῶν τῶν ἢ ἐπ' αὐτῆς τῆς Ῥώμης | [ἢ] ἐντὸς εἴκοσι μειλίων ἀπ{τ}ὸ τῆς πόλεως ὄντων τέσσαρας· ὁμοίως ἐκ τῶν στρατη||[γ]ικῶν πάντων τῶν ἐπ' αὐτῆς τῆς Ῥώμης ἢ ἐντὸς εἴκοσι μειλίων ἀπὸ τῆς πόλε||[ω]ς ὄντων τρῖς· ὁμοίως ἐκ τῶν ἄλλων συνκλητικῶν ἢ οἷς ἐπὶ τῆς συνκλήτου γνώ|μην ἀποφαίνεσθαι ἔξεστιν πάντων, οἳ ἂν τότε ἢ ἐπὶ Ῥώμης ἢ ἔνγειον εἴκοσι | μειλίων τῆς πόλεως ὦσιν, δύο· κληρούσθω δὲ μηδένα, ὃς ἂν ἑβ<δ>ομήκοντα ἢ | πλείω ἔτη γεγονὼς ἦι ἢ ἐπ' ἀρχῆς ἢ ἐπ' ἐξουσίας τεταγμένος ἢ ἐπιστάτης κριτη|ρίου ἢ ἐπιμελητὴς σειτομετρίας ἢ ὃν ἂν νόσος κωλύηι ταύτην τὴν λειτουργίαν || λειτουργεῖν ἀντικρὺς τῆς συνκλήτου ἐξομοσάμενος καὶ δοὺς ὑπὲρ τούτου | τρεῖς ὀμνύντας τῆς βουλῆς ἄνδρας, ἢ ὃς ἂν συγγενείαι ἢ οἰκηότητι προσή|κηι αὐτῶι ὥστε νόμωι Ἰουλίωι τῶι δικαστικῶι μαρτυρεῖν ἐπὶ δημοσίου δικαστη|ρίου ἄκων μὴ ἀναγκάζεσθαι, ἢ ὃν ἂν ὁ εὐθυνόμενος ὀμόσηι ἐπὶ τῆς συνκλήτου | ἐχθρὸν ἑατῶι εἶναι, μὴ πλείονας δὲ ἢ τρεῖς ἐξομνύσθω. οἳ ἂν ἐννέα τοῦ||τον τὸν τρόπον λάχωσιν, ἐκ τούτων ἄρχων, ὃς ἂν τὸν κλῆρον ποιήσηται, φροντι|ζέτω, ὅπως ἐντὸς δυεῖν ἡμερῶν οἱ τὰ χρήματα μεταπορευόμενοι καὶ ἀφ' οὗ ἂν | μεταπορεύωνται ἀνὰ μέρος ἀπολέγωνται, ἕως ἂν πέντε ὑπολειφθῶσιν. | ὃς ἂν τῶν κριτῶν τούτων, πρὶν ἂν κριθῆι τὸ πρᾶγμα, ἀποθάνηι, ἢ ἄλλη τις αἰτία διακωλύ|σῃ αὐτὸν κρίνειν, οὗ ἂν παραίτησις δοκιμασθῆι, ὀμοσάντων πέντε ἀνδρῶν τῶν ἐ||κ τῆς βουλῆς, τότε ὁ ἄρχων παρόντων τῶν κριτῶν καὶ τῶν τὰ χρήματα μεταπορευ|ομένων καὶ τούτου παρ᾽ οὗ ἂν μεταπορεύωνται, ἐπικληρούσθω ἐκ τούτων τῶν | ἀνδρῶν οἳ ἂν τῆς αὐτῆς τάξεως ὦσιν, καὶ τὰς αὐτὰς ἄρξαντες[3] ἀρχάς, ἣν ἂν τύ|χῃ ἄρξας ἐκεῖνος εἰς τοῦ τὸν τόπον ἐπικληροῦται, ἐφ᾽ ὧι μὴ ἐπικληρώ|σεται ἄνδρα ὃν κληροῦσθαι κατὰ τοῦ εὐθυνομένου τούτῳ τῷ δόγματι τῇ συν||κλήτῳ οὐκ ἔξεστιν. οἱ δὲ αἱρεθέντες κριταὶ περὶ τούτων μόνον ἀκουέ|τωσαν καὶ διαγεινωσκέτωσαν περὶ ὧν ἄν τις εὐθύνηται δημοσίαι ἢ ἰδίαι νε|νοσφισμένος, καὶ ὅσον ἂν κεφάλαιον χρήματος οἱ εὐθύνοντες ἀποδε⟨ί⟩|ξωσιν ἀπενηνέχθαι ἑαυτῶν ἰδίαι ἢ δημοσίαι, τοσοῦτον ἀποδιδόναι κελευέτω|σαν, ἐφ᾽ ὧι ἐντὸς τριάκοντα ἡμερῶν οἱ κριταὶ κρινοῦσιν. οὓς ἂν δέῃ ὑπὲρ || τούτων διαγεινώσκειν καὶ γνώμην ἀποφαίνεσθαι, οὗτοι μέχρι ὅτου ἂν διαγνῶσιν καὶ | τὴν γνώμην ἀποφήσωνται πάσης λειτουργίας δημοσίας ἐκτὸς ἱερῶν δημοσί|ων παρίσθωσαν. ἀρέσκειν δὲ τῆι βουλῆι τὸν ἄρχοντα τὸν τὴν κλήρωσιν | τῶν δικαστῶν ποιήσαντα ἤ, εἰ μὴ οὗτος δύναιτο, τῶν ὑπάτων τόν τε προηγοροῦν|τα ταύτης τῆς διαίτης προίστασθαι καὶ καταγγέλλειν μάρτυσιν τοῖς ἐπὶ τῆς Ἰτα||λίας οὖσιν ἐξουσίαν διδόναι, ἐφ᾽ ὧι τῶι μὲν ἰδίαι τι μεταπορευομένωι μὴ πλείο|σιν πέντε, τοῖς δὲ δημοσίαι μὴ πλείοσιν δέκα καταγγεῖλαι ἐπιτρέψει. ὁμοίως ἀρέσκειν τῆι βουλῆι κριτάς, οἳ ἂν ἐκ τούτου τοῦ ⟨δόγματος⟩ λάχωσιν, καθ᾽ ὃ ἂν αὐτῶν ἑκάστωι δόξηι, ἀναφανδὸν {ο} ἀποφαίνεσθαι, καὶ ὃ ἂν οἱ πλείους ἀποφήσωνται ἐὰν

[1] Ἕλληνας *inscr.*

[2] ἐπιφέρωσιν, ὅπως ἀκουσθῶσιν, ὁ ἄρχων *Oliverio.* ὅπως ⟨ὦσι κριταί⟩ *Oliver.*

[3] ἄρξαντας *inscr.*

312. Letter of Augustus to Cnidos, 6 B.C., Astypalaea. *Syll.*[3] 780.

[. . . | . . . δαμι]ωργοῦ δὲ Καιρογένεος Λευ[κα]θέου (?)

αὐτοκράτωρ Καῖσαρ θεοῦ υἱὸς Σεβαστὸς ἀρχιερεὺς | ὕπατος τὸ δωδέκατον ἀποδεδειγμένος | καὶ δημαρχικῆς ἐξουσίας τὸ ὀκτω{ι}καιδέκατον || Κνιδίων ἄρχουσι βουλῆι δήμωι χαίρειν· οἱ πρέσ|βεις ὑμῶν Διονύσιος β′ καὶ Διονύσιος β′ τοῦ Διονυ|σίου ἐνέτυχον ἐν Ῥώμηι μοι, καὶ τὸ ψήφισμα ἀποδόντες | κατηγόρησαν Εὐβούλου μὲν τοῦ Ἀναξανδρίδα τεθνει|ῶτος ἤδη, Τρυφέρας δὲ τῆς γυναικὸς αὐτοῦ παρούσης || περὶ τοῦ θανάτου τοῦ Εὐβούλου τοῦ Χρυσίππου. ἐγὼ{ι}| δὲ ἐξετάσαι προστάξας Γάλλωι Ἀσινίωι τῶι ἐμῶι φίλωι | τῶν οἰκετῶν τοὺς ἐνφερομένους τῆι αἰτίᾳ διὰ βα|σάνων ἔγνων Φιλεῖνον τὸν Χρυσίππου τρεῖς νύ|κτας συνεχῶς ἐπεληλυθότα τῆι οἰκίαι τῆι Εὐβού||λου καὶ Τρυφέρας μεθ' ὕβρεως καὶ τρόπωι τινὶ πολι|ορκίας, τῆι τρίτηι δὲ συνεπηιγμένον καὶ τὸν ἀδελ|φὸν Εὔβουλον, τοὺς δὲ τῆς οἰκίας δεσπότας Εὔβου|λον καὶ Τρυφέραν, ὡς οὔτε χρηματίζοντες πρὸς | τὸν Φιλεῖνον οὔτε ἀντιφραττόμενοι ταῖς προσ||βολαῖς ἀσφαλείας ἐν τῆι ἑαυτῶν οἰκίᾳ τυχεῖν ἠδύναν|το, προστεταχότας ἑνὶ τῶν οἰκετῶν οὐκ ἀποκτεῖ|ναι, ὡς ἴσως ἄν τις ὑπ' ὀργῆς οὐ[κ] ἀδίκου προήχθηι, ἀλ|λὰ ἀνεῖρξαι κατασκεδάσαντα τὰ κόπρια αὐτῶν· τὸν | δὲ οἰκέτην σὺν τοῖς καταχεομένοις εἴτε ἑκόντα || εἴτε ἄκοντα—αὐτὸς μὲν γὰρ ἐνέμεινεν ἀρνούμενο[ς]|—ἀφεῖναι τὴν γάστραν, [κα]ὶ τὸν Εὔβουλον ὑποπεσεῖν δικαιό|[τ]ερον ἂν σωθέντα τὰ{ι}δελφοῦ. πέπονφα δὲ ὑμεῖν καὶ α[ὐ|τ]ὰς τὰς ἀνακρίσεις. ἐθαύμαζον δ' ἄν, πῶς εἰς τόσον | ἔδεισαν τὴν παρ' ὑμεῖν ἐξετασίαν τῶν δούλων οἱ φ[εύ]||γοντες τὴν δίκην, εἰ μή ποι σφόδρα αὐτοῖς ἐδόξ[ατε] | χαλεποὶ γεγονέναι καὶ πρὸς τὰ ἐναντία μισοπόνη[ροι], | μὴ κατὰ τῶν ἀξίων πᾶν ὁτιοῦν παθεῖν, ἐπ' ἀλλο[τρίαν] | οἰκίαν νύκτωρ μεθ' ὕβρεως καὶ βίας τρὶς ἐπεληλυ[θό]||των καὶ τὴν κοινὴν ἁπάντων ὑμῶν ἀσφάλειαν [ἀναι]-||ρούντων ἀγαναχτοῦντες, ἀλλὰ κατὰ τῶν καὶ ἡ̣μ[ίκ' ἠ]|μύνοντο ἠτυχηκότων, ἠδικηκότων δὲ οὐδ' ἔστ[ιν ὅ, τι]. | ἀλλὰ νῦν ὀρθῶς ἄν μοι δοκεῖτε ποιῆσαι τῆι ἐμῆι [περὶ τού]|των γνώμηι προνοήσαντες καὶ τὰ ἐν τοῖς δημ[οσίοις] | ὑμῶν ὁμολογεῖν γράμματα. ἔρρωσθε

313. Letter of Iullus Antonius, proconsul of Asia, to Ephesus. Josephus, *Ant. Iud.* xvi. 172–3.

'Ιοῦλ‹λ›ος Ἀντώνιος ἀνθύπατος . . . 'Εφεσίων ἄρχουσι βουλῇ δήμῳ χαίρειν· οἱ ἐν τῇ Ἀσίᾳ κατοικοῦντες 'Ιουδαῖοι εἰδοῖς Φεβρουαρίοις δικαιοδοτοῦντί μοι ἐν 'Εφέσῳ ὑπέδειξαν Καίσαρα τὸν Σεβαστὸν καὶ Ἀγρίππαν συγκεχωρηκέναι αὐτοῖς χρῆσθαι τοῖς ἰδίοις νόμοις καὶ ἔθεσιν, ἀπαρχάς τε ἃς ἕκαστος αὐτῶν ἐκ τῆς ἰδίας προαιρέσεως εὐσεβείας ἕνεκα τῆς πρὸς τὸ θεῖον [. . .] ἀνακομιδῆς συμπορευομένους ποιεῖν ἀνεμποδίστως· ἤτουν τε ὅπως κἀγὼ ὁμοίως τοῖς ὑπὸ τοῦ Σεβαστοῦ καὶ Ἀγρίππα δοθεῖσιν τὴν ἐμὴν γνώμην βεβαιώσω· ὑμᾶς οὖν βούλομαι εἰδέναι ἐμὲ τοῖς τοῦ Σεβαστοῦ καὶ Ἀγρίππα βουλήμασι συνεπιτρέπειν αὐτοῖς χρῆσθαι καὶ ποιεῖν κατὰ τὰ πάτρια χωρὶς ἐμποδισμοῦ

314. Edict of Augustus. Josephus, *Ant. Iud.* xvi. 162–5.

Καῖσαρ Σεβαστὸς ἀρχιερεὺς δημαρχικῆς ἐξουσίας [. . .][1] λέγει· ἐπειδὴ τὸ ἔθνος τὸ τῶν 'Ιουδαίων εὐχάριστον εὑρέθη οὐ μόνον ἐν τῷ ἐνεστῶτι καιρῷ ἀλλὰ καὶ ἐν τῷ προγεγενημένῳ καὶ μάλιστα ἐπὶ τοῦ ἐμοῦ πατρὸς αὐτοκράτορος Καίσαρος πρὸς τόν δῆμον τὸν 'Ρωμαίων, ὅ τε ἀρχιερεὺς αὐτῶν 'Υρκανός, ἔδοξέ μοι καὶ τῷ ἐμῷ συμβουλίῳ μετὰ ὁρκωμοσίας γνώμῃ δήμου Ῥωμαίων τοὺς Ἰουδαίους χρῆσθαι τοῖς ἰδίοις ἐθισμοῖς κατὰ τὸν πάτριον αὐτῶν νόμον, καθὼς ἐχρῶντο ἐπὶ Ὑρκανοῦ ἀρχιερέως θεοῦ ὑψίστου, τά τε ἱερὰ εἶναι ἐν ἀσυλίᾳ καὶ ἀναπέμπεσθαι εἰς Ἱεροσόλυμα καὶ ἀποδίδοσθαι αὐτὰ τοῖς ἀποδοχεῦσιν Ἱεροσολύμων, ἐγγύας τε μὴ ὁμολογεῖν αὐτοὺς ἐν σάββασιν ἢ τῇ πρὸ ταύτης παρασκευῇ ἀπὸ ὥρας ἐνάτης. ἐὰν δέ τις φωραθῇ κλέπτων τὰς ἱερὰς βίβλους αὐτῶν ἢ τὰ ἱερὰ χρήματα ἔκ τε σαββατείου ἔκ τε ἀνδρῶνος, εἶναι αὐτὸν ἱερόσυλον καὶ τὸν βίον αὐτοῦ ἐνεχθῆναι εἰς τὸ δημόσιον τῶν Ῥωμαίων. τὸ δὲ ψήφισμα τὸ δοθέν μοι ὑπ' αὐτῶν ὑπὲρ τῆς ἐμῆς εὐσεβείας ἧς ἔχω πρὸς πάντας ἀνθρώπους καὶ ὑπὲρ Γαΐου Μαρκίου Κηνσωρίνου καὶ τοῦτο τὸ διάταγμα κελεύω ἀνατεθῆναι ἐν ἐπισημοτάτῳ τόπῳ τῷ γενηθέντι μοι ὑπὸ τοῦ κοινοῦ τῆς Ἀσίας ἐν Ἀγκύρῃ. ἐὰν δέ τις παραβῇ τι τῶν προειρημένων δώσει δίκην οὐχὶ μετρίαν

[1] *The Latin version of Josephus has here XI in the margin (= 13–12 B.C.).*

315. Oath of Gangra, 3 B.C., near Neapolis (Paphlagonia). *OGIS.* 532; *ILS.* 8781.

ἀπὸ αὐτοκράτορος Καίσ[αρος] | θεοῦ υἱοῦ Σεβαστοῦ ὑπατεύ[οντος τὸ] | δωδέκατον ἔτους τρίτου, π[ροτέραι] | νωνῶν Μαρτίων ἐν Γάγγροις ἐν [τ]ἀ[γορᾶι] ὅρ||κος ὁ τελεσθ[εὶς ὑ]πὸ τῶ[ν] κατοικ[ούντων Πα]|φλαγονία[ν καὶ τῶν πραγ]ματευομ[ένων πα]|ρ' αὐτοῖς Ῥ[ωμαίων]· |

ὀμνύω Δία Γῆν Ἥλιον θεοὺς πάντα[ς καὶ πά]|σας καὶ αὐτὸν τὸν Σεβασ[τ]ὸν εὐνοή[σειν Καί]||σαρι Σεβαστῶι καὶ τοῖς τ[έκ]νοις ἐγγό[νοις τε] | αὐτοῦ πάν[τ]α [τ]ὸν τοῦ [βίου] χρόνον κ[αὶ λό]|γωι [κ]αὶ ἔργωι καὶ γνώμ[ηι, φί]λους ἡγού[μενος] | οὓς ἂν ἐκεῖνοι ἡγῶντα[ι] ἐκχθρούς τε ν[ομίζων] | οὓς ἂν αὐτοὶ κρίνωσιν, ὑπέρ τε τῶν τ[ούτοις] || διαφερόντων μήτε σώματος φείσεσθ[αι μή]|τε ψυχῆς μήτε βίου μήτε τέκνων, ἀλ[λὰ παν]|τὶ τρόπωι ὑπὲρ τῶ[ν] ἐκείνοις ἀνηκό[ντων] | πάντα κίνδυνον ὑπομενεῖν· ὅτι τε ἂ[ν αἴσ]|θωμαι ἢ ἀκούσω ὑπεναντίον τούτ[οις λε]||γόμενον ἢ βουλευόμενον ἢ πρασσό[μενον], | τοῦτο ἐγμηνύσειν τε καὶ ἐχθρὸν ἔσ[εσθαι τῶι] | λέγοντι ἢ βουλευομένωι ἢ πράσσο[ντί τι τού]|των· οὕς τε ἂν ἐκχθροὺς αὐτ[ο]ὶ κρίν[ωσιν, τού]|τους κατὰ γῆν καὶ θάλασσαν ὅπλο[ις τε] || καὶ σιδήρωι διώξειν καὶ ἀμυνεῖσ[θαι]. | ἐὰν δέ τι ὑπεναντίον τούτωι τ[ῶι ὅρκωι] | ποήσω ἢ μὴ στοιχούντως καθὼ[ς ὤμο]|σα, ἐπαρῶμαι αὐτός τε κατ' ἐμοῦ καὶ σ[ώμα]|τος τοῦ ἐμαυτοῦ καὶ ψυχῆς καὶ βίου κα[ὶ τέ]||κνων καὶ παντὸς τοῦ ἐμαυτοῦ γέν[ους] | καὶ συνφέροντος ἐξώλειαν καὶ παν[ώλει]|αν μέχρι πάσης διαδοχῆς τῆς ἐ[μῆς καὶ] | τῶν ἐξ ἐμοῦ πάντων, καὶ μήτε σ[ώματα τὰ] |

τῶν ἐμῶν ἢ ἐξ ἐμοῦ μήτε γῆ μ[ήτε θάλασ]||σα δέξαιτο μηδὲ καρποὺς ἐνέγ[κοι αὐτοῖς]. |

κατὰ τὰ αὐτὰ ὤμοσαν καὶ οἱ ἐ[ν τῆι χώραι] | πάντες ἐν τοῖς κατὰ τὰς ὑ[παρχίας Σε]||βαστήοις παρὰ τοῖς βωμοῖ[ς τοῦ Σεβαστοῦ]· | ὁμοίως τε Φαζιμωνεῖται οἱ [τὴν νῦν Νεάπο]||λιν λεγομένην κατοικοῦν[τες ὤμοσαν σύμ]|παντες ἐν Σεβαστήωι παρὰ τ[ῶι βωμῶι τοῦ] | Σεβαστοῦ

316. I B.C., Nysa ad Maeandrum. *Syll.*³ 781.

[ἱ]ερέως Ῥώμης καὶ αὐτοκράτορος Καίσαρος Σεβαστο[ῦ Ἡρα|κλ]είδου τοῦ Ἡρακλείδου Μασταυρείτου· στεφανηφόρου | Διομ[ή]δους τοῦ Ἀθηναγόρου τοῦ Διομ[ή]δους ἱερ<έ>ως | [Δ]ιὸς Καπετωλίου διὰ βίου, μηνὸς Γορπιαίου ἐννεακαιδε||κάτῃ, πρὸ μιᾶς [ε]ἰδῶν Αὐγούστω<ν>, Κόσσῳ [Κ]ο[ρ]νηλίῳ Λεντύλῳ | καὶ Λευκίῳ Πείσωνι ὑπάτοις, ἐπὶ γραμματέως τοῦ δ[ή]μου Ἡλι|οδώρου τοῦ Μαιανδρίου τοῦ Θεοδότου ἱερέως Τιβερίου Κλαυ|δίου Νέρωνος διὰ βίου· Ἀρτεμίδωρος Δημητρίου Παπᾶς, | τῶν τῆς πόλεως στρατηγῶ<ν>, ἐπιμεληθεὶς ἀποκατέστη||σεν εἰς τὸ γραμματῆον τὰ ἱερὰ γράμματα περὶ τῶν θεῶν | καὶ τῆς ἀσυλίας αὐτῶν καὶ τῆ[ς] ἱκεσίας καὶ τῆς περὶ τὸ ἱε|ρὸν ἀτ[ε]λήας, ἐμφ[α]νίσας Γν[αί]ῳ Λέντλῳ Αὔγορι τῷ ἀνθυπ[ά]|τῳ καὶ ἀποδοὺς <τ>ὴν ὑπογεγραμμένην ἐπιστολή<ν>· | ἐπὶ Διομήδους τοῦ Ἀθηναγόρου μηνὸς Δαισίου ιζʹ. || [Γ]ναῖος Λέντλος Αὔγουρ ἀνθύπατος Νυσαέων ἄρχουσι· ἐ[π]|ηρώτ[ησε] Ἀρτεμίδωρος Δημητρίου Παπᾶς <ε>ἰ χρὴ | [. . . . .

317. Letter of proconsul to Chios, between A.D. 5 and 14, Chios. *Syll.*³ 785. Cf. Robert, *REG.* 1952, 128.

. . . . . .] | Σταφύλου ὑπαρχόντων πρὸς τοὺς Χείων πρέσβεις, ἀναγεινωσ[κόν]|των ἐπιστολὴν Ἀντιστίου Οὐέτερος τοῦ πρὸ ἐμοῦ ἀνθυπάτ[ου], | ἀνδρὸς ἐπιφανεστάτου, κατακολουθῶν τῇ καθολικῇ μου [προ]||θέ[σ]ει τοῦ [τ]η[ρ]εῖν τὰ ὑπὸ τῶν πρὸ ἐμοῦ ἀνθυπάτων γραφέντ[α, φυ]|λάττειν καὶ τὴν ὑπὲρ τούτων φερομένην ἐπιστολὴν Οὐέτε[ρος] | εὔλογον ἡγησάμην· ὕστερον δὲ ἑκατέρου μέρους ἐξ ἀντικα[τα]|στάσεως περὶ τῶν κατὰ μέρος ζητημάτων ἐν<τ>υχόντος διή[κου]|σα καὶ κατὰ τὴν ἐμὴν συνήθειαν παρʼ ἑκατέρου μέρους ἐπιμε[λέσ]||τερα γεγραμμένα ᾔτησα ὑπομνήματα· [ἃ λ]αβὼν καὶ κατὰ τὸ ἐπι[βάλ]|λον ἐπιστήσας εὗρον τοῖς μὲν χρόνο<ι>ς ἀρχαιοτάτου δόγμα[τος] | συνκλήτου ἀντισ[φρ]άγισμα, γεγονότος Λουκίῳ Σύλλᾳ τὸ δε[ύτε]|ρον ὑπάτωι, ἐν ᾧ μαρτυ[ρηθ]εῖσι τοῖς Χείοις, ὅσα ὑπὲρ Ῥωμαίων δι[έθη]|κάν τε Μιθριδάτην ἀνδραγαθοῦντες καὶ ὑπʼ αὐτοῦ ἔπαθον ἡ σύν[κλη]||τος εἰδικῶς ἐβεβαίωσεν ὅπως νόμοις τε καὶ ἔθεσιν καὶ δικαίοις [χρῶν]|ται, ἃ ἔσχον ὅτε τῇ Ῥωμαίων <φι>λίᾳ προσῆλθον, ἵνα τε ὑπὸ μηθ' ᾡτινι[οῦν] | τύπῳ ὦσιν ἀρχόντων ἢ ἀνταρχόντων, οἵ τε παρ' αὐτοῖς ὄντες Ῥω[μαῖ]|οι τοῖς Χείων ὑπακούωσιν νόμοις· αὐτοκράτορος δὲ θεοῦ υἱοῦ Σ[ε]|βαστοῦ τὸ ὄγδοον ὑπάτου ἐπιστολὴ⟨ν⟩ πρὸς Χείους γράφοντ[ος || . . .]ιεπεν τὴν πόλιν ἐλευθ[έραν . . .

318. Letter of Tiberius, A.D. 15, Cos. *IGRR.* iv. 1042; Paton and Hicks, *Inscr. of Cos*, no. 25.

Τιβέριος Καῖσαρ θεοῦ Σεβαστοῦ υἱὸς Σεβαστὸς δημαρχικῆς ἐξουσίας τὸ ἑπτακαιδέκατον αὐτοκράτωρ τὸ ζʹ Κῴων ἄρχουσι βουλῇ δήμῳ χαίρειν· ἀποδόντων μοι τῶν ὑμετέρων πρεσβέων τό τε ψήφισμα ὑμῶν καὶ ἃς ὑπέθεσθε αὐτοῖς πρὸς ἐμὲ ἐπιστολάς, τῆς μὲν διαθέσεως ὑμᾶς τῆς πρὸς ἐμαυτὸν ἐπαινῶ· διεκείμην δὲ καὶ πρότερον πρός τε τὴν πόλιν τὴν ὑμετέραν [. . . . . .

319. Letter of Tiberius, Aezani (Phrygia). *ILS.* 9463.

[ἀπὸ Β]ονωνίας τῆς ἐν Γαλλίᾳ ἐνεχθ[εῖσα ἐπιστολὴ Τιβερίου Καίσαρος]. Τιβέριος Καῖσαρ Αἰζ[ανειτῶν βουλῇ] δήμωι [χαίρειν]· ἀρχῆθεν ὑμῶν τὴ[ν εὐσέβειαν καὶ] πρὸς ἐμὲ συνπαθί[αν μαθὼν ἀπεδεξά]μην ἥδιστα καὶ ν[ῦν παρὰ τῶν ὑμε]τέρων πρεσβευτῶν [τὸ ψήφισμα τὸ] διαφαῖνον τῆς πό[λεως τὴν εἴς με εὔ]νοιαν· πειράσομαι [οὖν ὑμῖν ὅσον] ἂν ὦ δυνατὸς συν[αύξειν ἐν πᾶσι και]ροῖς οἷς ἀξιοῦτε τ[υχεῖν βοηθείας]

320. Two Edicts of Germanicus, A.D. 19, Papyrus. Hunt and Edgar, *Select Papyri*, ii, no. 211. Cf. Post, *AJP.* lxv (1944), 80.

(*a*) [Γερμανικὸς Καῖσαρ Σεβαστοῦ | υἱὸς θεοῦ Σεβαστοῦ υἱωνὸς | ἀνθύπατος λέγει· εἰς τὴν ἐμὴν | παρουσίαν νῦν ἤδη ἀκούων] || ἀ[γγα]ρ[είας . . . . πλοίων] | καὶ κτηνῶν γείνεσθαι καὶ | ἐπὶ σκηνώσεις καταλαμβά|νεσθαι ξενίας πρὸς βίαν καὶ | καταπλήσσεσθαι τοὺς ἰδιώτας, || ἀνανκαῖον ἡγησάμην δη|λῶσαι ὅτι οὔτε πλοῖον ὑπό τινος | ἢ ὑποζύγιον κατέχεσθαι βού|λομαι, εἰ μὴ κατὰ τὴν Βαιβίου | τοῦ ἐμοῦ φίλου καὶ γραμματέως || προσταγήν, οὔτε ξενίας καταλαμ|βάνεσθαι. ἐὰν γὰρ δέῃ, αὐτὸς Βαίβιος | ἐκ τοῦ ἴσου καὶ δικαίου τὰς ξενίας | διαδώσει· καὶ ὑπὲρ τῶν ἀγγαρευ|ομένων δὲ πλοίων ἢ ζευγῶν || ἀποδίδοσθαι τοὺς μισθοὺς κατὰ | τὴν ἐμὴν διαγραφὴν κελεύω{ι}. | τοὺς δὲ ἀντιλέγοντας ἐπὶ τὸν | γραμματέα μου ἀνάγεσθαι βού|λομ[αι ὃ]ς ἢ αὐτὸς κωλύσει ἀδι||κεῖσθαι τοὺς ἰδιώτας ⟨ἢ⟩ ἐμοὶ ἀναν|γελεῖ. τὰ δὲ διὰ τῆς πόλεως διατρέ|χοντα ὑποζύγια τοὺς ἀπαντῶν|τας πρὸς βίαν περιαιρεῖσθαι κωλύω. | τοῦτο γὰρ ἤδη ὁμολογουμένης || λῃστείας ἐστὶν ἔργον |

(*b*) Γερμανικὸς Καῖσαρ Σεβασ[τ]οῦ υἱὸς | θεοῦ Σεβαστοῦ υἱωνὸς ἀνθύπατος | λέγει· τὴν μὲν εὔνοιαν ὑμῶν, | ἣν ἀεὶ ἐπιδείκνυσθε ὅταν με εἴδ||ητε, ἀποδέχομαι, τὰς δὲ ἐπιφθόνου[ς] | ἐμοὶ καὶ ἰσοθέους ἐκφωνήσεις | ὑμῶν ἐξ [ἅ]παντος παραιτοῦμαι. | πρέπουσι γὰρ μόνῳ τῶι σωτῆρι | ὄντως καὶ εὐεργέτῃ τοῦ σύνπαντος || τῶν ἀνθρώπων γένους, τῷ ἐμῷ | πατρὶ καὶ τῇ μητρὶ αὐτοῦ ἐμῇ δὲ | μάμμῃ. τὰ δὲ ἡμέτερα ἔνλογα παρεπ[όμενά] | ἐστιν τῆς ἐκείνων θειότητος, ὡς | ἐάμ μοι μὴ πεισθῆτε, ἀνανκᾶτέ με || μὴ πολλάκις ὑμεῖν ἐνφανίζεσθαι

320a. A.D. 22–23, Egypt (near Sphinx). *SEG.* viii. 527.

[ἔτου]ς ἐνάτου Τιβερίου Καίσαρος Σεβα[στοῦ. . . | .] οἱ ἀπὸ Βουσίρεως [τ]οῦ Λητοπολίτου νο[μοῦ συνε|λ]θόντες ὁμοθυμαδὸν τάδε ἐψηφίσαν[το· ἐπεὶ]|| Γναῖος Πομπήϊος Σαβεῖνος ὁ στρατηγὸ[ς ἡμῶν] || οὐ διαλίπει πρὸς τοὺς ἀπὸ τοῦ νομοῦ ἐκτε[νῶς καὶ]| φιλανθρώπως διακείμενος, μάλιστα δὲ π[ροάγων[1] δι]|ὰ παντὸς ἐπ' εὐεργεσίαι τοὺς τὴν κώμ[ην κατοι|κ]οῦντας, ἔν τε ταῖς δικαιοδοσίαις κατ' ἴσον [ἀεὶ τὸ | δ]ίκαιον καθαρῶς καὶ ἀδωροδοκήτως κατὰ [τὴν τοῦ || θ]ειοτάτου ἡγεμόνος Γαΐου Γαλερίου βο[ύλησιν | ἀ]π[ο]νέμει, καὶ τὴν δὲ τῶν χωμάτων κατε[ργασίαν | ἐν τ]οῖς δέουσιν καιροῖς μετὰ πάσης ἐπιμε[λείας | π]οιεῖται ἀδεκάστως ἀναδεχόμενος πό[νον καὶ νυ|κτὸς] καὶ μεθ' ἡμέραν ἄχρι συνετέλεσεν, [ὥστε καὶ || τῶν] πεδίων πάνυ λιμνασθέντων ὑπέρ[μεγαν | σπ]ό[ρ]ον γεγονέναι, ἐποίησεν δὲ καὶ τοῖς [τὰ τῆς κώμ|ης] χώματα ἐργαζομένοις πρὸς τὸ ἀδι[αβόλους | καὶ] ἀσυκοφαντήτους εἶναι παρὰ τὸ πάλ[αι σπό|ρ]ον προεῖσθαι, ἔτι [δ]ὲ καὶ τὴν τῶν δημο[σίων διά||π]ρασιν ποιεῖται μετὰ πάσης ἐπεικείας, [ἄνευ τε βί|α]ς καὶ ἐπηρείας, ὃ [δ]ὴ μ[έ]γιστόν ἐστιν πρὸ[ς εὐδαιμο]|νίαν καὶ συνμον[ὴ]ν τῶν κωμῶν, καὶ [ἃ ἡ κώμη ὤφει]|λε ἄλλοις τοῖς τῆς [στρ]ατηγίας πραγμα[τικοῖς] | ἐπιτελῶν [τ]οὺς [γεωργοὺ]ς φυλάττει ἀνυ[πόπτους][2] || καὶ ἀζημίους [ὃν τ]ρόπον ἦν προσῆκον, [τούτων] | χάριν καὐτοὶ βουλ[όμεν]οι ἀμείβεσθαι χά[ρισιν, | ἐ]κρίναμεν τιμῆσαι τὸν π[ρο]γεγραμμένον Γν[αῖον | Π]ομπήϊον Σαβεῖνον τὸν στρατηγὸν στήλη[ι λι|θίν]ηι πε[ρ]ιεχούσηι τόδε τὸ ψήφισμα, ἣν κα[ὶ σ||τῆσ]αι ἐν τῶι τῆς κώμης ἐπισημοτάτωι τόπ[ωι, | ἀποδο]ῦναι δὲ αὐτῶι καὶ ἀντίγραφον [ὑπογ]εγραμμ[έ|νον ὑπὸ ὅσω]ν πλείστων, ὃ καὶ κύριο[ν ἔ]στ[αι]

[1] π[ροτιμῶν] or π[ροκρίνων] *Klaffenbach.* [2] ἀνυ[βρίστους] or ἀνυ[ποδίκους] *Wilhelm.*

321. Kierion (Thessaly). *IG.* ix. 2, 261.

(*a*) . . . . διαφέ]ρωνται πρὸς ἀ[λλή]λας οὐ | [. . . . . . .]ιη αἰτεῖται, ὅπως μεθ' ὅρκου κρυφα[ί|ως . . . . Μητ]ροπολειτῶν κρινόντων, βραβεύον|[τος . . . . τ]ε παρ' ὑμεῖν ὀφίλοντος, καθ' ἣν καὶ τῆς κρίσ[ε||ως . . . .]ν ἠνέχθησαν μεθ' ὅρκου ψῆφοι

Κιεριεῦσ[ι | διακόσιαι ἐνενήκοντα ὀκτώ, Μητρο]πολείταις τριάκοντα μία, ἄκυροι πέντε |

(*b*) [Γαΐῳ Ποππ]αίῳ Σαβείνῳ πρεσβευτῇ Τιβερίου Καίσαρ[ος | ὁ δεῖνα τοῦ δεῖνος γραμματε]ὺς τῶν συνέδρων πλεῖστα χαίρειν. ἔγρα-| [ψας ἡμῖν τὴν Κιεριέων καὶ Μητ]ροπολειτῶν ὑπόθεσιν ἣν εἶχον περὶ ὅρων, ὅ||[τι αὐτὴν ἠξίωσας τοὺς συνέδρου?]ς κρῖναι οὓς καὶ ἐδήλους μοι κατ' ὄψιν ἐν Αἴδε|[ψῷ· ἐμὲ δ' εὖ ἴσθι εὐθὺς οἴκαδε ἀ]ναγαγόντα προθεῖναι τὴν κρίσιν ἐν τῷ ἐνε|[στηκότι Θεσσαλῶν τῶν? ἐν Λα]ρίσῃ συνεδρίῳ τῷ ἐν τῷ Θύῳ μηνί· συνελθόντω[ν | δὲ καὶ ἀμφοτέρων ἐπὶ τὴ]ν κρίσιν καὶ λόγων ὑπ' αὐτῶν γενομένων, ἐνηνέ|[χθαι τὰς ψήφους κρυφαίως μεθ'] ὅρκου Κιεριεῦσιν μὲν διακοσίας ἐνενήκον[τα || ὀκτώ, Μητροπολείταις δὲ τριάκοντ]α μίαν, ἀκύρους πέντε. ταῦτα ἐπιτήδειον ἡγη|[σάμεθα γράψαι. ἔρρωσο.? Γαΐῳ Ποπ]παίῳ Σαβείνῳ πρεσβευτῇ Τιβερίου Καίσαρ[ος | ὁ δεῖνα τοῦ δεῖνος στρατη]γὸς Θεσσαλῶν χαίρειν· ἔγραψας κἀμοὶ καὶ το[ῖς | συνέδροις τὴν Κιεριέων τε καὶ Μ]ητροπολιτῶν ὑπόθεσιν, ἣν εἶχον περὶ ὅρων, ὅ|[τι τὸ συνέδριον τὴν περὶ τούτων] διάγνωσιν ἀνέπεμψεν. γείνωσκε οὖν εἰρημ[έ||νους τοὺς συνέδρους τοὺς ἐν τῷ Θύ]ῳ μηνὶ καὶ ἐνηνεγμένους μεθ' ὅρκου κρυφαί|[ως τὰς ψήφους Κιεριεῦσιν] μὲν διακοσίας ἐνενήκοντα ὀκτώ, Μητρ[ο|πολείταις δὲ τριάκοντα μίαν, ἀκύρους πέ]ντε· ταῦτα οὖν ἐπιτήδειον ἡγησ[ά|μεθα γράψαι, ὅπως ....]ον τὸ βέβαιον ἡ κρίσις ὑπό σου λάβῃ ἐπι|[.........

322. Imperial edict, Palestine (?). *SEG.* viii. 13; Robert, *Coll. Fröhner*, no. 70.

διάταγμα Καίσαρος. | ἀρέσκει μοι τάφους τύνβους | τε οἵτινες εἰς θρησκείαν προγόνων | ἐποίησαν ἢ τέκνων ἢ οἰκείων, || τούτους μένειν ἀμετακεινήτους | τὸν αἰῶνα· ἐὰν δέ τις ἐπιδίξῃ τι|νὰ ἢ καταλελυκότα ἢ ἄλλῳ τινὶ | τρόπῳ τοὺς κεκηδευμένους | ἐξερριφφότα ἢ εἰς ἑτέρους || τόπους δώλῳ πονηρῷ με|τατεθεικότα ἐπ' ἀδικίᾳ τῇ τῶν | κεκηδευμένων ἢ κατόχους ἢ λί|θους μετατεθεικότα, κατὰ τοῦ | τοιούτου κριτήριον ἐγὼ κελεύω || γενέσθαι, καθάπερ περὶ θεῶν | ε[ἰ]ς τὰς τῶν ἀνθρώπων θρησκ|κείας· πολὺ γὰρ μᾶλλον δεήσει | τοὺς κεκηδευμένους τειμᾶν. | καθόλου μηδενὶ ἐξέστω μετα||κεινῆσαι· εἰ δὲ μή, τοῦτον ἐγὼ κε|φαλῆς κατάκριτον ὀνόματι | τυμβωρυχίας θέλω γενέσθαι

Date disputed between the reigns of Augustus, Tiberius, and Claudius (see bibliography in SEG.*); cf. also de Visscher,* ADOA. *II (1953), 285. Oliver,* CP. *1954, 180.*

XIII

CITIES OF THE EMPIRE

For foundation of colonies see no. 187, for decrees of *municipia* and colonies 68, 69, 101, for magistracies 11, 131, 162, 224, 229–31, 234, 236–9, 244–7, 254, 256, for decrees of Greek cities 47, 99 (I), 102, 316, for a *conventus civium Romanorum* 111.

323. Fasti magistratuum, covering 34–28 B.C., Venusia. *ILS*. 6123.

......et be]lla facta a bello Marsico

P. Petinius P. Publilius aed.

L. Sempronius L. Scribonius
k. Iul. Paul. Aemilius
C. Memmius
k. Novem. M. Herennius
bellum Hilluricum
ex k. Iul. ad k. Iul.:
Q. Larcius C. Rumeius IIvir.
M. Metilius L. Annaeus aed.
hoc anno quaestores creati
ex k. Iul. ad k. Iul.:
C. Sulpicius C. Salvius Bubulcus q.

---

imp. Caesar II L. Volcacius
k. Ianuar. P. Autronius
k. Mais L. Flavius
C. Fonteius
k. Iul. M. Acilius
k. Septembr. L. Vinucius
k. Oct. ⟨Q.⟩ Laronius
ex k. Iul. ad k. Iul.:
C. Aemilius Q. Pontienus IIvir.
C. Valerius C. Turpilius aed.
L. Livius Ligus L. Cornelius q.

Cn. Domitius C. Sosius
k. Iul. L. Cornelius
k. Nov. M. Valerius
ex k. Iul. ad k. Sept. praefecti:
T. Licinius L. Cornelius
ex k. Sept. ad k. Febr.:
C. Plotius C. Annaeus IIvir.
ex k. Iul. ad k. Febr.:
C. Annius Sex. Vettius aed.
ex k. Iul. ad k. Iul.:
L. Scutarius M. Calpurnius q.

---

imp. Caesar III M. Valerius
k. Mais M. Titius
k. Oct. Cn. Pompeius
bellum Acti
ex k. Febr. ad k. Iul.:
Sex. Titius L. Geminius IIvir.
P. Sextilius Q. Luccius aed.
ex k. Iul. ad k. Ian.:
L. Scutarius T. Sepunius IIvir.
T. Antonius M. Valerius Mess. aed.
L. Annius C. Valerius q.

---

imp. Caesar IIII M. Licinius
k. Iul. C. Antistius
bellum Alexandreae
eid. Sept. M. Tullius
k. Nov. L. Saenius
ex k. Ian. ad k. Ian.:
L. Cornelius Q. Vettius IIvir.
C. Cassius C. Geminius Nig. [aed.]
[......................] q.

---

imp. Caesar V Sex. Appuleius L. Oppius L. Livius IIvir. q. M. Narius C. Mestrius aed. Q. Plestinus Sex. Fadius q. ———	imp. Caesar VI M. Agrippa II idem censoria potest. lustrum fecer. ex k. Ian. ad k. Iul.: L. Gavius C. Geminius Nig. IIvir. C. Caetronius C. Clodius aed.

324. Pompeii. *ILS.* 6361 b.

M. Holconio M. f. Rufo trib. mil. a popul. IIvir. i. d. V quinq. iter. Augusti Caesaris sacerd. patrono coloniae

325. A.D. 2, Pompeii. *ILS.* 6388.

P. Stallius Agatho minister d. d. imp. Caesare IX M. Silano cos.[1] [no]vatum P. Alfeno P. Vinicio cos., iussu M. Pomponi Marcelli, L. Valeri Flacci d. v. i. d., L. Obelli Lucretian[i, A. Perenni Merulini[2] d. v. v. a. s. p. p.][3]

[1] *25* B.C. [2] *Name from* ILS. *6392.* [3] d(uo) v(iri) v(iis) a(edibus) s(acris) p(ublicis) p(rocurandis) ?

326. 'mensa ponderaria', Pompeii. *CIL.* x. 793.

A. Clodius A. f. Flaccus, N. Arcaeus N. f. Arellian. Caledus d. v. i. d. mensuras exaequandas ex dec. decr.

The table has five cavities to contain specimen weights, with Oscan inscriptions which were later deleted.

327. Pompeii. *ILS.* 5053.

Clodia A. f. | sacerdos | publica | Cereris d. d. | Lassia M. f. | sacerdos | publica | Cereris d. d. | A. Clodius | M. f. Pal. scriba | magist. pag. Aug. | fel. sub.[1] | A. Clodius A. f. | Men. Flaccus IIvir | i. d. ter quinq. | trib. mil. a populo. | L. [G]ellius L. f. | Men. Calvos | decurio | Pompeis. | primo duomviratu Apollinarib. in foro pompam | tauros taurocentas succursores pontarios | paria III pugiles catervarios et pyctas ludos | omnibus acruamatis pantomimisq. | omnibus et | Pylade et HS n. CCIↃↃ in publicum pro duomviratu. | secundo duomviratu quinq. Apollinaribus in foro | pompam tauros taurarios succursores pugiles | catervarios; poster. die solus in spectaculis athletas | par. XXX glad. par. V et gladiat. par. XXXV et | venation. tauros taurocentas apros ursos | cetera venatione varia cum collega. | tertio duomviratu ludos factione prima adiectis acruamatis cum collega. | Clodia A. f. hoc monumentum sua impensa | sibi et suis

[1] fel(icis) sub(urbani)

328. 12 B.C., Capua. *ILS.* 3004.

I. o. m.[1] [P. Su]lpicio Quirin. C. Valg[i]o c[os]. Sex. Pontidio Basso M. Iunio Celere IIv[ir.] Sex. Helvio C. f. P. Titio Falerno aed. P. Rammius P. l. Chrestus navigator I. o. m. (*picture of a sailing ship*)

[1] I(ovi) o(ptimo) m(aximo)

329. Capua. *CIL.* x. 3903.

[quod . . . . . duoviri] verba fe[cerunt. | . . . . . . privatim e]t publice om[nibus honoribus ornare virum opti]mum dec[ere] quid de ea r[e] | fier[i placeret, de ea re haec auct]oritas facta e[st. | c]um L. An[tistius Campanus emeritis omnibu]s militiae stipe[ndis consecutus per gravissi]ma et periculo[si]ssima bella || iudicia dei C[aesaris et divi Augusti] deductusque a[b hoc in coloniam . . .] nostram adeo [pr]ivatim publi|ceque munifi-[centiam exercue]rit ut et patrimo[nium suum quodammodo partir]etur cum re p[ub]lica variis et | plurimis in[pendis in se receptis et] laetior sempe[r erogasse videretur quod in unive]rsos inpendis[set] quam quod | sibi ac suis i[nserviret et in cumulatio]ne officiorum r[ei publicae praestitorum co]nsenesceret ut [nu]nc quoque in | maximi[s nostris negotiis versaretur ips]e iam deficiens r[ei p. utili cura gravi tam]en annis suis [pl]acere conscri||ptis [civis honestissimi] atque utilissimi [memoriam . . . .]ae hisce honor[ib]us decorari | ut e for[o ad rogum funere per duov]iros alterum am[bosve locato . . . pro]batoque ferat[ur] vadimoniaque | eius diei dif[ferantur ne per quas r]es possit esse inped[itus populus quominus fun]us optimi et mu[ni]ficentissimi | princis (*sic*) v[iri quam maxime . . .] frequentet ut s[tatua . . . . . . i]naurata ei ex p[ub]lico ponatur | cum ins[cripto hoc . . . decurion]um decreto ubi l[ocum . . . L. Antistius Ca]mpanus filius [o]ptumus et || minist[erii eius atque munificen]tiae successor [elegerit . . . cete]risque statuis [cl]upeis donisque | quae ac[ceperit . . . .] in mortem et [quae post obitum ei d]ata sint locu[m] publice dari | quem L. [Antistius Campanus elegerit . . . . . .] secundum [via]m Appiam [. . . .

Further fragments cannot be restored.

330. Near Formiae. *ILS.* 1945.

M. Caelius M. l. Phileros accens. T. Sexti imp. in Africa Carthag. aed. praef. i. d. vectig. quinq. locand. in castell.

⊥XXXIII, aedem Tell. s. p. fec., IIvir Clupiae bis, Formis August. aedem Nept. lapid. varis s. p. ornav. Fresidiae N. l. Florae uxori viro opseq.[1] Q. Octavio Ɔ. l. Antimacho karo amico

[1] opseq(uentissimae)

331. Suessula (Campania). *Rivista Indo-Greco-Ital.* 1921, 76.

. . . . ?] Caes. Aug. f. C. Sallustius Epagathic. ob honorem Augustalit. l. d. d. d.

332. Rufrae (Campania). *ILS.* 5759.

M. Volcio M. f. Sabino tr. mil. quod aquam Iuliam pequnia sua adduxit Rufrani vicani

333. Decree of the Town Council, A.D. 26, Veii. *ILS.* 6579.

centumviri municipii Augusti Veientis | Romae in aedem Veneris Genetricis cum convenis|sent, placuit universis, dum decretum conscriberetur, | interim ex auctoritate omnium permitti || C. Iulio divi Augusti l. Geloti, qui omni tempore | municip. Veios non solum consilio et gratia adiuverit | sed etiam inpensis suis et per filium suum celebrari | voluerit, honorem ei iustissimum decerni, ut | Augustalium numero habeatur aeque ac si eo || honore usus sit, liceatque ei omnibus spectaculis | municipio nostro bisellio proprio inter Augus|tales considere cenisque omnibus publicis | inter centumviros interesse, itemque placere | ne quod ab eo liberisque eius vectigal municipii || Augusti Veientis exigeretur |

adfuerunt C. Scaevius Curiatius | L. Perperna Priscus IIvir. | M. Flavius Rufus q. | T. Vettius Rufus q. || M. Tarquitius Saturnin. | L. Maecilius Scrupus | L. Favonius Lucanus | Cn. Octavius Sabinus | T. Sempronius Gracchus || P. Acuvius P. f. Tro. | C. Veianius Maximus | T. Tarquitius Rufus | C. Iulius Merula. | Actum || Gaetulico et Calvisio Sabino cos.

334. Falerii. *ILS.* 5373.

honoris imp. Caesaris divi f. Augusti pont. maxim. patr. patriae et municip., magistri Augustales C. Egnatius M. l. Glyco, C. Egnatius C. l. Musicus, C. Iulius Caesar. l. Isochrysus, Q. Floronius Q. l. Princeps, viam Augustam ab via Annia extra portam ad Cereris silice sternendam curarunt pecunia sua pro ludis

335. Asculum. *ILS.* 6565.

d. m. M. Valerio col. l. Vernae sexvir. Aug. et Tib.[1] Ianuarius [c]ol. di[sp.] qui fuerat [arc]arius[2] eiu[s, i]tem Vibia Primil[l]a uxo[r s]ib[i e]t po[ste]ris eorum

[1] Aug(ustali) et Tib(eriali) [2] *Or possibly* [vic]arius

336. Iguvium. *ILS.* 5531.

[C]n. Satrius Cn. f. Rufus IIIIvir iur. dic. [b]asilicas sublaqueavit trabes tecti ferro suffixit lapide stravit podio circumclusit sua pec. et dedit

decurionatus nomine	HS IↃↃ∞
in commeatum legionibus	HS ∞∞∞∞CCCCL
in aedem Dianae restituendam	HS IↃↃ∞CC
in ludos Victoriae Caesaris August.	HS IↃↃ∞∞∞DCCL

337. Umbria. *ILS.* 1901.

[. . . . . l]io Vibi f. Clu. patri | [. . . . .]lio Ti. f. Clu. fratri | [. . . . .]ciae matri | [. . . . .]lius Ti. f. Pup. Clemens scr. XXVI[vir. | tr. mi]l. a populo IIvir iure dicundo Carsulis sex [dier. | circ. se]x scen. primus munus gladiatorium municipio [edidit]

338. 23–20 B.C., Augusta Praetoria. *ILS.* 6753.

imp. Caesa[ri] divi f. August. cos. XI imp. VI[II] tribunic. pot. Salassi incol. qui initio se in colon. con[t.] patron.

339. Arch, Pola. *ILS.* 2229.

L. Sergius C. f. aed. IIvir
Salvia Postuma Sergi
L. Sergius L. f. Lepidus aed. tr. mil. leg. XXIX
(*vac.*)
Cn. Sergius C. f. aed. IIvir quinq.
Salvia Postuma Sergi de sua pecunia

339a. Bronze coin, Halaesa (Sicilia). Grant, *FITA.* 195.

Obv. Head of Augustus. HALAESA ARCHONIDA
Rev. Wreath. *Inside*: AVG. *Round*: M. PACCIVS MACXV. FLAME. (*or* M. PAC. MAX. IIVIR AVG. DES.)

339b. Bronze coin, Caralis (Sardinia). Grant, *FITA.* 149.

Obv. Two male busts. ARISTO MVTVMBAL RICOCE SVF.
Rev. Temple. KAR. VENERIS

340. Mediolanum Santonum (Gaul). *ILS.* 7040.

[C. Iulio] C. Iuli Ricoveriugi f. Vol. Marino [flamini? Augus]-tali primo c. c. R.[1] quaestori verg[obreto, Iulia] Marina filia p[osuit]

[1] c(uratori) c(ivium) R(omanorum)

341. Altar, Lutetia Parisiorum. *ILS.* 4613 d; cf. *Revue des études latines,* xviii (1940), 33.

Tib. Caesare Aug. Iovi optum[o] maxsumo nautae Parisiac[i] publice posierun[t]

342. Bronze coin, Caesaraugusta (Tarraconensis). Heiss, p. 201, no. 18; Vives, p. 79, no. 24.

Obv. Three vexilla. AVGVSTO DIVI F. LEG. IV LEG. VI LEG. X

Rev. TIB. CLOD. FLAVO PRAEF. GERMAN. L. IVVENT. LVPERCO IIVIR C. C. A.[1]

[1] c(olonia) C(aesar) A(ugusta)

343. Bronze coin, Emerita. Heiss, p. 400, no. 18; Vives, p. 63, no. 23.

Obv. Head of Augustus. PERM. CAES. AVG.

Rev. Legionary eagle between standards. C. A. E.[1] LE. V X

[1] c(olonia) A(ugusta) E(merita)

343a. Bronze coin, Italica. Heiss, p. 380, no. 8; Vives, p. 127, no. 9.

Obv. Head of Tiberius. IMP. TI. CAESAR AVGVSTVS PON. MAX.

Rev. Altar, inscribed: PROVIDENTIAE AVGVSTI round: PERM. DIVI AVG. MVNIC. ITALIC.

343b. Bronze coin, Babba (Mauretania). Grant, *FITA.* 222.

Obv. Head of Augustus. CAESAR AVGVSTVS

Rev. Three-arched bridge. L. POMPON[I] L. IVLI. IIVIR. Q. [C. C.] I. B.[1]

[1] duovir(i) q(uinquennales) c(oloniae) c(ampestris) I(uliae) B(abbae)

344. A.D. 32–33, near Membressa (Africa). *Bull. arch. comité des travaux hist.* 1907, xiii.

Ti. Caesari Aug. f. Aug. pon. max. cos. V imp. VIII trib. pot. XXXIIII C. Septumius C. f. Saturninus fla. col(umnas) IIII d. s. p. f. cur(atore) L. Lurio Q. f. Rufo

345. A.D. 36–37, Thugga. *Nouv. archives des missions,* 1913, 38.

imp. Ti. Caesari divi Aug. f. Aug. pontif. maximo tribunic. potest. XXXVIII cos. V | L. Manilius L. f. Arn. Bucco IIvir dedicavit. | L. Postumius C. f. Arn. Chius patron. pag. nomine suo et Firmi et Rufi filiorum | forum et aream ante templum Caesaris stravit aram Aug. aedem Saturn. arcum d. s. p. f. c.

346. Architrave with Latin and Neo-Punic inscription, A.D. 1–2, Lepcis Magna. *ITrip.*, no. 321.

imp. Caesare divi f. Aug. pont. max. tr. pot. XXIV cos. XIII patre patr. Annobal Rufus ornator patriae amator concordiae flamen sufes praef. sacr. Himilconis Tapapi f. d. s. p. fac. coer. idemq. dedicavit

347. Salonae. *ILS.* 7160.

L. Anicio L. f. Paetinati IIIIvir. iure dic. quinquennal. prae. quinq. Drusi Caesar. Germanici praefec. quinq. P. Dolabellae pontifici flamini Iuliae Augustae praef. fabr. praefectur. Phariac. Salonitan.

347a. Dalmatia. *Bull. inst. arch. bulgare*, 1950, 235.

divo Augusto et Ti. Caesari Aug. f. Aug. sacrum veterani pagi Scunastic. quibus colonia Naronit.[1] agros dedit

[1] Naronit(ana)

348. Chersus (Dalmatian island). *ILS.* 5516.

Ti. Caesari Aug. f. Augusto pon[t.] max. C. Aemilius Volso. f. Oca L. Fonteius Q. f. Rufus IIviri porticum curiam d. d. faciundum curaver. eid.que probav[ere]

348a. Bronze coin, 43–42 B.C., Cassandrea. Grant, *FITA*. 272.

Obv. Head of Iuppiter Ammon. HAMMON

Rev. Two corn-ears. HORT. COL. D.[1]

[1] Hort(ensius) col(oniam) d(eduxit)

349. Corinth. *Corinth*, viii. 2, no. 81.

T. Manlio T. f. Col. Iuvenco aed. praef. i. d. IIvir. pontif. agonothet. Isthm. et Caesareon qui primus Caesarea egit ante Isthmiạ hieromnemonẹ[s]

350. Gytheum (Laconia). *SEG.* xi. 924.

C. Iulium Lacharis f. Euryclem cives Romani in Laconica qui habitant negotiantur benefici ergo

Γάϊον Ἰούλιον Λαχάρους υἱὸν Εὐρυκλέα Ῥωμαῖοι οἱ ἐν ταῖς πόλεσιν τῆς Λακωνικῆς πραγματευόμενοι τὸν αὐτῶν εὐεργέτην

351. Asopus (Laconia). *IG.* v. 1, 970.

ἁ πόλις Γάϊον Ἰούλιον Εὐρυκλέ[α τὸ]ν ἑαυτᾶς εὐεργέ[τ]αν ἀνθέντα τὸ [ἔ]λαιον ε[ἰς] τὸν αἰῶνα

352. Cyzicus. *SEG.* iv. 707 and *IGRR.* iv. 144.

ἐπὶ Πανσανίου τοῦ Εὐμένους τὸ [β' ἱππ]άρχεω, μηνὸς Καλαμαιῶνος, | ἔδοξεν τῆι βουλῆι καὶ τῶι δήμωι· Πανσανίας Εὐμ[ένους] Αἰγικορεὺς μέσης ἐπὶ Δημητρίου εἶπεν· ἐπεὶ | Ἀντωνία Τρύφαινα βασιλέως Πολέμωνος καὶ β[ασιλίσ]σης Πυθοδωρίδος θυγάτηρ τὸν αἰώνιον τοῦ μεγίστο[υ] | θεῶν Τιβερίου Σεβαστοῦ Καίσαρος οἶκον καὶ τὴν ἀθάν[ατον ἡ]γεμονίαν αὐτοῦ διὰ παντὸς εὐσεβοῦσα συγκαθιέρωσ[ε] || τῆι Πολιάδι Ἀθηνᾷ ἄγαλμα τῆς μητρὸς αὐτοῦ Σεβαστ[ῆς Νει]κηφόρου καὶ λαβοῦσα παρὰ τῆς πόλεως ἱερητείαν αὐτῆ[ς] | ἐν τῆι πέρσυ ἀγομένῃ ἀτελείᾳ τῶν Παναθηναίων, τ[οῖς Σε]βαστοῖς πάντα μὲν τὰ πρὸς εὐσέβειαν τῶν θεῶν κα|[τὰ] τὸ ἔθος αὐτῆς ἐκπρεπῶς <θυσιῶ>ν πολλῶν ἱερουργ[ουμένω]ν ἐξεπλήρωσεν, τῆι δὲ ἐνφύτωι φιλανθρωπίᾳ πρός | τε τοὺς ἐνχωρίους καὶ τοὺς ξένους ἐχρήσατο, ὡς <θαυμάζεσθαι> ὑπὸ τ[ῶν ἐπιδη]μού<ν>των ξένων μετὰ πάσης ἀποδοχῆς ἐπί τε εὐσε|βείαι καὶ ὁσιότητι καὶ φιλοδοξίᾳ, ἐν δὲ τῶι κατ' ἔτος [ἐνιαυτῶ]ι ἀπούσης μὲν αὐτῆς, πάντων δὲ συντετελεσμένων || ἐκπλέως κατὰ τὴν ἐκείνης εὐσέβειαν, καὶ τῶν ἀπὸ τῆς οἰ[κουμέν]ης ἐνπόρων καὶ ξένων τῶν ἐληλυθότων εἰς τὴν πανή|γυριν βουλομένων ἀναθεῖναι αὐτῆς ὅπλον εἰκονικὸν ἐπ[ίχρυσ]ον καὶ διὰ τοῦτο ἐπεληλυθότων ἐπί τε τὴν βουλὴν καὶ τὸν | δῆμον καὶ ἀξιούντων συνχωρηθῆναι αὐτοῖς ποιήσασθαι τὴν ἀνάθεσιν· δεδόχθαι τῆι βουλῆι καὶ τῶι δήμωι· | συγκεχωρῆσθαι αὐτοῖς ἀναθεῖναι τὸ ὅπλον ἐν τῶι τῆς Πολίαδος ναῶι, ἐφ' ὧι καὶ ἐπιγράψαι· οἱ ἀπὸ τῆς Ἀσίας ἐργασταὶ | ἀφειγμένοι εἰς τὴν πανήγυριν καὶ ἀτέλειαν τὴν ἀγομένην ἐν Κυζικῶι τοῖς Σεβαστοῖς καὶ τῆι Πολιάδι Ἀθηνᾷ || Ἀντωνίαν Τρύφαιναν βασιλέως Πολέμωνος καὶ βασιλίσσης Πυθοδωρίδος Φιλομήτορος θυγατέρα, ἱερήαν Σεβασ|τῆς Νεικηφόρου, διά τε τὴν περὶ τὸν τοῦ μεγίστου θεῶν Τιβερίου Σεβαστοῦ Καίσαρος οἶκον εὐσέβειαν καὶ διὰ τὴν | ἐν πᾶσι σεμνότητα καὶ εἰς ἑαυτοὺς εὐεργεσίαν

353. Thyateira (Asia). *RPh.* 1913, 294.

οἱ ἀλειφόμενοι ἐν τῶι τρίτωι γυμνασίωι ἐτείμησαν Γάϊον Ἰούλιον Μάρκου υἱὸν Λέπιδον τὸν ἀρχιερέα τῆς Ἀσίας καὶ ἀγωνοθέτην διὰ βίου γυμνασιάρχοντα τὸ ε̅ ἐπιμεληθέντος Ἀρτεμιδώρου τοῦ Ἀρτεμιδώρου γραμματέως

353a. Bronze coin, *c.* 42–41 B.C., Lampsacus. Grant, *FITA.* 246.

Obv. Head of Caesar. C. G. I. L.[1]

Rev. Man ploughing. Q. LVCRETIO L. PONTIO IIVIR. COL. DED. P.[2]

[1] C(olonia) G(emina ?) I(ulia) L(ampsacus)
[2] IIvir(is) col(oniae) ded(uctae) p(rimis)

353b. Bronze coin, Parium. *BMC. Mysia,* p. 103, no. 84.

Obv. Head of Octavian. M. BARBATIO MAN. ACILIO IIVIR. C. G. I. P.[1]

Rev. Man ploughing. P. VIBIO SAC. CAES. Q. BARBA. PRAEF. PRO IIVIR.

[1] *See no. 353a.*

354. Tessera patronatus, probably A.D. 28, near Brixia. *ILS.* 6099.

L. Silano flamin[e] Martiali C. Vellaeo Tutore cos. non. Decembr. senatus populusque Siagitanus hospitium fecerunt cum C. Silio C. f. Fab. Aviola trib. mil. leg. III Aug. praefecto fabrum eumque posterosque eius sibi posterisque suis patronum coptaverunt. C. Silius C. f. Fab. Aviola eos posterosque eorum in fidem clientelamque suam recepit. agente Celere Imilchonis Gulalsae filio sufete

355. Tessera patronatus, 12 B.C., Africa. *ILS.* 6095.

P. Sulpicio Quirinio C. Valgio cos. senatus populusque civitatium stipendiariorum pago Gurzenses hospitium fecerunt quom L. Domitio Cn. f. L. n. Ahenobarbo procos. eumque et postereis (*sic*) eius sibi posterisque sueis patronum coptaverunt, isque eos posterosque eorum in fidem clientelamque suam recepit. faciundum coeraverunt Ammicar Milchatonis f. Cynasyn., Boncar Azzrubalis f. Aethogursensis, Muthunbal Saphonis f. Cui. Nas. Uzitensis

356. Tessera patronatus, A.D. 15–17, Rome. *Bull. Comm.* 1912, 113.

[coloni coloniae Iuliae Assuritanae hos]pitium fec[erunt cum A. Vibio Habito] pro cos. liber[is posterisque eius eumque] rogarunt uti [se liberos posterosque] suos in fidem clie[ntelamque reciperet]. A. Vibius Habitus pro [cos. colonos coloniae] Iuliae Assuritanae [liberos posterosque eorum] in fidem et clientel[am suam suorumque] recepit. [egerunt] M. Canin[ius . . . .]

356a. A.D. 6, Emerita. *Emerita*, 1948, 46.

[M. Aemilio Lepid]o L. Arrun[tio] cos. decuriones et municipes Martienses qui antea Ugienses fuerant hospitium fecerunt cum decurionibus et colonis coloniae Augustae Emeritae sibi liberis posterisq. eorum. egerunt legati P. Mummius P. f. Gal. Ursus M. Aemilius M. f. Gal. Fronto

XIV

VARIA

357. A husband's eulogy of his wife (formerly called *Laudatio Turiae*), between 8 and 2 B.C., Rome. *ILS*. 8393 and p. cxc. M. Durry, *Éloge funèbre d'une matrone romaine* (1950). Gordon, *AJA*. 1950, 223 (col. I, ll. 1–24, 42–52; II, ll. 1–20, 66–79 are here omitted).

cesserunt constantiae tuae neque amplius rem sollicitarunt: I. 25
quo facto [reverentiae in patrem], | pietatis in sororem, fide[i]
in nos patrocinium succeptum sola peregisti. | rara sunt tam
diuturna matrimonia finita morte, non divertio in[terrupta;
nam contigit] | nobis, ut ad annum XXXXI sine offensa per-
duceretur. utinam vetust[um ita extremam sub]|isset muta-
tionem vice m[e]a, qua iustius erat cedere fato maiorem. ||

domestica bona pudici[t]iae opsequi comitatis facilitatis lani- 30
ficiis tuis [adsiduitatis religionis] | sine superstitione o[r]natus
non conspiciendi cultus modici cur [memorem? cur dicam de
tuorum cari]|tate familiae pietate, [c]um aeque matrem meam
ac tuos parentes col[ueris eandemque quietem] | illi quam tuis
curaveris, cetera innumerabilia habueris commun[ia cum omni-
bus] | matronis dignam f[a]mam co[l]entibus? propria sunt tua,
quae vindico ac [quorum pauci in] || similia inciderunt, ut talia 35
paterentur et praestarent, quae rara ut essent [hominum] |
fortuna cavit. |

omne tuom patrimonium acceptum ab parentibus communi
diligentia cons[ervavimus], | neque enim erat adquirendi tibi
cura, quod totum mihi tradidisti. officia [ita par]|titi sumus, ut
ego tu[t]elam tuae fortunae gererem, tu meae custodiam sust[i-
neres. multa] || de hac parte omittam, ne tua propria mecum 40
communicem; satis sit [hoc] mi[hi tuis] | de sensibus [indi]-
casse. |

acerbissumum tamen in vi[ta] mihi accidisse tua vice fate- II. 21
bo[r, reddito iam non inutili] | cive patriae benificio et i[ud]icio
apsentis Caesaris Augusti [quom per te] | de restitutione mea
M. L[epi]dus conlega praesens interp[ellaretur et ad eius] |
pedes prostrata humi, n[on] modo non adlevata, sed tra[cta et
servilem in] || modum rapsata, livori[bus c]orporis repleta, fir- 25
missimo [animo eum admone]|res edicti Caesaris cum g[r]atula-

tione restitutionis me[ae, auditisque verbis eti]|am contumeliosis et cr[ud]elibus exceptis volneribus pa[lam ea praeferres], | ut auctor meorum peric[ul]orum notesceret. quoi noc[uit mox quod fecit]. |

quid hac virtute efficaciu[s]? praebere Caesari clementia[e locum et cum cu]||stodia spiritus mei not[a]re inportunam crudelitatem [egregia tua] | patientia? |

sed quid plura? parcamu[s] orationi quae debet et potest e[xire, ne viliter maxi]|ma opera tractando pa[r]um digne peragamus, quom pr[o documento] | meritorum tuorum oc[ulis] omnium praeferam titulum [vitae servatae]. ||

pacato orbe terrarum, res[titut]a re publica quieta deinde n[obis et felicia] | tempora contigerunt. fue[ru]nt optati liberi, quos aliqua[mdiu sors invi]|derat. si fortuna procede[re e]sset passa sollemnis inservie[ns, quid utrique no]|strum defuit? procedens a[et]as spem [f]iniebat. quid agitav[eris propter hoc quae]|que ingredi conata sis, f[or]sitan in quibusdam feminis [conspicua et admirabi]||lia, in te quidem minime a[dmi]randa conlata virtutibu[s tuis reliquis, praetereo]. | diffidens fecunditati tuae [et d]olens orbitate mea, ne tenen[do in matrimonio] | te spem habendi liberos [dep]onerem atque eius caussa ess[em infelix, de divertio] | elocuta es, vocuamque [do]mum alterius fecunditati t[e tradituram, non alia] | mente nisi ut nota con[co]rdia nostra tu ipsa mihi di[gnam con]||dicionem quaereres p[ara]resque, ac futuros liberos t[e communes pro]|que tuis habituram adf[irm]ares, neque patrimoni nos[tri quod adhuc] | fuerat commune, separa[ti]onem facturam, sed in eodem [arbitrio meo id] | ei si vellem tuo ministerio [fu]turum; nihil seiunctum, ni[hil separatum te] | habituram, sororis soc[rusve] officia pietatemque mihi d[einceps praestituram]. ||

fatear necessest adeo me exa[rsi]sse, ut excesserim mente, adeo [exhorruisse ac]|tus tuos, ut vix redderer [mi]hi. agitari divertia inter nos [ante quam | f]ato dicta lex esset, poss[e te a]liquid concipere mente, qua[re viva desineres] | esse mihi uxor, cum paene [e]xule me vita fidissuma perman[sisses]. |

quae tanta mihi fuerit cu[pid]itas aut necessitas habendi li[beros, ut propterea] || fidem exuerem, mutare[m c]erta dubiis? sed quid plura? [permansisti] | aput me; neque enim ced[er]e tibi sine dedecore meo et co[mmuni infelici]|tate poteram. | tibi vero quid memorabi[lius] quam inserviendo mihi o[peram dedisse te] | ut, quom ex te liberos ha[b]ere non possem, per te tamen [haberem et diffi]||dentia partus tui alteriu[s c]oniugio parares fecunditat[em] ? |

utinam patiente utriusqu[e a]etate procedere coniugium [potuisset, donec e]|lato me maiore, quod iu[sti]us erat, suprema mihi praesta[res, antea vero super]|stite te excederem orbitat[e f]ilia mihi supstituta. |

praecucurristi fato. delegast[i] mihi luctum desiderio tui nec libe[ros habentem solum vi]||rum reliquisti. flectam ego quoque sensus meos ad iudicia tu[a, a te destinatam adoptans] |

358. Via Appia. *ILS.* 1949.

M. Aurelius Cottae | Maximi l. Zosimus, | accensus patroni. |
libertinus eram, fateor; || sed facta legetur |
patrono Cotta nobilis umbra mea. |
qui mihi saepe libens census donavit | equestris,
qui iussit natos | tollere, quos aleret ||
quique suas commisit opes | mihi semper, et idem
dotavit | natas ut pater ipse meas, |
Cottanumque meum produxit | honore tribuni,
quem fortis || castris Caesaris emeruit. |
quid non Cotta dedit? qui nunc | et carmina tristis
haec dedit | in tumulo conspicienda meo. |
Aurelia Saturnia Zosimi

358a. 21 January, A.D. 31, Lusitania. *CRAcInscr.* 1952, 472.

Ti. Caesare V L. Aelio Sei⟨a⟩no cos. XII k. Febr.

Q. Stertinius Q. f. Bassus Q. Stertinius Q. ⟨f.⟩ Rufus L. Stertinius Q. f. Rufinus hospitium fecerunt cum L. Fulcinio Trione leg. Ti. Caesaris liberis posterisque eius

L. Fulcinius Trio leg. Ti. Caesaris Q. Stertinium Q. f. Bassum Q. Stertinium Q. ⟨f.⟩ Rufum L. Stertinium Q. f. Rufinum liberos posterosq. eorum in fidem clientelamq. suam liberorum posterorumq. suorum recepit

359. Near Corfinium. *ILS.* 2682.

. . . .] | Nigri, annos XXXVIIII u[n]i | nupta viro summa cum | concordia ad ultumum || diem pervenit, tres ex [e]o | superstites reliquid libero[s], unum maximis municipi honorib. | iudiciis August. Caesaris usum, | alterum castresibus eiusdem | Caesaris August. summis [eq]u[es]||tris ordinis honoribus et iam | superiori destinatum ordini, | filiam sanctissimam probissimo viro coniunctam et ex ea duos | [nepotes . . . .] dedit [. . . . .] | quas [. . . . .]||rib[. . . . .

360. Celeia (Noricum). *ILS.* 1977.

C. Iulius Vepo donatus civitate Romana viritim et inmunitate ab divo Aug. vivos fecit sibi et Boniatae Antoni fil. coniugi et suis

360a. March, 2 B.C., Coptos–Berenice road, Egypt. Meredith, *Chronique d'Égypte*, no. 58 (1954), 281; cf. *JRS.* 1953, p. 39.

C. Numidius Eros hic fuit anno XXIIX Caesaris exs Ind⟨i⟩a red⟨i⟩e⟨n⟩s menos P⟨h⟩amen(oth)

360b. 2–5 July, A.D. 6, same place as 360a. *JRS.* 1953, p. 38.

Λυσᾶς Ποπλίου Ἀννίου Πλοκάμου ἥκω{ι} Lλε *Καίσαρος ἐπεὶφ η̄*
Lysa P. Anni Plocami veni anno XXXV III Non. Iul. [. . .

361. A.D. 11–12, Nisyra (Lydia). Keil u. Premerstein, *Denkschr. Ak. Wien* 1911, no. 192.

[ἔτους] ϛϙʹ[1] *οἱ [Νισυρ]έων κάτοικ[οι ἐτ]είμη[σ]αν Γάιον Αἰμίλιον Γέμινον Καίσαρος Σεβαστοῦ κεντορίωνα λεγιῶνος ζʹ ἀρετῆς ἕνεκεν πάσης καὶ εὐχαριστίας τῆς ὑπὲρ Μάρκου Ἀντωνίου τοῦ αὐτῶν κατοίκου*

[1] *Year 96 of Sullan era.*

362. A.D. 15, Rome. *ILS.* 9349.

Druso Caesar[e] C. Norbano Flacco [co]s. Menander C. Comini Macri et C. Corneli Crispi, bigarius vincit ludis Mart. q. f.[1] cos. eq.[2] Basilisco Rustico, ludis Victor. Caesar. q.f.[1] P. Cornelius Scip. Q. Pompeius Macer pr. eq.[2] Histro Corace

[1] q(uos) f(ecerunt) [2] eq(uis)

363. 35 B.C., Polis (Ithaca). *BCH.* 1930, 490.

Epaphroditus Novi
ungentarius de sa-
cra via hic fuit
k. Oct. quo anno
L. Cornuficius
Sex. Pompei-
us cos. fue-
runt

APPENDIX

363a. Between 1 and 25 Jan., A.D. 47, Feltria (Venetia). *ILS.* 208.

Ti. Claudius Drusi f. Caesar Aug. Germanicus pontifex maximus tribunicia potestate VI cos. IV imp. XI p. p. censor viam Claudiam Augustam quam Drusus pater Alpibus bello patefactis derex[e]rat, munit ab Altino usque ad flumen Danuvium. m. p. CCCL

364. Lex de imperio Vespasiani, Rome. *ILS.* 244.

. . . .] foedusve cum quibus volet facere liceat, ita uti licuit divo Aug. | Ti. Iulio Caesari Aug. Tiberioque Claudio Caesari Aug. Germanico. |

utique ei senatum habere relationem facere remittere senatus | consulta per relationem discessionemque facere liceat, || ita uti licuit divo Aug. Ti. Iulio Caesari Aug. Ti. Claudio Caesari | Augusto Germanico. |

utique, cum ex voluntate auctoritateve iussu mandatuve eius | praesenteve eo senatus habebitur, omnium rerum ius perinde | habeatur servetur, ac si e lege senatus edictus esset habereturque. ||

utique quos magistratum potestatem imperium curationemve | cuius rei petentes senatui populoque Romano commendaverit, | quibusque suffragationem suam dederit promiserit, eorum | comitis quibusque extra ordinem ratio habeatur. |

utique ei fines pomerii proferre promovere, cum ex republica || censebit esse, liceat, ita uti licuit Ti. Claudio Caesari Aug. | Germanico. |

utique quaecunque ex usu reipublicae maiestate divinarum | huma⟨na⟩rum publicarum privatarumque rerum esse {e} | censebit, ei agere facere ius potestasque sit, ita uti divo Aug. || Tiberioque Iulio Caesari Aug. Tiberioque Claudio Caesari | Aug. Germanico fuit. |

utique quibus legibus plebeive scitis scriptum fuit, ne divus Aug. | Tiberiusve Iulius Caesar Aug. Tiberiusque Claudius Caesar Aug. | Germanicus tenerentur, iis legibus plebisque scitis imp. Caesar || Vespasianus solutus sit, quaeque ex quaque lege rogatione | divum Aug. Tiberiumve Iulium Caesarem Aug.

Tiberiumve | Claudium Caesarem Aug. Germanicum facere oportuit, | ea omnia imp. Caesari Vespasiano Aug. facere liceat. |

utique quae ante hanc legem rogatam acta gesta || decreta imperata ab imperatore Caesare Vespasiano Aug. | iussu mandatuve eius a quoque sunt, ea perinde iusta rataq. | sint ac si populi plebisve iussu acta essent |

sanctio.

si quis huiusce legis ergo adversus leges rogationes plebisve scita | senatusve consulta fecit fecerit, sive quod eum ex lege rogatione || plebisve scito s.ve c. facere oportebit, non fecerit huius legis | ergo, id ei ne fraudi esto neve quit ob eam rem populo dare debeto | neve cui de ea re actio neve iudicatio esto neve quis de ea re apud | [s]e agi sinito

No. 365 of the first edition is now no. 94a.

ADDENDA

365. Cumae. Sherk, *Roman Documents from the Greek East*, no. 61.

[*Α*]*ὐτοκράτωρ Καῖσαρ Θεοῦ υἱὸς Σεβαστὸς* [ ] | [*Μ*]*ᾶρκος Ἀγρίπας Λευκίου υἱὸς ὕπατοι ν ε*[. . .]. | [*Εἴ*] *τινες δημόσιοι τόποι ἢ ἱεροὶ ἐν π̣ό̣λεσ*[*ι*. .] | [*π*]*όλεως ἑκάστης ἐπαρχείας εἰσὶν εἴτε τι*[*νὰ ἀναθή*]-| *ματα τούτων τῶν τόπων εἰσὶν ἔσονταί τ*[*ε, μηδεὶς*] || [*τ*]*α̣ῦτα αἱρέτω μηδὲ ἀγοραζέτω μηδὲ ἀπο*[*τίμημα*] | [*ἢ*] *δῶρον λαμβανέτω. ὃ ἂν ἐκεῖθεν ἀπενη*[*νεγμένον*] | [*ἢ ἠ*]*γορασμένον ἔν τε δώρῳ δεδομένον ᾖ,* [*ὃς ἂν ἐπὶ τῆς*] | [*ἐ*]*παρχείας ᾖ ἀποκατασταθῆναι εἰς τὸν δημ*[*όσιον λόγον*] | *ἢ ἱερὸν τῆς πόλεως φροντιζέτω, καὶ ὃ ἂν χρ*[*ῆμα ἐνεχύρι*]-|| [*ο*]*ν δοθῇ, τοῦτο μὴ δικαιοδοτείτω* {*ι*} *vacat* |
[.] Vinicius proc(onsul) s(alutem) d(at) mag(istratibus) Cumas. Apollonides L. f. No[race(us) | c(ivis) v(ester)] me adeit et demostravit Liberei Patris fanum nom[ine | ven]ḍitiones possiderei ab Lusia Diogenis f. Tucalleus c(ive) [v(estro), | et c]ụm vellent thiaseitae sacra deo restituere iussu Au[gu-||s]ti Caesaris pretio soluto quod est inscreiptum fano, | [. .]berei ab Lusia. E(go) v(olo) v(os) c(urare), sei ita sunt, utei Lusias quod | [est] positum pretium fano recipiet et restituat deo fa-|[num e]t in eo inscreibatur Imp. Caesar Deivei f. Augustu[s] re[sti-|tuit. Sei] autem Lusia contradeicit quae Apollonides pos[tu-||lat, vadi]monium ei satisdato ubi ego ero. Lusiam prom[it-|tere magi]s probo. *Ἐπὶ πρυτάνεως Φανίτου vacat* | [. . . *ος*] *Οὐινίκιος χαίρειν λέγει ἄρχουσι Κυμαίων. Ἀ*[*πολ*]-|[*λωνίδ*]*ης Λευκίου Νωρακεῖος πολείτης ὑμέτερό*[*ς μοι*] | [*προσῆλ*]*θεν καὶ ὑπέδειξεν Διονύσου ἱερὸν ὀνόμ*[*ατι*] || [*πράσεως κ*]*α̣τ̣έ̣χ̣ε̣σθαι ὑπὸ Λυσίου τοῦ Διογένους* [*Τυκάλ*]-|[*λεως πολείτου ὑμετέρο*]*υ, καὶ ὅτε ἠβού*[*λοντο οἱ θιασεῖ*]-|[*ται*. . . . .
. . . .] |

366. Laudatio Agrippae. P. Colon. inv. nr. 4701. Cf. *ZPE.* v (1970), 217 ff.; vi (1970), 227 ff.

Ἡ [*γ*]*ά̣ρ τοι δημαρχική σοι ἐξουσία εἰς πέν*|*τε ἔτη κατὰ δόγμα συνκλήτου* | *Λέντ*⟨*λ*⟩*ων ὑπατευόντων ἐδόθη καὶ* | *πάλιν αὔτη εἰς ἄλλην Ὀλυμπιάδα* | [*ὑ*]*πατευόντων Τιβερίου Νέρωνος* || *καὶ Κυιν*⟨*τι*⟩*λίου Οὐάρου γαμβρῶν τῶν* | *σῶν προσεπεδόθη. καὶ εἰς*{*s*} *ἃς δήπο*|*τέ σε ὑπαρχείας τὰ κοινὰ τῶν Ῥω*|*μαίων ἐφέλκοιτο,* μηθενὸς ἐν ἐ|κείναις ἐξουσίαν μ̣ε̣ί̣ζ̣ω ⟨εἶναι⟩ τῆς σῆς ἐ̣ν̣ || νόμωι ἐκυρώθη. α[....]ε̣ι̣σ̣....[...]|ὑψους καὶ ἡμετέραι [..........] | ταῖς ἰδίαις {ἰδ̣ίαις} κα[..........] | πάντων ἀνθρώπων[...

367. Lucus Feroniae. *JRS.* lxi (1971), 143 (=*AE.* 1972, 174); *Hermes* c (1972), 461ff,

[L. Volusio L. f. Q. n. Sa]turnino cos. | [augur sodalis Augustal]is Titi proc[os. Asiae | legatus divi Aug. item Ti. Caesa]ris Aug. pro praetore ịṇ [provinciis | --- et Dalmatia pra]efectus urbis fuiṭ. [Cum in praefectura | sua nonagesimum et tertium] annum agens de[cessit senatus || auctore Caesare Augusto German]ịc̣o funere pubḷịc̣ọ [eum efferi | censuit vadimoniis exsequi]arum [ei]us c̣ạusa dilatis item statuas ei | [ponend]ạṣ ṭṛ[ium]fales ịṇ foro Augusti aeneam in templo noṿo divi Augus{s}ti | [mar]ṃoreas [du]as consulares unam in templo divi Iuli alteraṃ ịṇ | [P]a[l]atio intra Tripylum tertiam in aria Apolinis in conspectum curiae || ạuguralem in regia equestrem proxime rostra sella curuli residentem at | theatrum Pompeianum in porticu Lentulorum.

368. Tuzla. J. M. Crook, *The Troad*, p. 412, no. 50. Cf. *ZPE.* xiii (1974), 161 ff.

C. Fabricio C. f. | Ani. Tusco, IIvir., augur., | praef. cohort. Apulae et | operum quae in colonia iussu | Augusti facta sunt, trib. mil. leg. III || Cyr. VIII, trib. dilectus ingenuorum | quem Romae habuit Augustus et | Ti. Caesar, praef. fabr. IIII, praef. equit. | alae praet. IIII, hasta pura et corona | aurea donatus est a Germanico || Caesare imp. bello Germanico | d. d.

369. Caesarea. *AE.* 1963, no. 104. Cf. *Rend. Acc. Linc.* xix (1964), 59 ff.

imperatori | Tiberieum | Pon|tius Pilatus | [pr]aefectus Iudae || d. d.

370. Alba Fucens. *AE.* 1957, no. 250.

Q. Naevius Q. f. Fab. Cordus Sutorius Macro | praefectus vigilum praefectus praetori | Ti. Caesaris Augusti testamento dedit.

371. Rome. *AE.* 1946, no. 94.

L. Iulio L. f. Ani. | Graecino | tr. pl., pr. | M. Iulius L. f. Ani. | Graecinus || quaestor f.

372. Fasti Ostienses, A.D. 6 (*Inscriptiones Italiae*, XIII. i. 183)

[M. Aemilius Lepidus, L. Arruntius | k. Iul. L. N]onius Asprenas | Agrippa Caesar [abdicatus est? | IIvir(i) c(ensoria) p(otestate) q(uinquennales)] A. Egrilius Rufus, L. Cre[pereius? ...]

373. Tabarka (Tunisia). *AE*. 1959, no. 77.

M. Lepido imp. | tert. pont. max. | III vir r. p. c. bis cos. | iter. patrono. | ex d. d.

374. Vatican Obelisk, Rome. *AE*. 1964 no. 255. Cf. *JRS*. lxi (1971), 146.

Iussu Imp. Caesaris Divi f. | C. Cornelius Cn. f. Gallus | praef. fabr. Caesaris Divi f. | forum Iulium fecit.

375. Via Salaria, near Vicus Novus. *AE*. 1964, no. 107. Cf. *JRS*. lvi (1966), 119.

... | praefe]ctus castrorum a[nnis?... | sub Tib.] Caesare Augusti [f. item | sub C. Ca]esare Augusti f. i[n Hispa|nia] Ilurico Arm[enia | item sub?] Agrippa

376. *CIL*. vi. 1743. Cf. *Bonner Jahrb*. clxv (1965), 88 ff.

Munatio | Planco | Paulino | v. c. Praesidi | Pann. per ann. XVII || Crepereius Amantius v. c. | et Ca(e)onia Marina C. f. eius | ababo | suo.

377. *Forschungen in Ephesos*, iv. 3 (1951), p. 280, no. 24. Cf. *JRS*. lxiii (1973), 55.

]θέλετε κελεύετε ἵνα Μᾶρκος Ἀν[... | ...]εἶτέ τι ὑπὲρ ταύτης ἱερωσύνης τε[... | ...]νημονήαν θεοῦ Ἰουλίου μετὰ πο[... | ...]τε ποῇ μήτε τις τούτων τινα τῶν[... | ...]ων πρὸς ταύτην τὴν ἱερομνημ[ο.. || ...]ρέχειν τούτων τῶν διδόντων ἢ ὑ[... | ...]ην τὴν ἐρώτησιν ποιήσῃ ἢ γ[... | ...]ρι μόνῃ τε αἰτίαι πάντω[ν.. | ...] ταρχο[...

378. (*a*) Athens (*b*) Callatis. *CP*. lxii (1967), 41–2.

(*a*) Ἡ ἐξ Ἀ]ρήου [πάγου βουλὴ | Σέξτον Αἴλιο]ν Κάτον [πρεσβευτὴν Καίσαρος | Σεβαστοῦ καὶ ἀν]θύπα[τον Μακεδονίας ἀρε|τῆς ἕν]εκα καὶ ε[ὐνοίας]

(*b*) Ὁ δ[ᾶμος] | Ποπλίῳ Οὐνικί[ῳ πρεσβεύτᾳ καὶ ἀντι]|στρατάγῳ τῶ πά[τρωνι καὶ εὐεργέτᾳ | τᾶς τῶν Καλλα]τι[ανῶν πόλιος]

379. Oxyr. Pap. 2435. (*?Acta Alexandrinorum.*)

Recto

].[

[ο] εξηγητης επεδωκ αυτω αυτοκρατωρι αμφο[τερα]
τα ψηφισμαται   ο αυτοκρατωρ εγωι πεμφθ[ει]ς
[υπο του] π̣[α]τ̣ρ̣ο̣ς ανδρες Αλενξανδρεις
[οι] οχλοι εφωνησαν ουα κυρι επ αγαθωι
[δ]ε̣ξη̣ι̣ των αγαθων   ο αυτοκρατωρ· περι πολλου
[μεν ουν] ποιησαμενοι   ανδρες Αλεξα̣ν̣[δρεις]
[δ]ιαλεχθηναι με υμειν ανασχεσθε ιν οταν επιτελε-
[σ]ω τα προς εκασται των επισζητουμενων τοτε επι-
[σ]ημανησθαι εγω πεμφθεις ως εφη⟨ν⟩ υπο του πατρος
[ε]πι το καταστησασθαι ταις περαν θαλασης επαρχιας
[ε]χων χαλεπο̣τ̣α̣τον προσταγμα προτον μεν δια τον
πλουν κα`ι´ δια το απεσπασθαι πατρος και μαμμης
[κ]αι μητρος και αδελφων και τεκνων και οικιω̣ν̣ [ ]
προκιμεν... [..προ]σ̣τ̣αγμα το̣ν.[.].ον.η̣[.....]
[.]κοντητον[.].[.]σ̣πασαμην το οικ̣ιον πολυμ[......]
[κ]αινην δε θ̣αλα̣σ̣αν ειναι προτον μεν ειδω την η̣[με-]
[τ]εραν πολιν   οι [οχ]λοι εφωνησαν επ αγαθωι̣
[αυ]τοκρατωρ ηδ̣η δε ηγησα̣μενος αυτην ειν̣[αι]
[λ]αμπροτατο̣ν̣ θεαμαι το μεν προτον δια τ̣[ον]
[η]ρωα και κτ[ισ]την προς τον κυνη τι εστιν ο[φ]ε̣ι̣[λημα]
[το]ις τ̣ων α̣υ̣τ̣[ων] αντεχωμενοις επιτα δια τας ευ̣ε̣[ρ-]
[γε]σιας τας εμου παππου Σεβαστου και πατρος εστιν
[.].τ̣η̣σεις ως οιμιν προς εμε δικαιον και σιοπω μεν ο⟨υ⟩ν
[οι οχλ]οι εφωνη̣σα⟨ν⟩ ιο ζω̣ης επι πλιο̣ν̣ ο αυτ̣ο̣κρατω̣ρ̣
[α] ο̣ι̣δ ε̣κ̣α̣[σ]τ̣ος εμεμνημην δε̣ και ως ταυτ̣α̣ πολλ̣α̣-
[πλ]α̣σειονα τεθησαυρισμεναι ε̣ν ταις υμετεραις
[ευ]χαις ευρον εγραφη μεν γαρ ψηφισμα̣τ̣αι
[εν]τιμαι συνηλε̣γμενων και ολιγων ανδρων [

Verso

[τομ(ου)..] κ̣[ο]λ̣(ληματος) π ετο[υ]ς μβ Καισαρος   ε̣ιφ.ν̣ναι.[
[.....] .δ⁻ ωρας θ⁻ εκαθισεν ο Σε-
[βαστος] εν τωι του Απολλωνος ι̣ερω
[εν τη Ρ]ωμαικη βυβλιοθηκηι και δι-
[ηκουσ]ε̣ν των πρεσβευτων ⟨των⟩ Αλεξα̣ν̣-

[δρεων] συνκαθημενο̣υ̣ αυτω̣ι Τ̣ι̣β[ε]ριου
[Καισαρ]ο̣ς̣ και Δ[ρ]ουσου του Κ̣α̣ι̣σ̣α̣ρος
[και Ουα]λ̣[ε]ρ̣ιου Μ̣ε̣σσαλινου̣ Κυρβ̣ι̣ν̣ου
[......]υ̣ και Τ̣ι..[..]ος̣ Δ̣ε̣ν̣[..]ο̣υ̣.σ̣τορος
[.......]ου Μα[σ]ω̣[νι]ου Τιτου ......ι̣ν̣ου
[.......]ω̣ν̣ος Μ̣αρκ[ο]υ Αυηδιου Οργ⟨ολ⟩ανιου
[.......]σ̣ι̣α̣ν̣ου Τ̣.δ̣... ανεδωκεν τα
[ψηφισ]μαται Αλ̣ε̣ξ̣α̣[νδ]ρος και ειπ̣εν
[.....]ειας π⟨ρ⟩ο̣επεμψε με η πολεις
[.....]οντα της ..ι̣σ̣ης παρασ̣τ̣ησα⟨ι⟩ σοι
[.....]ην και α̣ν̣α̣δ̣ι̣[δο]ν̣α̣ι̣ τ̣α̣ι̣ ψ̣η̣φισματ̣α̣ι̣
[.....]ε̣νπο̣[.....]ν̣ον δε κ̣α̣ι̣ Λ̣ι̣βιας
[........] κ̣α̣ι̣ [Τιβε]ρ̣ι̣ο̣υ̣(?) [Καισ]α̣[ρο]ς̣ δ̣ι̣[....]
[......]δ̣[.]ακο̣[15]ρ̣[..]α̣ς
[....το]σ̣αυτα̣ι̣ αλλ.....κεχ....α̣ι̣ο̣υ̣
[πρεσβ]ευτων μ̣ετ̣α̣ξυ δε ου το[.]...[.......]
[.....]ς ων̣.δ̣ι̣κα̣ι̣[......ε]γνωκ̣α̣ς̣ α̣ξιου-
[.....]α σε .....ε.θης̣ τη νικη .ι̣σ̣α̣ς̣ ελ-
[.....]σ) ο Σ̣ε̣β̣α̣στος ειδεν αυτην
[..... ε]π̣ α̣γ̣α̣θωι επ αγαθωι μετα δε
[ταυτ ειπε] Τιμο̣ξ̣ε̣νος ρητωρ οσην και τοις
[.....]στοις υ̣[.]ο̣.....ιοις παραχησις ουδε̣ν̣
[.....]ευ̣.ομ[....... κ]υριε Σεβαστε τοσαυ̣-
[την και] τοις [σ]ο[ις] Α̣[λ]ε̣ξανδρευσι δεομε-
[θα πα]ρασχε[ιν] σημερο̣ν λογω γαρ υμεις
[ικετε]υ̣σαντες παρεσμεν το δ αληθος
[.....]απασι α σ̣πουδην την συνιεροτατην
[τυχην] π̣ρ̣οσκυνησασα̣ν̣ ετυγχανε⟦ιν⟧ οι δε με̣λ̣

COMPARATIVE TABLE

A. INSCRIPTIONS

		E. and J.
Abbott and Johnson, *Municipal Administration*		
no. 32		20
ADOA.		
ii, 1953	p. 285	322
AJA.		
1950	p. 233	357
AJP.		
1948	p. 436	81a
1954	225	94a
	248	94b
Ann. ép.		
1899, no.	153	65
1904	173	165
1907	154	344
1910	207	232
1912	213	167
1913	40	356
	216	275
1914	87	135
	172	345
	190	353
1920	43	75
	82	308
1921	2	108
1922	40	86
	95	296
	120	331
1923	70–71	156
	72	155
1924	55	259
1925	93	270
	94	90
1927	139	283
1928	15	12
	49–50	76
1929	99–100	102
1930	66	150
	70	216
1932	22	363
1933	84	168
	204	269
1934	90	226
	151	80
1935	46	114
	47	148
1936	18	268
	110	174
	157	291
1937	114	12
	168	169
1938	3	346
	83	89
1938	110	236
	149	163
	173	233
1939	113	107
	142	103
1940	68	43
	69	291
1941	61	297
	64	145
	105	225
1945	19	132
1946	201	112
1948	1	218a
	8	105a
	198	77b
1949	176	63a
	215	94a
1950	44	347a
1951	2	357
	205	105b
1952	49	356a
	164	94a
1953	88	358a
	225	p. 45
APont.		
1938	53	301
Arch. Anz.		
1938	106	107
1940	521	225
Ἀρχ. Ἐφ.		
1932	3	268
Ath. Mitt.		
1911	287	167
1912	180	167
BCH.		
1923	87	259
1926	447	76
1927	253	176
1930	490	363
1932	203	168
1934	300	114
	449	148
BFC.		
1904	89	165
Bolletino di archeol. e di storia dalmatica		
1914	104	86
E. Breccia, *Catalogo del museo d'Alessandria. Iscr. Gr. e Lat.*		
49		285
Bruns, *Fontes Iuris Romani Antiqui* (ed. septima)		
no. 22		279
29		105
43		299
46		30
47		278
48		37
56		364
69		302
74		31
77		282
BSA.		
1918–19	35	108
1947	222	115
Bull. Comm.		
1899	141	65
1912	113	356
1928	298	150
	318	216
1933, App.	17	226
1939	13	297
	24	145
Bulletin archéol. du comité des travaux historiques		
1907	XIII	344
Bulletin de l'association des musées de Slovénie		
1937	134	233
Bulletin de l'institut archéol. bulgare		
1950	235	347a
Bulletin de la soc. historique du Périgord		
1941	402	132
Bulletino del museo dell' impero romano		
iii (1932)	17	226
Chronique d'Égypte		
no. 58, 1954	281	360a
CIG.		
3285		143
3642		129
CIL.		
ii.	no. 194	131
	473	112

CIL. (*cont.*)		*E. and J.*
ii.	474	74
	2038	123
	2107	60
	2916	263
	3414	204
	3417	162
	4701	289
	5807	263
iii.	455	189
	551	202
	605	234
	1698	267
	1741	208
	2709	257
	2908	265
	3148	348
	3158	43a
	3198	292
	3200	266
	3201	293
	5232	360
	6418	258
	6627	261
	6687	231
	6703	284
	7107	144
	7156–7	63
	7452	255
	10131	348
	10156	292
	10158	266
	10159	293
	14147, 5	21
	14401c	294
	14625	9
	14712	347
	p. 785	202
	1651	266
iv.	no. 1553	p. 41
	2105	235
v.	50	339
	525	57
	862	193
	1838	243
	2501	254
	3340	222
	4329	210
	4348	211
	4910	241
	4922	354
	5027	58
	7231	166
	7567	230
	7817	40
	8002	363a
	p. 1022	57
vi.	no. 251	133
	385	39
	386	36
	446	139
	456	41
	712	14
	761	141
	873	17
	874	297
	876	23
	899	63a
vi.	909–10	92
	913	96
	930	364
	1244	281
	1266	298
	1317	194
	1360	192
	1364	212
	1460	188
	1501	196
	1527	357
	1799	183
	1815	151
	1921a	250
	1963	147
	2023b	p. 41
	2169	230a
	2489	251
	2782	250
	2993	253
	3530	240
	3673	215
	3835	195
	3881	149
	3919	146
	4222	125
	4351	159
	4776	154
	5180	147
	5197	158
	5730–1	152
	8409c	153
	8881	149
	8927	277
	9005	157
	10213	53
	21771	219
	30856	215
	30975	142
	31541h	295
	31561k	280
	31670	357
	31713	191
	31857	223
	32323	30–32
	37053	357
	39207	63a
viii.	68	355
	10023	290
	14603	260
	15775	111
	22786f	264
ix.	41	274
	422	323
	1125	221
	1456	161
	2142	55
	2342	213
	2443	79
	2845–6	197
	3044	244
	3158	359
	3305	205
	5645	207
	5811	22
x.	793	326
	830	324
x.	884	325
	1074	327
	1613	110
	1624	50
	3357	272
	3358	273
	3804	328
	3903	329
	4833	332
	4842	282
	4843	283
	4862	245
	4868	246
	4872	242
	5393	229
	5713	247
	6087	187
	6101	237
	6104	330
	6305	121
	7501	126
xi.	365	286
	367	82
	623	11
	1362	206
	1420	68
	1421	69
	3083	334
	3200	104
	3303	101
	3805	333
	3872	85
	4170	51
	4575	337
	4654	271
	5820	336
	6011	228
	7283	220
	7553	198
xii.	257	276
	1849	97
	3179	256
	4333	100
	6038	105
xiii.	1041	269a
	1048	340
	1541	120
	1550	160
	3026d	341
	3570	44
	4635	137
	8648	45
xiv.	2264	188
	2298	358
	2954	249
	3472	248
	3602	214
	3606	200
	3613	199

Corinth

		E. and J.
viii. 2, no.	15	130
	16	73
	81	349
	110	113

		E. and J.
CP.		
1954	180	322
CRAcInscr.		
1903	608	62
1913	680	135
1919	332	75
1939	99	43
	104	291
1952	472	358a
A. Degrassi, *Epigrafia romana*		
i.	79	63a
Doxa		
1949	79	63a
M. Durry, *Éloge funèbre d'une matrone romaine*		
		357
Emerita		
xvi. 1948	46	356a
E. Espérandieu, *Inscriptions latines de Gaule (Narbonnaise)*		
no. 633		217
FIR.		
no. 14		279
22		105
38		299
40		30
41		278
42		37
55		301
57		31
67		282
Forschungen in Ephesus		
iii. 52		71
Fouilles de Delphes		
iii. 1, 532		218
E. Groag, *Die röm. Reichsbeamten von Achaia*		
20		198
Hesperia		
1937	464	89
1947	68	64
1948	41	81a
E. Hohl, *Sitzungsber. d. Deutschen Akademie*		
1952		p. 45
IBM.		
iv. 1, no. 894		98a
IG.		
ii.² no.	3233	81a
	3238	128
	3250	64

		E. and J.
ii.²	3257	136
	3430	175
	3436	164
	3437–8	176
	3439	164
	3440	178
	3445	164
	4118	190
	4126	202
v. 1,	970	351
ix. 2,	261	321
xii. 2,	35	307
	168	67
	212	95
	537	63
	540	94
xii. 5,	940	203
IGRR.		
i. no.	874	170
	879	172
	901	171
	1109	62
	1359	186
iii.	719	72
	721	88
	895	177
iv.	9	63
	11	94
	33	307
	68	67
	144	352
	180	129
	206	93
	219	227
	1042	318
	1300	95
	1375	361
	1392	144
	1444	143
	1756	99
ILS.		
no.	76	55
	77	57
	81	17
	82	22
	83	23
	84	286
	86	58
	88	36
	89	104
	91	14
	94	166
	95	39
	96	60
	98	281
	99	41
	102	289
	103	42
	105	232a
	107	61
	112	100
	113	82
	120	127

	E. and J.
121	126
130	74
139	68
140	69
147	79
151	290
154	101
156	50
157	51
158	52
159	85
168	92
176	92
182	96
189	97
208	363a
244	364
840	162
842	183
847	241
886	187
887	188
891	189
901	191
903	192
906	193
909	194
911	195
914	196
915	197
916	198
918	199
921	200
928	202
932	205
935	206
937	207
938	208
940	210
942	211
943	212
944	213
950	214
1314	240
1320	230a
1335	221
1336	222
1337	223
1349	243
1514	158
1795	157
1802	159
1847	146
1877	149
1901	337
1926	151
1945	330
1948	147
1949	358
1977	360
2014	250
2021	242
2028	251
2226	247
2229	339
2231	271
2243	254

ILS. (*cont.*)	*E. and J.*
2244	45
2252–3	257
2259	258
2267	256
2270	255
2280	265
2281	267
2305	260
2454–5	263
2478	266
2483	261
2531	269a
2637	248
2672	11
2676	235
2678	234
2682	359
2683	231
2684	249
2688	246
2689	244
2690	245
2691	228
2703	239
2817	272
2818	273
2819	274
2822	276
2823	277
3004	328
3090	142
3308	141
3320	43b
3612	139
3783	215
3806	161
4613d	341
4995	125
5050	31–32
5053	327
5373	334
5516	348
5531	336
5743	282
5744	283
5746	280
5759	332
5828	294
5829	292
5829a	293
5923d	295
5935	297
5939	298
6044	53
6080	133
6095	355
6099	354
6123	323
6285	237
6286	229
6361b	324
6388	325
6565	335
6579	333
6747	230
6753	338
6774–5	111
6892	112
6896	131
6964	105
7040	340
7041	120
7160	347
7848	219
7888a, b	152
8393	357
8781	315
8784	77
8810	190
8815	218
8893	9
8894	38
8897	71
8898	44
8965	43a
8995	21
8996	220
9007	224
9250	140
9349	362
9370	285
9371	288
9375	264
9463	319
9483	209
9494	252
9495	106
9503	238

Inscriptions de Délos

		E. and J.
no. 1586		179

Inscriptions latines de Gaule (Narbonnaise)

		E. and J.
no. 633		217

IPEux.

		E. and J.
ii. no. 25		170
36		172
354		171

Istituto di studi romani di Africa romana

		E. and J.
1935	238	291

ISyr.

		E. and J.
iii. 1, no. 718		301

ITrip.

		E. and J.
no. 319		105b
321		346
324a		105a
330		218a
930		291

Iura

		E. and J.
I (1950)	280	94b

JdS.

		E. and J.
1938	73	236
	74	126

JRS.

		E. and J.
1949	17	279
1953	38	360b
	39	360a

Keil u. Premerstein, *Denkschr. Akad. Wien* 1911

		E. and J.
no. 192		361

Krenker u. Schede, *Tempel in Ankara*

		E. and J.
p. 52		109

Le Bas et Waddington, *Voyage archéol. en Grèce et en Asie*, II

		E. and J.
no. 442–3		20
1039		93

Mélanges d'archéol. et d'hist. (École franç. de Rome)

		E. and J.
1936	98	12

Mélanges Boissier

		E. and J.
p. 419		109

Mélanges Gautier

		E. and J.
p. 332		163

MemAmAcR.

		E. and J.
1949	105	311

Mémoires des musées archéol. provençaux

		E. and J.
1943	45	112

Mnemosyne

		E. and J.
1919	263	308

NdS.

		E. and J.
1913	24	275
1921	260	296
1922	417	156
	418	155
1924	514	90
1926	437	283
1933	460	80
1938	5	103
1947	49	94a
	66f.	94b

Nouvelles archives des missions

		E. and J.
1913	38	345

OGIS.

		E. and J.
no. 197		164
357		175
363		176
377		173
378		48
414		178
417		179

OGIS. (*cont.*)	*E. and J.*
453–5	299
458	98
463	203
532	315
533	109
583	134
598	138
606	180
659	116
767	47

Paton and Hicks, *Inscriptions of Cos*

25	318

Petersen u. Luschan, *Reisen in Lykien*

43	72

Proceedings of the Society for Biblical Archaeology

1909	323	232

Quarterly of the Dept. of Antiquities in Palestine

1938	p. 1	138

RA.

1926	i.	40	135
1935	ii.	140	174
1952	i.	48	22

		E. and J.
REG.		
1952	128	317
Revue biblique		
1921, p. 263		138
RFil.		
1942	125	307
RhM.		
1952	95, 97	45
Rivista Indo-Greco-Italica		
1921	76	331

L. Robert, *La collection Fröhner*

no. 70	322

L. Robert, *Les gladiateurs dans l'orient grec*

p. 135	109

RPh.		
1913	294	353
Sardis		
vii. 1, no. 8		99
SEG.		
iv. no. 102		270
	490	98

		E. and J.
iv.	709	352
vi.	646	201
viii.	13	322
	527	320a
ix.	6	47
	8	311
	63	46
xi.	922–3	102
	924	350

Studi offerti a E. Ciaceri

p. 254	77b

Syll.[3]

no. 768	303
780	312
781	316
782	78
785	317

Syria

1932	275	269

Tibiletti, *Principi e magistrati repubblicani* (1953)

p. 188	213
passim	94a

Θρακικά

1935	302	169

B. PAPYRI

AJP.		
1944	80	320
BGU.		
iv. no. 1108		262
FIR.		
no. 56		302

Hunt and Edgar, *Select Papyri*

ii, no. 211	320

Pap. Oxyrh.

ii, no. 240	117

Preisigke, *Sammelbuch griechischer Urkunden*

i, no. 1570	184
4224	300
7738	320a

Wilcken, *Chrestomathie*

no. 112	118
462	302

C. COINS

Acta Divi Augusti, ed. Reg. accad. ital. Pars prior.

p. 93, no. 74	181
77	342
p. 94, no. 82	124
83	343

BMC.

Galatia	
101	181
158, no. 53	185
Lydia	
139, no. 13	189a
251, no. 104	130a
Mysia	
103, no. 84	353b
Troas	
146, no. 24	190b

Grant, *Asp.*

p. 8, no. 20		209a
10	27	209c
14	42 ff.	134a

Grant, *FITA.*

p. 149		339b
195		339a
206		2a
222		343b
224		190a
246		353a
272		348a
362		77a
382, no. 2		219a

Grueber

p. 370		1
372, nos.	104 ff.	2
401	67 f.	7
411	102 ff.	56
471	38 ff.	3
480	68 ff.	4
500	131	8
525	179 ff.	10
560	7 ff.	5

Head, *HN.*[2]

p. 888, fig. 399	162a

Heiss

p. 124, no. 56		107a
183	21	50a

Heiss (*cont.*)		*E. and J.*
p. 201,	no. 18	342
380,	8	343a
393,	2	124
393,	4	93a
400,	18	343

Mattingly		*E. and J.*
p. 1,	nos. 2 ff.	29
3	10 ff.	26
4	18 ff.	28
13	69	33
15	79 ff.	287
17	90	34
	91 ff.	35
23	112 ff.	70
26	124 f.	25
29	134 ff.	19
54	298 ff.	58a
59	322	24
	323 ff.	6
73	427 ff.	27
87	506 ff.	81
88	513 ff.	66
92	548 ff.	119
101	617 ff.	16
105	647 ff.	13
106	650 ff.	15
112	691 ff.	18
114	705 ff.	122
115	707 ff.	59
129	70 ff.	49
130	76 ff.	87
131	79 f.	83
	81 ff.	84
133	95 ff.	91
141	146 ff.	54
162	104	182

Numism. Chronicle	*E. and J.*
1950 p. 45, nos. 4 ff.	209b

Numism. Notes and Monographs	*E. and J.*
109 (1947)	96a

Sydenham	*E. and J.*
nos. 1041 ff.	1
1045	2
1171 ff.	7
1210	10
1287 ff.	3
1301	4
1329	56
1344 f.	5
1356 f.	8

Vives		*E. and J.*
p. 56, no.	17	50a
63	23	343
79	24	342
124	3	124
	4	93a
127	9	343a
131	12	107a

D. LITERARY SOURCES

Frontinus, *de aquis urbis Romae*	
ch. 100, 104, 106	278
108, 125, 127	278
129	279

Josephus, *Antiqu. Iudaicae*	
xvi, §§ 162–5	314
166	304
167–8	309
169–70	310
171	305
172–3	313

Macrobius, *Saturnalia*	
i. 12, 35	37

Philo, *Legatio ad Gaium*	
40, § 315	306

Pliny, *Nat. Hist.* iii,	
§§ 136–7	p. 62, no. 40

Stein, *Röm. Inschriften in der antiken Literatur*	
p. 34	40

N 0 19 814819 4

N 0 19 814819 4